W9-AGO-967

The Student Teaching Experience

Cases from the Classroom

SECOND EDITION

Patricia J. Wentz

University of West Florida

Merrill
Prentice Hall

Upper Saddle River, New Jersey
Columbus, Ohio

43864423

10-3-01

LB
2157
U5W46
2001

c.1

Library of Congress Cataloging-in-Publication Data

Wentz, Patricia J.
  The student teaching experience : cases from the classroom / Patricia J. Wentz—2nd ed.
    p. cm.
Rev. ed. of: Student teaching casebook for supervising teachers and teaching interns. ©1994.
Includes bibliographical references and index.
ISBN 0-13-026100-9
  1. Student teaching—United States—Case studies. 2. Student teachers—Supervision
of—United States—Case studies. I. Wentz, Patricia J. Student teaching casebook for
supervising teachers and teaching interns. II. Title.

LB2157.U5 W46 2001
370'.71—dc21

00-03995

Vice President and Publisher: Jeffery W. Johnston
Editor: Debra A. Stollenwerk
Editorial Assistant: Penny S. Burleson
Production Editor: Mary Harlan
Design Coordinator: Diane C. Lorenzo
Cover Design: Eric Flegel
Cover art: Kenneth Henson
Text Design: Clarinda Publication Services
Production Coordination: Patricia Noble, Clarinda Publication Services
Production Manager: Pamela D. Bennett
Director of Marketing: Kevin Flanagan
Marketing Manager: Amy June
Marketing Services Manager: Krista Groshong

This book was set in Garamond by The Clarinda Company. It was printed and bound by
R. R. Donnelley & Sons Company. The cover was printed by Phoenix Color Corp.

Previous edition, entitled *Student Teaching Casebook for Supervising Teachers and
Teaching Interns,* copyright © 1994 by Macmillan Publishing Company.

Copyright © 2001 by Prentice-Hall, Inc., Upper Saddle River, New Jersey 07458. All rights reserved.
Printed in the United States of America. This publication is protected by Copyright and permission should be
obtained from the publisher prior to any prohibited reproduction, storage in a retrieval system, or transmission in
any form or by any means, electronic, mechanical, photocopying, recording, or likewise. For information regarding
permission(s), write to: Rights and Permissions Department.

10 9 8 7 6 5 4 3 2
ISBN: 0-13-026100-9

Preface

This book addresses the practical, day-to-day induction into the classroom of the beginning student teacher. It guides the student teacher from day one in the assigned classroom through the adjustments of beginning to teach in the classroom and on to the certification and job application processes. Portions of the text are presented for the benefit of the classroom cooperating teacher. It is anticipated that the university supervisor also would make use of this text to assist in the professional induction and successful assignment of the student teacher.

Special recommendations are listed as guidelines; they are meant as suggestions that may stimulate the process of induction and give more confidence to both the student teacher and the cooperating teacher. In this book, the term *cooperating teacher* is used to indicate the classroom teacher who will host the student teacher in his or her classroom for the student teaching assignment. The term *university supervisor* is used to designate the individual from the university who is assigned to visit, support, and evaluate the student teacher throughout the school term.

The case studies presented in each chapter introduce real-life school experiences for the student teacher. These cases should stimulate discussion and afford opportunities for small and large group discussions and role playing. Although some of these cases appear to be extreme, most have actually occurred.

Topics within chapters have been clustered chronologically, from beginning to completion, according to the stage and subject topic of student teaching. The limited time of both supervisors and student teachers demands a practical how-to book on moving through the experience successfully. The writing is compact and to the point and has been proven practical. Although the cooperating teacher, the university supervisor, and the student teacher cannot possibly accomplish all of the suggestions that are given, these suggestions can be used as springboards for discussion.

The current annotated bibliography found at the end of each chapter offers references for the student teachers and the coordinators seeking additional ideas and sources of research, additional suggestions, and student teacher-related information.

This book attempts to bring together the necessary ingredients for a meaningful student teaching experience. I recommend this book for undergraduate and graduate classes dealing with general methods, the preparation for student teaching, and the supervision of student teaching. This material has been used successfully for the training of supervising teachers, and it would benefit in-service and staff development programs in public and private school districts as well.

ACKNOWLEDGMENTS

I wish to thank the many students, student teachers, cooperating teachers, and university supervisors who have given us feedback on these cases and on the first edition of this text. Of special note are the following reviewers: Elaine Chakonas, Dominican University; Manina Urgolo Dunn, Seton Hall University; Susan Hahn, St. Mary's College of California; Michael Perl, Kansas State University; and Marilyn Ward, Carthage College.

I want to especially thank Dr. James Yarling, my co-author in the first edition of this book, for the investment of his time, energy, expertise, and professional dedication. Dr. Yarling is legendary among his student teachers for his knowledge, tact, diplomacy, and professionalism.

Most of all, I want to thank my husband, Dr. Charles H. Wentz, for his patience and encouragement. Charles fed the cats, walked the dogs, took time from his own exciting professional endeavors, and did all those things I would be doing if I had not been revising this text. I am grateful for his personal and professional support.

DISCOVER THE COMPANION WEBSITE ACCOMPANYING THIS BOOK

The Prentice Hall Companion Website: A Virtual Learning Environment

Technology is a constantly growing and changing aspect of our field that is creating a need for content and resources. To address this emerging need, Prentice Hall has developed an online learning environment for students and professors alike—Companion Websites—to support our textbooks.

In creating a Companion Website, our goal is to build on and enhance what the textbook already offers. For this reason, the content for each user-friendly website is organized by topic and provides the professor and student with a variety of meaningful resources. Common features of a Companion Website include:

For the Professor—

Every Companion Website integrates **Syllabus Manager**™, an online syllabus creation and management utility.

- **Syllabus Manager**™ provides you, the instructor, with an easy, step-by-step process to create and revise syllabi, with direct links into Companion Website and other online content without having to learn HTML.
- Students may logon to your syllabus during any study session. All they need to know is the web address for the Companion Website and the password you've assigned to your syllabus.
- After you have created a syllabus using **Syllabus Manager**™, students may enter the syllabus for their course section from any point in the Companion Website.
- Clicking on a date, the student is shown the list of activities for the assignment. The activities for each assignment are linked directly to actual content, saving time for students.
- Adding assignments consists of clicking on the desired due date, then filling in the details of the assignment—name of the assignment, instructions, and whether or not it is a one-time or repeating assignment.
- In addition, links to other activities can be created easily. If the activity is online, a URL can be entered in the space provided, and it will be linked automatically in the final syllabus.
- Your completed syllabus is hosted on our servers, allowing convenient updates from any computer on the Internet. Changes you make to your syllabus are immediately available to your students at their next logon.

For the Student—

- **Topic Overviews**—outline key concepts in topic areas
- **Electronic Bluebook**—send homework or essays directly to your instructor's email with this paperless form
- **Message Board**—serves as a virtual bulletin board to post—or respond to—questions or comments to/from a national audience
- **Chat**—real-time chat with anyone who is using the text anywhere in the country—ideal for discussion and study groups, class projects, etc.
- **Web Destinations**—links to www sites that relate to each topic area
- **Professional Organizations**—links to organizations that relate to topic areas
- **Additional Resources**—access to topic-specific content that enhances material found in the text

To take advantage of these and other resources, please visit the *The Student Teaching Experience: Cases from the Classroom* Companion Website at

www.prenhall.com/wentz

Contents

P A R T

1

A Professional Entrance

1

Getting Off to a Good Start

Many people in universities, communities, and schools are involved in the cooperative venture of training teachers. They spend much time and effort on teacher training programs and take their responsibilities very seriously.

The basic purpose of any student teaching program is to provide a situation in which student teachers learn and practice varied techniques of teaching while working with "real students" under the direction of a certified teacher in a public or private school. The length of student teaching has normally been one quarter or semester, although some programs are now yearlong internships.

The actual placement of student teachers is usually done through a cooperative arrangement between the university and the school district, resulting in a placement that meets the needs of that particular student teacher as closely as possible. The director of Student Teaching at the university meets with the designated individual representing the school district and reviews the individual applications, keeping in mind those teachers in the school district who have been designated as appropriate for the role of cooperating teacher. The next step in the placement is to request that the principal at the school of the suggested cooperating teacher review the application and discuss with the cooperating teacher the likelihood of accepting that student teacher. If all agree, the student teacher is notified and encouraged to visit the classroom to become accustomed to the setting.

The general atmosphere in every school is different. In most schools, student teachers receive a warm welcome from the staff, but if a cooperating teacher is assigned a student teacher without having the opportunity to volunteer for the assignment, problems can result that affect the student teacher. Normally, a cooperating teacher is quite eager to have the opportunity to work with a student teacher who will bring fresh ideas into the classroom. Student teachers usually begin by wondering whether they will be able to complete the assignment satisfactorily. The possibility of failure does exist. Some of the questions in the mind of the beginning student teacher are: Will I perform satisfactorily for my cooperating teacher? Will we have a personality conflict? Will I be able to be myself, or must I become a clone of my cooperating teacher? Will I be able to control a classroom full of students? Will my cooperating teacher assist me in filling in the gaps? Will the pupils accept me as a teacher or see me as a student?

The cooperating teacher, especially if this is his or her first student teacher, also has questions in mind: Will the student teacher be critical of my teaching? Will I perform as a satisfactory cooperating teacher? Will I be able to turn my class over to a student teacher? How will my pupils feel about having another adult in the classroom? How will I get along with my new student teacher? Will the student teacher be competent enough to work with my class? How will I get along with the university supervisor?

The decision to become a professional educator carries with it the responsibility to appear professional both in appearance and in habits. Dress and physical appearance are important when working in a teaching role. Most school districts have written dress codes, and the student teacher should comply with these codes cooperatively and completely.

Subject matter and classroom equipment often dictate types of clothing student teachers should wear. Technical education teachers frequently find a necktie to be a safety hazard, and science teachers and art teachers sometimes find that loose-fitting clothes with floppy sleeves or long scarves can be dangerous in a laboratory. Female kindergarten teachers often discover that wearing a skirt or dress is impractical.

It is imperative that student teachers understand the importance of the personal impression that they make on all who see them. This includes not only the faculty, students, staff, and administration of the school but also the community citizens who may be volunteering in the school and the parents of the school's students. The physical appearance and the neat, clean grooming and appearance are of primary importance. Holding a close second to appearance is the punctuality and attendance of the student teacher. Being on time doesn't mean getting to class breathless just in time; it means being there early and maintaining a calm demeanor.

The first few weeks of student teaching are crucial for the student teacher. First impressions are often unchanged. Student teachers begin their student teaching with an orientation period during which they become acquainted with the community, school, staff, and students.

It is critical that student teachers get to know the community and the kinds of homes their students come from. This information will be valuable to aid them in their understanding of why some children get sleepy about midmorning and why the school may have a breakfast program. A drive through the community, noting the addresses of the students, is a good beginning. During the semester, if the occasion arises, the student teacher and the cooperating teacher may visit the homes of the students on a "just getting to know you" basis. This kind of visit is a major positive public relations technique that some schools are using to improve communication between home and school, and being able to visit with the cooperating teacher will be an asset. Another way the student teacher can get to know the community is to visit grocery stores, drugstores, and gas stations to get a reference point on the culture of the students who attend that school.

It is important that student teachers and cooperating teachers believe that student teaching is going to be worthwhile and even enjoyable. This is absolutely true in most student teaching assignments. Cooperating teachers are usually pleased with the addition of two adult hands, and student teachers find that student teaching is the most beneficial experience they have had in college.

From beginning to end of the student teaching experience, most student teachers will accumulate questions throughout the day. These should be written, and at the end of the school day, the cooperating teacher can sit with the student teacher and answer that day's questions. The next day will bring new questions, and frequently, some of the same questions may appear in a couple of weeks. This problem can be eliminated by the student teacher's keeping a record of the questions and answers in a notepad designated for that purpose. The cooperating teacher will appreciate such a plan; it saves many questions from having to be answered more than once.

GUIDELINES FOR THE STUDENT TEACHER

- **Go into student teaching with a positive attitude and a determination to do your very best**. Although you still consider yourself a student, you are well on your way to becoming a professional. An average performance will not be good enough.
- **Be determined to show enthusiasm and to prove you have definite contributions to make to the teaching profession**. If you do not feel good about yourself, chances are your impression on others will be negative.
- **Consider student teaching a full-time task**. Part-time jobs, heavy social engagements, and college courses should be avoided if at all possible. You owe it to your pupils to be available to concentrate on student teaching.
- **Make specific preparations prior to student teaching**. This could involve reading through pertinent curriculum guides or preparing teaching units that your cooperating teacher has suggested. Such preparations would impress your cooperating teacher and make you feel more confident.
- **Try to be congenial at all times**. Pleasant student teachers make the best impressions. Make the most of each day's opportunities.
- **Keep in mind that you are about to enter a very noble profession, one that involves the responsibility of guiding young lives to their optimum**.
- **Look the part of a professional. Determine what is considered appropriate dress in your particular school**. By all means, be neat and clean. As a teacher-to-be, you must be an example to your pupils.
- **Learn the names of your pupils**. The pupils will be impressed if you call them by name within the first few days. It will also work to your advantage if you learn the names of the school staff.
- **Follow the rules of the school**. Be punctual and call if you will be tardy or absent. Be at school when you are supposed to be there, if not before. Under

normal conditions, it would be good to remain at school until your cooperating teacher is ready to leave.

- **Attend all required meetings: faculty, grade level, PTA, and others involving your cooperating teacher**. These meetings can be informative and can help give you the total picture of the teaching profession.
- **Become familiar with instructional materials**. This is time-consuming but a necessary task.
- **Be an alert observer**. While observing your cooperating teacher, take notes for use at later conferences. Cooperating teachers become upset if you spend time observing but fail to see what is taking place.
- **As you start student teaching, look interested and be curious**. Look for ways to be helpful in the classroom. Volunteer special assistance for individual students or small groups. Your involvement should be active rather than passive.

GUIDELINES FOR THE COOPERATING TEACHER

- **Consider it an honor to be assigned a student teacher**. Not only your pupils but also your student teacher will adopt some of your ideas and concerns in life.
- **Approach this opportunity with confidence and trust**. If you consider your student teacher as a worthy, unique individual, you should do well as a cooperating teacher. Student teachers produce better results if you express confidence in them.
- **Enter the student teaching experience with the frame of mind that you are going to have another teacher in the classroom**. Let your student teacher know that you hope to pursue the "we" process. Effective team teaching can use the strengths of both individuals and can benefit your pupils.
- **Consider your student teacher a beginner**. There are many tasks a student teacher has not yet experienced in the process of teaching; only experience can fill these gaps.
- **Prepare your pupils for the student teacher**. Explain to them that they are going to have the benefit of another teacher. In the beginning, student teachers usually think of themselves as students rather than teachers.
- **Show warmth and openness when you first meet your student teacher**. Your attitude toward the student teacher will be easily detected at this meeting.
- **Specify to your student teacher what you expect**. A good early project is to decide jointly on a lesson plan and journal format (see sample formats in Appendixes C, D, E, & F) and to stress to the student teacher the need to keep a journal. Planning should be done carefully and creatively.
- **Involve your student teacher early and gradually**. Assign routine tasks and encourage work with individual pupils or small groups. Allow routines to vary to provide for the special needs and abilities of your student teacher.

- **Provide your student teacher with a table or desk.**
- **Encourage creative thinking by your student teacher and pupils.** Student teachers should be expected to show initiative and to try out their ideas.
- **Provide for planned and unplanned conferences.** Suggest that your student teacher keep notes during observations and give your guidelines for taking notes that will be discussed at the next conference.
- **Strive for open communication with your student teacher to assure professional growth.** This can happen only in an environment of mutual trust and helpfulness.

CASE STUDIES

C   A   S   E
1-1   Mrs. Van Dyke's student teacher Camille has been approximately a half hour late each of the first 3 days of her second-grade teaching assignment. Camille appears to be quite upset over the matter but feels she has a legitimate excuse. Her 2-year-old has the flu, and she considers home responsibilities her first obligation.

Mrs. Van Dyke has strong feelings that a student teachers's first responsibility is the student teaching assignment. She is a conscientious cooperating teacher and expects her student teacher to arrive at school on time. She and Camille discuss the matter, and emotions run high. Each party holds her ground, and the problem is not resolved.

Camille calls the university supervisor.

1. What reaction do you feel the university supervisor will have?
2. What steps could the university supervisor take?
3. Do you feel that Mrs. Van Dyke has been fair with her student teacher? Explain.
4. How could Camille have planned for unforeseen emergencies such as this before beginning her student teaching?
5. Should Camille have called the university supervisor in the first place?
6. Under what conditions should the principal be consulted?

C   A   S   E
1-2   Tom is in his 2nd week as a student teacher in a fifth-grade classroom. His cooperating teacher encourages him to look for ways to get more involved in classroom activities and suggests he work with individual students having difficulty with mathematics.

One week goes by, and Tom shows little or no involvement. He appears listless and constantly complains about his lack of knowledge in certain subjects, especially mathematics.

The cooperating teacher contacts Tom's university supervisor to discuss the problem.

1. What do you consider to be Tom's problem?
2. If you were Tom's university supervisor, what would you do?
3. If Tom does not show more interest, in what ways would his student teaching program be affected?
4. What options are available to the coordinating teacher?
5. How could this problem be avoided for student teachers in the future?

C A S E

1-3   Mrs. Chang's student teacher Anna is very sure of herself during the 1st week of student teaching. She has been one big smile from the very start, giving the impression that she is living in another world. The fact is that three of Mrs. Chang's seventh-grade social studies classes are most difficult to handle, even for an experienced teacher.

Mrs. Chang wonders how Anna will ever win the respect of her classes. Anna seems to have decided that teaching is all sugar and cream and that negative factors should be overlooked.

Of course, the giggly seventh graders think the student teacher is very amusing. Some are quite eager to assist her in losing her smile. Mrs. Chang knows from experience that the seventh graders will make life unbearable for Anna when she begins teaching unless some changes are made. However, Mrs. Chang does not want to discourage her student teacher's positive attitude.

1. A positive attitude is an asset in a student teacher. What do you see to be the problem with Anna?
2. How should Mrs. Chang address Anna's problem?
3. What changes could Anna make to be more successful?
4. How could the university supervisor help define the problem for Anna?
5. How would teachers you have known have dealt with such a problem?

C A S E

1-4   Paul began his student teaching as a loner. He avoided talking to teachers and, in fact, had difficulty communicating with his coordinating teacher, Mr. Evans. Although Mr. Evans suggested that Paul work with individual students and assume minor classroom chores, Paul has avoided all types of responsibility.

Most of Paul's comments are negative. Paul hints periodically that he really does not know whether teaching is what he wants to do. Mr. Evans is quite alarmed when Paul mentions that he has not gotten anything out of his college methods classes.

1. What could cause Paul to be so negative?
2. What steps can Mr. Evans take to change Paul's pattern?
3. How can a teacher have a negative disposition and still be effective?

4. What effect would more involvement with other student teachers have on Paul's attitude?
5. Why should a cooperating teacher spend time trying to train someone to be a teacher when the person is not sure that he or she wants to be one?

C A S E

1-5   Beth has entered student teaching with a great deal of enthusiasm. She projects much more self-confidence than the typical student teacher.

During her introduction to the class, she states that she has a few rules she expects to enforce. One of the rules is in definite conflict with the cooperating teacher's procedures.

1. How could Beth be approached tactfully?
2. Should a student teacher ever be permitted to be in conflict with the cooperating teacher's procedures? Why or why not?
3. Most student teachers are quite cautious at the beginning. Why do you think Beth started with such confidence?
4. What could the cooperating teacher have done to have avoided this situation?
5. How could this problem indicate possible related difficulties in the future?

C A S E

1-6   Marilee is student teaching in a suburban high school, and her academic preparation seems to be satisfactory. The major problem with Marilee is the way she dresses; she always looks like a fashion model, and this disturbs both the students and the faculty. The students think some of her clothes are amusing, and members of the faculty consider some of her outfits to be too revealing.

Although Marilee always wears the latest fashion, she is dressing inappropriately for the classroom and for teaching.

1. How could Marilee's apparel affect the students?
2. What should the cooperating teacher do?
3. How can the cooperating teacher avoid hurting Marilee's feelings?
4. Would she seem envious if she suggests that Marilee tone down her wardrobe?
5. To what extent should the university supervisor be involved?

RECOMMENDED READING

Boyer, E. (1990). Teaching in America. In M. L. Kysilka (Ed.), *Honor in teaching: Reflections* (pp. 3–6). West Lafayette, IN: Kappa Delta Pi. *Boyer implores us to accord teaching the dignity it deserves. Reading this essay will give student teachers a zest for entering the profession and encouragement to assist with the profession's renewal.*

Deal, T. E., & Chatman, R. (Spring 1989). Learning the ropes alone: Socializing new teachers. *Action in Teacher Education, 11*(1), 21–30. *Deal and Chatman give specific examples of how to assist in the orientation of new teachers. These techniques can be used in acclimating the student teacher.*

Morris, J. E., Pannell, S. K., & Houston, W. R. (1988). Standards for professional laboratory and field experiences: Review and recommendations. In J. Sikula (Ed.), *Action in teacher education* (pp. 147–152). Reston, VA: Association of Teacher Educators. *The authors provide an analysis of the current standards for laboratory and field experiences which have originated primarily from historically successful practices. The discussion and set of recommendations speak to the improvement of teacher education through a revision of the standards.*

Odel, S. J. (1990). Support for new teachers. In T. M. Bey & C. T. Holmes (Eds.), *Mentoring: Developing successful new teachers* (pp. 3–23). Reston, VA: Association of Teacher Educators. *An explanation of the mentoring concept, a table that gives mentoring roles from literature, and methods of applying the mentoring concept to the beginning teacher/experienced teacher team are given. The importance of the careful choice of a mentor and the maintenance of such a relationship are stressed.*

Rand, M. K. (1999). *Voices of student teachers: Cases from the field.* Upper Saddle River, NJ: Merrill/Prentice Hall. *This text contains actual cases written by student teachers and offers the beginning student teacher a preview of what the classroom may hold for him or her and shows the marriage of theory and practical reality.*

Redman, G. L. (1999). *Teaching in today's classroom: Cases from elementary school.* Upper Saddle River, NJ: Merrill/Prentice Hall. *This casebook gives 22 critical components of teaching in the elementary school in the domains of planning and preparation, creating an environment for learning, instruction, and professional responsibilities.*

Redman, G. L. (1999). *Teaching in today's classrooms: Cases from middle and secondary school.* Upper Saddle River, NJ: Merrill/Prentice Hall. *Relevant to preservice and inservice teachers in Grades 6 through 12 across subject areas, the cases in this text are problem-based and reflect authentic classroom situations.*

Sorenson, V. M., & Veele, M. L. (1978). The student teaching team. *In Student teacher's handbook* (pp. 3–14). Holmes Beach, FL: Learning Publications. *This overview gives the student teacher a good idea of the responsibilities of the student teaching team and where the student teacher fits into the team. The school administrator is included as a member of the team in addition to the university supervisor, the cooperating teacher, and the student teacher.*

Tyler, R. (1990). Placing teaching in the proper perspective. In M. L. Kysilka (Ed.), *Honor in teaching: Reflections* (pp. 15–18). West Lafayette, IN: Kappa Delta Pi. *This brief essay by Ralph Tyler, the father of curriculum development in modern education, speaks to the honor of the profession of teaching. Tyler refers to the value of teaching to our civilization and indicates that the public should understand and respect more of what teachers currently do.*

Wong, H. K., Wong, R. T. (1996). *The first days of school: How to be an effective teacher.* Columbus, OH: National Middle School Association. *The Wongs are favorites of teachers everywhere and in this text they combine research, practical techniques, and common sense.*

Getting to Know Administration, Faculty, and Staff

Becoming acquainted with the total school administration, faculty, and staff is a wise move for the student teacher (see Appendix A for staff organization). Getting to know the individual qualities and characteristics of everyone who works at the school will not only make the student teacher feel more at home but also help the student teacher to know who to turn to if she needs something. Student teachers will probably meet the administrative team of principal, assistant principal, dean, and curriculum coordinator on their first visit to the school. These are individuals whose names they should remember and whom they should get to know if time permits. These individuals can be very helpful later in the job-hunting process.

It is likely that any of these administrators may invite the student teacher in for an interview. The student teacher should take advantage of such an audience and can expect an interview to follow the following general agenda: some social conversation (hometown, favorite sports teams, hobbies, etc.) to make the student teacher feel comfortable, some information about the school furnished by the administrator to help acclimate the student teacher, some questions about the student teacher's background and learning theory preferences, and finally some assurances that this will be an outstanding professional opportunity to student teach in the administrator's school.

The student teacher should use every opportunity appropriate to meet and talk with other faculty members from the first observation day until the last day of the assignment. Professional relationships are likely to develop that both encourage and assist the student teacher. Additionally, knowing the name of the school secretary, the counselor, the nurse, and the custodian is a valuable professional practice. It is also advantageous for the student teacher to become acquainted with the teacher aides and other paraprofessionals.

The number of people on the school faculty can determine the number and quality of interactions the student teacher shares with faculty. In a small school, the student teacher could get to know all the faculty and be known, at least on a speak-in-the-hall basis. The student teacher should speak to everyone, smile, and make some appropriate comment if possible. In a large school, there may be faculty the student teacher will never meet. Every effort should be made by the student teacher to get to know and observe the teachers in the same grade level or in the same department.

During the initial visitations to the student teaching assignment, the student teacher should have the opportunity to meet a small circle of teachers. This group includes the cooperating teacher, other teachers in the department or grade level, the department chairperson or grade level chairperson, the teachers across the hall and next door to the assigned classroom, the assistant principal, and the principal.

Although in many elementary schools the teacher eats with the class, some schools offer a special dining area for faculty that provides an excellent opportunity for the student teacher to get to know other faculty. Prudence dictates that the student teacher listen more than talk during such times. It is necessary to be friendly, listen courteously, and contribute to the conversation when appropriate. Just as this is an excellent opportunity for the student teacher to get to know the faculty, so is it a good opportunity for the faculty to get to know the student teacher. The student teacher should be careful to avoid seeming hostile even though he or she may have hostility toward some ideas discussed.

The student teacher should also avoid appearing to profess beliefs that run counter to those generally accepted by the community. By expressing unpopular ideas or by appearing to be discourteous, crude, or hostile, the student teacher will probably lose any opportunity of being offered a permanent position in that school or in any other school in the community. The host school always retains the right of having the student teacher removed from the student teaching assignment. A lack of ability to get along with faculty is sufficient reason for the cooperating teacher or the administration to request withdrawal.

The teachers' lounge is another good place to get to know faculty. The lounge offers a haven and refuge to tired teachers. Some teachers feel the lounge is a center to pick up on the latest news; others see it as a place to put their feet up and relax for 5 minutes before the next class with a cold beverage or a cup of coffee.

Student teachers should recognize the teachers' lounge as a place to relax momentarily, to meet new people, to discover more about the profession of teaching, and even to discuss student-related problems that there may otherwise be no time to discuss, provided confidentiality is observed. Many times, teachers may relate ideas and concerns about students from a prior year to student teachers that will greatly aid in developing individual programs for particular students. Usually the teachers' lounge contains a bulletin board, which should be checked frequently.

The student teacher should be careful about the impression being made on other teachers and should never criticize the cooperating teacher, other teachers, or the administration, even though others in the group appear to criticize openly with no qualms. Remember that those teachers already have a job. Should the conversation become unprofessional, the student teacher can tactfully bring up a new topic, appear to be engrossed in the plan book, or generally ignore the situation.

During their college training, future teachers are often advised to beware of the teachers' lounge, to stay out of "that place." However, in the best professional and personal interest of the student teacher, appropriate use of the teachers' lounge may be suggested by the cooperating teacher.

Even after eating lunch at the faculty table and spending the morning break (if there is one) in the teachers' lounge, there may be some teachers whom the student teacher will not have met. At the first faculty meeting held after the beginning of the student teaching term, the principal will probably introduce the student teacher to the entire faculty group.

As the student teacher makes each acquaintance at the school, it is advisable to avoid trying to establish identical rapport with everyone. It will become obvious that the desirable rapport can be established based on the relationship that the student teacher will be developing with each individual. For instance, some teachers will be closer in assignment to what the student teacher is doing, and others will be closer in age, social activities, and personal preferences. The student teacher should gauge the relationship and fashion the appropriate rapport with each individual, remaining genuine to all.

GUIDELINES FOR THE STUDENT TEACHER

- **The last thing a teacher needs is a permanent shadow, so do not become one for your cooperating teacher.** Stand on your own two feet.
- **Avoid following your cooperating teacher around all day.**
- **It is appropriate for the two of you to go to lunch together,** but allow some other teachers to sit next to the cooperating teacher.
- **Just as the cooperating teacher needs a break from the students during the day,** so do the student teacher and cooperating teacher need a break from each other.
- **It is your responsibility to make of yourself a congenial, outgoing person that the other teachers enjoy being around.**
- **Do your best to remember teachers' names when you are introduced.**
- **Remember something interesting about each teacher you meet.** As time goes on, you may find you have developed friendships that will last for a long time.
- **Shyness is often interpreted as aloofness.** A safe general rule is to become acquainted with members of the faculty and have friendly conversations.
- **Indicate an interest in the activities of the school.** If wisely and carefully used, this interest can be one of your best resources for information on school activities as well as on individual students.
- **Be extremely careful; do not gossip.** Never let yourself be guilty of unflattering conversation about anyone—student or professional—either stated or implied.
- **Confidentiality is expected of any professional.** In schools located near the college or university, the students taught by the student teacher may be children

of faculty members at the school or college. In many cases, parents and community residents are classroom volunteers. You should maintain professional discretion while developing cordial relationships with all school employees.

- **You are a guest in the school and should not appear otherwise.**
- **Keep in mind that the teachers with whom you are associating already have contracts and you do not.** You have to prove yourself; people are watching you and your reactions to practically everything to judge your professional development.
- **If there are several student teachers in your building, be careful not to cluster.** Mix with the teachers, learn from them, and do not be afraid to ask their advice.
- **Use the teachers' lounge at appropriate times, during scheduled breaks and before and after school.** This will give you the opportunity to let the staff know that you are friendly.
- **When you go to the lounge, avoid imposing your attitudes on education to those teachers who are seeking a moment's rest.**
- **Be aware of the time you are spending in the lounge.**
- **Occasionally, particularly in the case of teachers with no homeroom,** the lounge becomes a workroom—a place to grade papers, make out tests, check homework, and develop lesson plans. Try to avoid disturbing those people at work.
- **If your lounge is used continuously during the day for relaxing and social types of activities,** find a corner in the library or the cafeteria (or some place your cooperating teacher suggests) to work on your professional responsibilities. Trying to accomplish such tasks where others are relaxed tends to make you less productive.
- **The people you meet in the lounge may be good contacts for future job references, so behave accordingly.**

GUIDELINES FOR THE COOPERATING TEACHER

- **Prior to the arrival of the student teacher, discuss with your fellow teachers the fact that you will be having a student teacher in your classroom.** Make a special point of discussing this with those faculty members who are teaching the same subject.
- **If there are faculty members from the same hometown or region as the student teacher,** tell them about your student teacher.
- **Ask some of your fellow teachers for permission for your student teacher to visit in their classrooms to observe.**
- **Before taking the student teacher with you to the first teachers' meeting,** check with the principal for approval and give any information necessary for the introduction of the student teacher.
- **Find some congenial teachers who are in the teachers' lounge at the same time your student teacher is there and ask that they help make the student teacher feel welcome at your school.**

- **Location of the bathroom facilities in the teachers' lounge is part of the initial information the student teacher should have.**
- **Explain to your student teacher school customs involving use of student bathroom facilities and the teachers' lounge.**
- **Names of teachers with similar interests would be appreciated by the student teacher.**

CASE STUDIES

C A S E

2-1   Mazie was the new student teacher in Mrs. Pollock's junior high math classes. Eager to become accepted as part of the school faculty, Mazie made a point of getting to know as many of the faculty as possible. A major part of her plan was for the faculty to get to know her. Early in the term, Mazie began to get to school a half hour earlier than the other teachers so that she could get her work organized and begin visiting with the other teachers as they arrived at school. Lengthy visitations cut into the other teachers' work time, and the teachers mentioned this to Mrs. Pollock.

1. What action should Mrs. Pollack take?
2. What responsibilities do the people who were being bothered have?
3. How might Mrs. Pollack help Mazie to accomplish her goal in more acceptable methods?
4. In what ways could the other teachers help resolve this situation?
5. What lessons can Mazie learn from this kind of behavior?

C A S E

2-2   Manuel was assigned as a student teacher in U.S. government with Ms. Soltice. Manuel held promise of becoming a good, strong teacher; however, his enthusiasm for his subject carried itself too far for some of his lunch-table teacher friends. At times that enthusiasm would turn to aggression and hostility. As Manuel realized the situation had occurred, he would carefully apologize. Another teacher told Ms. Soltice that some of the lunch group were unhappy with Manuel's aggression and hostility and were trying to avoid him.

1. What actions should Ms. Soltice take to help Manuel get along with the other teachers?
2. How could Ms. Soltice help Manuel maintain his enthusiasm about his subject?
3. What help could other members of the lunch group contribute?
4. Are there other avenues toward which Ms. Soltice could help Manuel channel this enthusiasm?
5. How could the guidance counselor help ameliorate this situation?

C   A   S   E

2-3   The faculty at Meadowbrook Elementary were always happy to welcome student teachers, and their acceptance of Henry was no exception. Henry was to student teach in Mrs. Lassiter's fourth-grade classroom and he appeared to be eager to get to work. At first, Mrs. Lassiter thought that Henry was just shy about being new in the classroom because he never talked to the children. She further observed that when possible, Henry avoided talking with students and faculty, although he did not seem nervous about working closely with her.

After 2 weeks in his assignment, Henry still had not visited the teachers' lounge or the school cafeteria. Mrs. Lassiter felt that immediate action was necessary.

1. What effect will Henry's aloofness have on his student teaching experience?
2. How could the university supervisor be involved with this problem before the next scheduled visit?
3. How could Mrs. Lassiter involve other cooperating teachers in resolving this situation?
4. What kind of involvement with the children could Mrs. Lassiter prescribe?
5. How could a personality characteristic such as shyness be diagnosed prior to student teaching?

C   A   S   E

2-4   James, the new student teacher in math at the high school, enjoys smoking cigarettes, but the high school has a smoke-free environment rule. Having been accustomed to smoking between classes at the university, James felt that it would be impossible for him to live through the entire school day without smoking a cigarette. Because he felt that a nonsmoker would not understand his problem, he hesitated to mention it to his cooperating teacher.

As his drive for a smoke grew during the 1st week of student teaching, James became inattentive and irritable.

1. Why would the cooperating teacher assume that the problem with James was the student teaching assignment?
2. What should James do?
3. What clues should the cooperating teacher watch for?
4. How could James resolve this situation?
5. How should he approach other teachers or student teachers to determine how they get through the day without smoking?

C   A   S   E

2-5   Ella was thoroughly enjoying her student teaching. The faculty was happy with her and all aspects of her student teaching seemed progressive and appropriate. One day, one of the female teachers who happened to be recently divorced and quite attractive was alone with Ella in the teachers' lounge when the principal entered. Ella noticed innuendoes and began to feel uncomfortable in the presence of these two people, who obviously would have liked a few minutes alone.

1. What should Ella do?
2. How could she have pretended to be oblivious to what was happening?
3. For what reasons should she confide in her cooperating teacher?
4. What effect could a discussion of this situation with anyone have on her chances of being hired to teach in this school?
5. What future actions would you suggest?

C A S E

2-6   Bob is student teaching in a large high school that has a number of young teachers. As Bob began using the teachers' lounge, one of the young male teachers seemed to take Bob under his wing, trying to help in any situation, be available to answer all questions, and generally be helpful. After a few weeks of such attention, Bob sensed that this particular young male teacher had interests other than professional ones. Having realized that most of the faculty had seen them working together and talking to each other a great deal of the time, Bob knew that he was likely to be labeled in a way he considered inappropriate.

1. What are Bob's options?
2. How could he explain this to his cooperating teacher (a female)?
3. Why should he go to the administration with this problem?
4. What is likely to happen if he decides to discuss this with any other male faculty member?
5. What advice would you give Bob?

C A S E

2-7   Lu dearly loved working with the children in her first-grade class and was excited about the prospects of a career in education. She considered her cooperating teacher to be one of the very best and felt privileged to have this particular assignment. She was so impressed with her cooperating teacher that she became her shadow. The cooperating teacher began to feel confined. The student teacher, not wanting to miss a chance to learn from her, felt compelled to go with her to the lounge and continue dialogue there. The cooperating teacher was at her wit's end.

1. How could the cooperating teacher periodically free herself of the student teacher?
2. What should the cooperating teacher do about this situation?
3. How could the university supervisor help?
4. Would the principal be the appropriate person to assist with the solution?
5. How could the cooperating teacher enlist the help of other teachers with supervisory experience?

RECOMMENDED READING

Conley, S., & Cooper, B. (Eds.). (1991). *The school as a work environment: Implications for reform.* Boston: Allyn & Bacon. *This book is based on how teachers work in their schools and opportunities for future development related to their work. The student teacher can more easily understand the faculty and staff with whom he works by having a background knowledge in such topics as teachers' work cultures, in-school influence, and teacher commitment.*

Drayer, A. M. (1979). Problems of adjustment to school personnel. In *Problems in middle and high school teaching: A handbook for student teachers and beginning teachers* (pp. 211–242). Boston: Allyn & Bacon. *The author lists practical, useful suggestions for developing good relationships with school personnel. Points for discussion are given, and each is illustrated by a problem from student teaching experiences.*

Gauss, J. (1985). Fellow employees. In *So you wanna teach, huh?* (pp. 25–36). Boston: University Press of America. *The author gives practical advice with a touch of humor on how to succeed in school by knowing what happens behind the scenes. He recommends that the new teacher immediately get to know (in this order): the custodian, the school secretary, the principal, the vice principal, the school nurse, the counselor, the librarian, the cafeteria director, the grounds people, and fellow teachers.*

Gose, M. D. (1999). *Creating a winning game plan.* Thousand Oaks, CA: Corwin Press. *Considered required reading for student teachers, this book will take you successfully through the survival stage of beginning teaching and offers a wealth of strategies for the classroom.*

Lovell, J. T., & Wiles, K. (1983). Organization and operation of the faculty. In *Supervision for better schools* (5th ed.) (pp. 248–268). Englewood Cliffs, NJ: Prentice Hall. *Although this material is written for the educator in a supervisory position, it benefits the student teacher and the cooperating teacher to discuss how and whether these concepts apply in their school. This chapter speaks to structuring the group and good uses of communication within the group.*

Zimpher, N. L., & Grossman, J. E. (1992). Collegial support by teacher mentors and peer consultants. In C. D. Glickman (Ed.), *Supervision in transition: 1992 yearbook of the Association for Supervision and Curriculum Development* (pp. 141–154). Alexandria, VA: Association for Supervision and Curriculum Development. *Zimpher and Grossman examine both the teacher mentor model and an alternative approach to assisting students just beginning to teach. This alternative model is the peer assistance and review (PAR) model. Such a comparison of models highlights the decision of whether to have the same person responsible for both formative assistance and summative evaluation.*

Becoming Familiar With School Property

When a student teacher arrives at the assigned school, time can be saved if he or she knows how to move quickly from one area of the school to another. A tour of the school building should be one of the first orders of business and should include the location of the library, teachers' lounge, physical education area, music room, general offices, guidance office, medical clinic, auditorium, gymnasium, cafeteria, and restrooms for students and for adults.

Knowing the whereabouts of the custodial and maintenance staff is another must. These important people can be valuable help in keeping a classroom running smoothly. Student teachers should know the necessary procedures for obtaining their assistance and be introduced to them at the beginning of student teaching.

Classes in the elementary schools often have different procedures. It is necessary to know where to deliver or pick up students for physical education, music, art, and other special classes. When and where the pupils arrive and depart on the school buses must also be well understood; where pupils are delivered can often be different from where they are picked up, based on school outdoor traffic flow patterns. Student teachers must also be informed about rainy day or snow day schedules. Procedures for fire drills and other emergencies need to be studied, as confusion can result if the recommended procedures are not followed.

Student teachers assigned to middle or high schools might easily be assigned hall duty during their student teaching term. Student teachers should expect to be assigned such duties that are normally given to classroom teachers.

The use of the media center or library in the assigned school could be a major factor in the success of the student teacher. Ample time should be given for a new student teacher to meet the people in charge of these sites and to look over what is available there. If the school district maintains a central media center or production lab, it is a good idea for the student teacher to arrange a visit.

The boundaries of school grounds are often not fenced. It is helpful to know these boundaries in order to participate in such activities as observation walks and recess periods. Off-limit areas in the middle and high schools should be pointed out to the student teacher.

GUIDELINES FOR THE STUDENT TEACHER

- **On your first visit to the school, report to the office of the principal.** Teachers often have to sign in at this office at the start of the day. Someone will take or direct you to the classroom or office of your cooperating teacher.
- **Take an early interest in touring the school building.** This will probably be arranged for you by your cooperating teacher. If not, suggest such a tour.
- **Study a floor plan of the building.**
- **If you drive to school, inquire about the proper place to park.** Schools often have restricted parking spaces for faculty and student teachers.
- **If you smoke, inquire from your cooperating teacher as to where, when, or whether this can be done.** It might be but don't assume that it is, permissible to smoke in the teachers' lounge. Ask your cooperating teacher first before smoking.
- **Find answers to the following questions:**

  1. What are the school practices with regard to supervising corridors, group movement within the building, and space assignment on the playground?
  2. What are the teachers' responsibilities before and after school?
  3. What are the teachers' duties during lunch periods?
  4. What are the responsibilities of teachers for outdoor and indoor play periods?
  5. What are the other special duties of teachers in the building in which you teach?

- **Study the procedures for fire drill, tornado/hurricane, earthquake alerts for your classroom.** It might be that your cooperating teacher is out of the room when the first such drill takes place. It could be disastrous if there was a real fire and you were unprepared.
- **If you are an elementary student teacher, you should be eager to assist pupils getting to and from the buses.** You should also show initiative in the supervision of restroom breaks for students. Line-up areas and methods should be noted.
- **Hold your phone calls to a minimum.** Only emergency calls could be appropriate. Many phone calls are received by schools in a given day, and you should not be responsible for tying up the lines. Those calling you could ask to have a message placed in the mailbox of your cooperating teacher.

GUIDELINES FOR THE COOPERATING TEACHER

- **Arrange a tour of the school for the student teacher at the beginning of student teaching.**

- **This is an excellent initial contact between your principal and student teacher.** Principals are usually proud of their buildings and appreciate the opportunity to show them off.
- **Try to get a map of the school for your student teacher; there is probably an emergency drill map.** If there is not one available, sketch one yourself. Fire drill and other emergency procedures should be explained as soon as possible. Your student teacher can be a big help during emergencies if properly trained.
- **Explain the pick-up and delivery system in operation for students in your class.** Student teachers can be involved from the start in moving the pupils about the school; put them to work the 1st day.
- **If your school district has a central media center or production laboratory, arrange for your student teacher to spend some time there.** In addition, plan for your student teacher to spend at least part of a day in the school library or media center.

CASE STUDIES

C A S E   3-1

DeLos had been a student teacher for 3 weeks in a high school English assignment and appeared to have gotten off to a good start. There was only one concern that bothered his cooperating teacher: DeLos was a heavy smoker who thought he must have a cigarette at each class break. His first pattern was to go into the rest room of the teachers' lounge to do his smoking, because the lounge was near his classroom.

There was an unwritten law that the principal did not want any smoking on the school grounds—by students or teachers. After receiving complaints from other teachers about DeLos's smoking, DeLos's cooperating teacher asked him to quit. DeLos continued to disappear for a few minutes at each class break. It was evident that he was not going to the lounge; his cooperating teacher suspected that he was going to the nearest pupils' restroom to smoke.

1. What action should the cooperating teacher take?
2. How can DeLos justify his actions?
3. What responsibility does the cooperating teacher have to the principal? To the university supervisor?
4. At what point should the university supervisor be brought into the picture?
5. What options are open to DeLos?

C A S E   3-2

Margaret arrived at school the 1st day of student teaching and had difficulty finding a place to park. She felt lucky when she found a space near the front entrance. She continued to park in the same spot for the first week of school. The next Monday morning, the principal confronted Margaret and suggested that she find another space to park because she had been parking in a space that had customarily been taken by one of the regular teachers. Margaret was embarrassed and upset.

1. How important an issue is this?
2. Should a student teacher be given all of the privileges of the regular teachers? Explain.
3. Why would it have been wise for Margaret to have inquired about where student teachers should park?
4. In what way could Margaret appease the teacher whose parking space she had taken?
5. How could the cooperating teacher help Margaret with this embarrassing situation?

C A S E

3-3   Gerry was a student teacher assigned to a seventh-grade social studies class. All middle school student teachers were asked to visit the school district's central media center on the 2nd day of student teaching. At a group meeting held on the university campus registration day, the student teachers were given precise directions on how to get to the media center. Gerry decided to drive alone to the center. He did not give himself enough time, got lost, and missed more than half of the session.

The next day, Gerry's cooperating teacher asked about his experiences at the media center. She was noticeably upset when Gerry explained what had happened. She asked Gerry if this episode was indicative of how he would perform in her classroom. Her lecture concerning the importance of promptness was long but to the point. Gerry was upset. What a way to begin student teaching!

1. How could this situation have been prevented?
2. Why would Gerry's cooperating teacher make such a big deal out of this matter?
3. What chances do you think Gerry has of being successful in this assignment?
4. What do you think Gerry should do now?
5. In what ways could the university supervisor assist Gerry?

C A S E

3-4   Marty was in her 3rd week as a student teacher in an eighth-grade English assignment. She was in the middle of her third-period class when the fire drill bell rang. Marty did not know what to do with her class; she did have the insight, however, to ask the students, because the cooperating teacher was out of the classroom. They were able to get out of the building in a reasonable time, so they were not conspicuous. Marty thought about the possibilities of a real fire and was upset with herself for not knowing the fire drill routes.

1. Why was it inexcusable for a student teacher not to know fire drill procedures?
2. Whose responsibility was it to inform Marty of the fire drill routes?

3. How should Marty react to any comments by the students about her lack of information?
4. What can Marty do to show that she has learned a lesson from this event?
5. What could have resulted if this had been a real fire?

C A S E

3-5   Rocky met his ninth-grade physical education class in the gymnasium for his first session. His cooperating teacher was called to the office, causing Rocky to feel pressured and anxious. As planned, Rocky was to take this class to the athletic field for a game of soccer. A busy four-lane highway had to be crossed to get to the field; what Rocky did not know was that an overpass was to be used. Instead, Rocky led the students across the busy highway, causing the passing motorists to be frustrated. Rocky was quite embarrassed when he found out about the overpass.

1. In what ways would Rocky have been liable if a student had been injured while crossing the highway?
2. What responsibility should the cooperating teacher accept for Rocky's failure to use the overpass?
3. How could this dangerous situation have been avoided?
4. What can Rocky do to regain the confidence of his cooperating teacher and students?
5. How could this experience be of value to Rocky in years to come?

RECOMMENDED READING

Cohen, L., & Manion, L. (1983). Extra-curricular activities. In *A guide to teaching practice* (pp. 237–242). New York: Methuen & Company. *The authors include good suggestions for planning and implementing extracurricular activities. Responsibility, safety, and travel activities are highlighted.*

Cohen, L., & Manion, L. (1983). The school as an organization. In *A guide to teaching practice* (pp. 9–13). New York: Methuen & Company. *Both formal and informal school structure are explained in this material. Methods of organizing activities and the use of time for successful classroom experiences are also included.*

Lovell, J. T., & Wiles, K. (1983). The supervisory team at the local school. In *Supervision for better schools* (5th ed.) (pp. 232–247). Englewood

Cliffs, NJ: Prentice Hall. *This chapter may help the student teacher to more readily understand that the supervisory structure serves as an instructional support team. The authors review the responsibilities of this team in assisting with planning and resources.*

Machado, J. M., & Meyer, H. C. (1984). Understanding home and school interactions. In *Early childhood practicum guide: A sourcebook for beginning teachers of young children* (pp. 175–182). Albany, NY: Delmar Publishers. *The authors discuss the procedure for planning and making a home visit. Other home/school interactions discussed include parent conferences (formal and informal) and written communication.*

Tracey, K. (1980). Affiliation. In D. R. Cruickshank (Ed.), *Teaching is tough* (pp. 75–111). Englewood Cliffs, NJ: Prentice Hall. *This material has probably already been experienced by the cooperating teacher. The in-depth explanation of these topics is excellent for discussions. Affiliation usually is perceived only peripherally by student teachers, but* *having access to Tracey's work will assist in the process of assimilating the student teacher into the social and academic structure of the school. Activities and checklists are included.*

Becoming Familiar
With School Policies

Dealing with students in a school without being familiar with school policy is rather difficult and dangerous. The student teacher should obtain from the cooperating teacher or the school secretary copies of school and district policies and should read them thoroughly.

The administration expects all personnel to be aware of school policies and usually is happy to discuss policies with the student teacher, provided sufficient time is available. The student teacher who feels that there are too many rules to remember should discuss this with the cooperating teacher, and time should be spent on those needs that appear to be most pressing and that arise most often. Any rule or policy covering emergencies should be committed to memory immediately.

Early awareness of school and district rules pays huge dividends for the student teacher. Frequently, student teachers see such rules as an encumbrance just for the sake of having a rule. It is helpful for them to understand that state laws pertaining to education are translated into rules by the state department of education. Each school district within the state must abide by these rules.

Accordingly, each school within a district must abide by the district rules (which must include the state rules and may include additional district rules). By the time these rules get passed along to the individual school, the original laws have been enhanced by additions at the state department level and the district level. Most schools also add rules that apply specifically to their situations. Therefore, by the time the original law gets interpreted and translated through the various levels of school government, a great deal of encumbrance may have been added.

An urban district may have some rules different from those of a rural district because of the needs of the area. The student teacher can feel confident that a strong familiarity with the policies of the assigned school is a good foundation for the knowledge of any set of school policies in the region.

The student teacher should take advantage of the opportunity to become familiar with specific school rules relating to student behavior, parental interactions, governance of the school faculty, and school board issues that may affect the school, the faculty, or the community. One rule that can get student teachers in trouble if they're unaware of it is the rule on photographing or videotaping students without their parents' permission. Most school boards forbid any videotaping or photographing without the parents' written permission. This is a particularly serious case for the student teacher who has a digital camera and wishes to develop a home page on the Web for the class. Without written parental permission as to specific kinds of photo work, the student teacher would have a problem.

Occasionally, the student teacher may ask questions that receive a shake of the head or a shrug of the shoulders. It is important to know of whom to ask questions. If the student teacher's questions get a rebuff, no answer, or no satisfactory answer, the student teacher should ask the cooperating teacher. If the answer is still not clear, the student teacher should ask the university supervisor.

GUIDELINES FOR THE STUDENT TEACHER

- **Some of the most important materials to be read at the beginning of your student teaching assignment are policy handbooks, both of the individual school and of the school district.**
- **You should be aware that most elementary and secondary schools have developed school policy handbooks and student handbooks.** These books are distributed to each student the 1st day of school. Most students know the school rules, and they expect the student teacher to also know them.
- **As you read, make notes for future reference.**
- **Set priorities for your own use of those policies most applicable to you and your students.**
- **Ask your cooperating teacher about those policies that seem strange, unnecessary, or impractical.**
- **Policies may be a topic of conversation for the teachers' lounge, and the student teacher can profit from this provided he or she remains neutral.** Specific examples of situations offered by other teachers may cause the policies to be more easily remembered.
- **Interviews with the dean and the guidance counselor are profitable in terms of helping the student teacher apply policies and rules to particular situations.** This knowledge also assists the student teacher to see the practicality and usefulness of many of the policies.
- **Take care of district and school handbooks and return them to the right people at the appropriate time.** Your principal may have an extra copy of the school handbook so that you can have a personal permanent copy.
- **Situations may arise during the term in which the cooperating teacher and the student teacher must explain school policy to parents.** In some areas, the

district and school dress codes are routinely challenged by some parents and students, particularly in secondary school. It is important that you know the rules.

- **You will have opportunities to reinforce school regulations during discussions with students.** This is another reason to be thoroughly familiar with the policies.
- **If you visit with the cooperating teacher before the beginning of the term, try to read all available policy materials before student teaching begins.**

GUIDELINES FOR THE COOPERATING TEACHER

- **Most school administrators keep a copy of the district handbook in the school and give each teacher a copy of the new school handbook at the beginning of the school year.** Obtain a copy of the district handbook as well as a copy of the school handbook for the student teacher. If extra copies are not available, share your copies with the student teacher for use during the term.
- **As early in the student teaching assignment as possible, discuss at length with the student teacher those school policies that are most critical,** such as those concerning questions of legality and the health and safety of the individual students.
- **If it appears the policy manuals have not been studied, impress on the student teacher the need to do so.**
- **You may have the student teacher prepare a notebook with copies of procedures,** such as those for fire drills, checking out students, parents as visitors, caring for sick children, and escorting children off school grounds.
- **Test and double test your student teacher on knowledge of emergency procedures.** This may save a life.

CASE STUDIES

C   A   S   E

4-1   Edward, the new student teacher in Mrs. Schmidt's classroom, had appeared well-dressed each day for the 1st week of his student teaching assignment. Mrs. Schmidt had observed that Edward had begun associating with two of the male teachers who were usually not well-dressed and she was aware of their growing influence on him.

As Mrs. Schmidt expected, Edward appeared at school the 2nd week wearing clothes that were more casual and looking less well groomed.

1. What kinds of advice about this type of problem could Mrs. Schmidt have given Edward at the beginning of his 1st week of the assignment?
2. What action could Mrs. Schmidt take at this point?

3. How could her suggestions be seen by Edward as jealousy?
4. In what ways could Mrs. Schmidt enlist the help of the two male teachers?
5. Because this was not a breach of a particular school policy, should Mrs. Schmidt mention it to Edward at all?
6. To what extent should Mrs. Schmidt feel a responsibility for Edward's success after completing his work in her classroom?

C A S E

4-2   Denise, a first-grade student, suddenly became ill during the day and Cashay, the student teacher, called the child's mother to ask her to come get Denise and take her home. This occurred while the cooperating teacher was in the library working on a resource unit. The student teacher had suggested that Denise's mother drive her car right up to the door and Cashay would take Denise out to the car. The cooperating teacher arrived on the scene as Cashay was reentering the building and Denise and her mother were driving away.

1. What action should the cooperating teacher take?
2. What were the legal responsibilities of the cooperating teacher? Of Cashay?
3. How should the cooperating teacher discuss with Cashay the problem caused when she had allowed Denise to leave school without her mother's signature on the sign-out pad and without a note?
4. Should the cooperating teacher bring this to the attention of the principal? Are there legal requirements that she do so? If so, what?
5. How effective would it be to have the mother return the following day and document the sign-out sheet?

C A S E

4-3   Beverly, the new English student teacher, was working with the yearbook staff and discovered that ad sales were not completed. She invited four seniors on the yearbook advertisement sales staff to work on ad sales during her planning period; the students were to accompany her in her automobile. Beverly had excused herself from the cooperating teacher by saying she had some work that needed to be done that period. Her trip with the students did pay off in five ad sales but the cooperating teacher discovered that all four students had left school without permission.

1. How should the cooperating teacher approach Beverly?
2. How severe is this infraction of school policy?
3. Should the university supervisor be called?
4. Should the parents of the four students be involved?
5. What action do you think the principal will take?

C A S E

4-4   During the 10-minute break following lunch for his students, Russell rested in the faculty lounge before reporting to his newly assigned student teaching classroom. As he listened to other teachers discuss school policies relative to teachers' hours, he became aware that a number of the teachers did not observe school regulations but instead seemed to come and go from the campus at their leisure during their planning period and immediately after school was out.

It seemed to Russell as if some of these faculty members arrived barely in time to get to their classrooms ahead of the students. Russell realized that he must have had a puzzled look on his face because one of the teachers leaned over to him and said quietly, "They just use the east entrance and don't go through the front door."

After rest time was over, Russell returned to his class of 10th-grade biology students. During class, he began thinking of errands he might be able to take care of during the school day by leaving school for only a few minutes each day or immediately after school.

1. What responsibility does Russell have to stay at school during school hours?
2. What options does he have if he wants to run those errands during the school day?
3. As a student teacher, how would he be expected to maintain school policy?
4. How should the cooperating teacher handle this situation?
5. What are the best sources of advice relative to school policy during student teaching?

C A S E

4-5   Brian enjoyed student teaching in Mrs. Hargroves's chemistry class. He was an intelligent young man and the college was proud of his record. He felt that every problem could be handled in a logical, rational method. As Brian became more and more acquainted with school policy, he felt that some of the policies were outdated or inappropriate, and his expressions of his opinion were not always to people who understood that he was a developing professional and had not yet learned levels of discretion.

1. How should Mrs. Hargroves approach this situation?
2. How can Brian be led to understand the need for established school policy and his responsibility to the school board?
3. To what extent should the administration of the school be involved in this situation with Brian?
4. Could an informational discussion with the assistant principal be of any help to Brian? What kinds of things should the assistant principal discuss?
5. What assistance can the university supervisor give to the cooperating teacher? To Brian?

RECOMMENDED READING

Glasser, W. (1990). Building a friendly workplace. In *The quality school: Managing students without coercion* (pp. 122–133). New York: Harper & Row. *Glasser discusses control theory in terms of rules. He advocates few rules, nonadversarial rules, and the use of student-developed rules. This is helpful reading for the student teacher.*

Greene, M. (1989). Social and political contexts. In M. C. Reynolds (Ed.), *Knowledge base for the beginning teacher* (pp. 143–154). New York: Pergamon Press. *Cooperating teachers may find this material valuable to share with student teachers in view of understanding the social and political contexts of schooling, policies, and rules. This material is helpful for the advanced student teacher or the graduate student with an in-depth background in the sociological foundations of education.*

Hevener, F., Jr. (1981). Learning the community and school. In *Successful student teaching: A handbook for elementary and secondary student teachers* (pp. 18–23). Palo Alto, CA: R.&E. Research Associates. *In this chapter, Hevener stresses the importance of getting to the student teaching placement site early by arranging a preteaching conference with the cooperating teacher. He emphasizes such details as learning the bell schedule, referral procedures, nonteaching responsibilities, and information about the faculty and department meetings.*

Lunenburg, F., & Ornstein, A. C. (1991). Local school districts. In *Educational administration: Concepts and practices*. Belmont, CA: Wadsworth. *The authors give a good overview of state and local policy and the implementation of school policy by the local school superintendents and school boards. Although this text is written for those pursuing administrative careers, it gives the cooperating teacher and the student teacher an opportunity to discuss the implications of local school district activities.*

McCarty, D. J. (1989). The school district: A unique setting. In M. C. Reynolds (Ed.), *Knowledge base for the beginning teacher* (pp. 155–162). New York: Pergamon Press. *This material carefully explains the power structure in typical school districts, the governance and management of schooling within the district, and the impact of the school district itself on what happens in the classroom. The rules and policies under which a student teacher works are developed through the community power structures, political pressures, administrators, and unions.*

5

Discovering School Referral Services

The size of the school district, not the size of the school, normally determines the number and kinds of referral services available to students. Most referral services fall within the categories of physical and mental health support, although social services (family and economic) are usually available also. School policy frequently dictates that actual referrals are made by only one school official, usually the principal, on recommendation of the guidance counselor. It is critical for the student teacher to be aware of what is available so that as indications of needs become apparent, such needs can be relayed to the appropriate school authority after discussion with the cooperating teacher.

The guidance departments of various schools offer a variety of services to children and youth. The student teacher should be informed of the services available through this department. Although the variety of services available depends on the financial capability of the school district and the cooperativeness of local public health officials, most students can receive help when needed. Sometimes such help is the result of the action of the individual teacher searching for free services available for the student when parents are unable to pay.

In addition to the school district offering services, communities frequently offer assistance through Community Mental Health, Pregnancy Consultation Services, and the Division of Youth Services. Some schools have school nurses, and the student teacher, with the consent of the cooperating teacher, can make an immediate referral when needed. When students are aware of the availability of a school nurse, the students themselves sometimes ask for a pass to see the nurse. If a student frequently requests this service, the student teacher should consult with the school nurse regarding the nature of the student's problem. Follow-up evaluation sheets also provide this information.

Smaller schools may share a school nurse, and some schools have the services of only a county or parish health department nurse. Schools may maintain an infirmary, usually consisting of a cot or two where students who are ill can be made comfortable with some isolation while waiting for someone to pick them up from school.

Under no condition should a student teacher administer medication to a student. If it is necessary for a student to take medication during school hours, the school nurse or the person legally designated by the principal is the appropriate person to dispense medication. This ruling applies to all medication, including aspirin, as some students are allergic to aspirin. With regard to students with health problems or physical impairment, the student teacher needs to understand the following three strategies:

1. Consider the safety of these students first.
2. All medication should be administered by the school nurse. In the event there is no school nurse available, the office of the principal is the only entity that has the legal right to administer medication to a student.
3. Become aware of referral agencies that can assist the student. Work with the cooperating teacher on this.

All teachers and student teachers should be aware of the nature of acquired immune deficiency syndrome (AIDS) or any other communicable disease. They should obtain the most recent statistical data from the local city, county, or parish health department. Students, teachers, administrators, or student teachers may have AIDS and should never be discriminated against because of having this condition, just as one would not discriminate against a person who had a broken arm. AIDS cases in schools are usually identified to the principal only; no one else in the school except for the school nurse has the legal right to know which students have AIDS. It is the responsibility of the principal to determine who, if anyone, in that school has a need to know such information.

Health department officials have indicated to classroom teachers that every individual with whom a person works in the public sector should be treated as if that individual had AIDS. This attitude avoids discrimination. With very young children who bite, or with students who are injured in the biology lab or in physical education class, the student teacher may question how to handle the flow of blood or other body fluids. This text cannot be completely prescriptive in this matter; however, it is important that student teachers be aware of the most current and realistic information available.

Family problems of students is another area of concern to the student teacher. Traumatic experiences in their family life can affect the performance of students in the classroom to a great extent. The student teacher should be aware of such possibilities and develop special patience and consideration for those students whose home life is in upheaval. Frequently, such students need special counseling. The student teacher should work very closely with the cooperating teacher in such instances; care should be taken to remain objective yet kind and supportive. Students can have life-altering experiences and sometimes have no one but a teacher with whom to discuss their problems. Experiences such as a death or separation in the family, being witness to an accident or a crime, being a victim of crime, being a victim of abuse in the home, or poverty can permanently damage a student's self-image and ability to work successfully at school. Within the range recommended by the cooperating teacher, the student teacher may effect a change for the positive in the life of a student.

For those chronic cases needing medical attention but not sufficiently acute to send immediately to the school nurse, the student teacher should discuss the history of the case and the current situation with the cooperating teacher and with the school nurse. The nurse may make the appropriate referral to a doctor.

Referrals for dental needs are sometimes more difficult to discover. Unexplained changes in behavior, a droopy head, unusual grouchiness, and general inattentiveness may indicate some otherwise hidden dental-related pain or illness.

Mental health problems are usually handled differently. The student teacher should discuss the situation with the cooperating teacher and with the guidance counselor. If the school has no guidance counselor, the situation should be discussed with the principal or the designated faculty member in charge of student services. That person will help the teacher deal with the problem and may aid in referring the situation to a district psychologist or area psychiatrist. Keeping a daily log of the behavior of the student helps in explaining the problem to the referral professional. Such a record is frequently required to initiate a referral to a psychologist.

Children with special needs are often dependent on the skill of the regular classroom teacher in identifying their problems, developing the necessary remediation, and initiating a referral for assistance.

Another important topic that should be discussed with the student teacher is that of child abuse and how to recognize it. Some have a broad knowledge about signs of such abuse; others know very little about such things. Suspected abuse victims must be referred to the proper authorities.

Students with economic needs frequently appear in some schools and almost never appear in others. The student teacher should discuss with the cooperating teacher such cases. In one school, a second grader never wore shoes to school and claimed that he had none. Arrangements were made to purchase a pair of shoes for the boy. Faithfully, the boy thereafter carried his shoes to school in his arms every morning and took them home again in the afternoon, all the while remaining barefoot. Such a case is an illustration of the need for follow-through by the referral agency.

Some students are irritable and disgruntled in class because they are hungry. Free lunch programs and food stamps for the families of such students should be investigated. Frequently, local churches maintain clothes closets, and the student who has insufficient clothes can go or be taken there for fitting. Student teachers must sometimes deal with family pride, and when suggesting referrals for economic services, this family pride as well as the pride of the student must be handled carefully and discreetly.

GUIDELINES FOR THE STUDENT TEACHER

- **Read all school and district policies concerning referrals of kind.** Discuss them with your cooperating teacher. You may remember cases from your own school days and how critical such referrals can be to students.

- **Discussing problems with other professionals helps place these problems in the right perspective.**
- **Any classroom management problems or any changes in student behavior should be investigated as potential health concerns or economic needs.**
- **Be especially alert to the needs of the students who are sleepy and lethargic,** are quiet and afraid to speak, suddenly exhibit erratic behavior, or seem to find concentration difficult.
- **Discretion is paramount.** The student teacher should never discuss any referral in the presence of other students or uninvolved faculty.
- **Be aware of information of health or learning problems available in the students' cumulative folders.**
- **The school nurse can offer materials that help you recognize particular symptoms and needs, including those related to prescribed medication as well as covert drug usage.**
- **Discuss with the school nurse the appropriate first aid measures expected of you in the classroom.**
- **Although you may have no need during student teaching,** find from your cooperating teacher the appropriate referral action and similar advocate agencies for child abuse.
- **One of the best resources in discovering school referral services can be the cooperating teacher.**

GUIDELINES FOR THE COOPERATING TEACHER

- **Use wisdom and experience in deciding just how much information you wish to disclose immediately to your student teacher about your students and their needs.** The student teacher will be concerned with those cases occurring during the term.
- **If the student teacher is not sufficiently perceptive to notice situations as they develop in the classroom among the students, point out those situations.** The student in the class is the top priority in student teaching, and occasionally the cooperating teacher must intervene to avoid problems for the students.
- **Help the student teacher to understand that teachers are to be patient** and should not become discouraged over the amount of paperwork and red tape involved in obtaining services for a child.
- **Explain to your student teacher the backgrounds of the children with special needs in your classroom.** Your student teacher might have taken a course or courses dealing with special-needs students but some student teachers are completely unaware of this element.
- **Introduce your student teacher to the guidance department, making sure to include contact with a guidance counselor.**

- **Discuss with your student teacher your experiences with abused an/or neglected children,** a topic that is very much on the minds of all teachers today.

CASE STUDIES

C A S E **5-1** Eloise, a 10th grader, has missed English class for 4 days with alleged health problems. On checking with Eloise's other teachers, the English student teacher discovered that Eloise has reported to other classes with no problems.

1. What could cause the student to miss this class so frequently?
2. What action should the student teacher take?
3. What should be the advice and actions of the coordinating teacher?
4. Whose responsibility is it to contact the parents?
5. How could a 10th grader miss these classes undetected by school staff?

C A S E **5-2** George is a high school senior who appears to mix well with his peers. He is rather quiet and seldom speaks. His grades are barely average, although his written work is consistently turned in on time. He is a clean, well-groomed student who listens attentively and appears to understand. The student teacher is warned by the cooperating teacher not to call on George in class because of his stuttering.

1. Should the student teacher do nothing and just concentrate on getting written answers from George?
2. In what way can the guidance counselor help the student teacher?
3. What would be the advantage or disadvantage of bringing up the subject of George in the teachers' lounge?
4. What are some appropriate actions for the student teacher?
5. How do you think George feels about never being called on?

C A S E **5-3** Donald, a fourth grader, is smaller than most of his classmates and he never seems to have much energy. Mornings he seems cranky and weak and watches the clock until lunchtime. He receives free lunches which he devours immediately and gets large second helpings from the cafeteria staff. After lunch, he is sleepy in class and seems to get revived about the time school is out.

1. Have you observed similar situations in your previous experiences? Explain.
2. How should the student teacher approach Donald's problem?
3. What role should the cooperating teacher play, considering the fact that this situation existed prior to the arrival of the student teacher?

4. What other individuals should be involved in the solution to Donald's problem?
5. Who should be involved in a home visit in this case?

C A S E

5-4   Cheryl, a first-grade girl from a middle-class home, was always vivacious and alert to classroom happenings until the morning she came in and confided to the student teacher that she was afraid to go home that day because her stepfather had threatened to beat her up the next time he saw her.

The student teacher discreetly mentioned this to the cooperating teacher, who replied that Cheryl had told her about such threats before. Because the stepfather was on the school board, the teacher had not mentioned it for fear of making him upset with the school and of losing her job.

1. Would it be wise or unwise to ignore the cooperating teacher's advice? Explain.
2. Should the university supervisor be involved?
3. What actions should the student teacher take to protect Cheryl from violence and further threats?
4. How could the cooperating teacher be more professional in this case?
5. The fact that Cheryl brought this matter to the student teacher tells us what about this situation?

C A S E

5-5   Student teaching in middle school geography was a happy experience for Molly who enjoyed her students, her subject, and even working with her cooperating teacher.

She was floored one day when one of the girls in her eight-grade class came up to her privately and asked for help. Assuring the student that she would try to help, Molly prepared to listen patiently. The student proceeded to explain that she thought she might be pregnant and did not know what to do, where to go, or with whom to talk. This was not a situation Molly had been trained to deal with and she was momentarily at a loss for a response.

1. What should be Molly's first response to the student?
2. How much of the conversation with the student should Molly share with the cooperating teacher?
3. What recommendations should Molly make to the student?
4. How should Molly implement a school referral? Through whom? To what agency?
5. Should Molly attempt any type of follow-up of this situation? Why?
6. In what way do you think Molly's university experience could have prepared her for this situation?

C A S E

5-6   Salina was the new student teacher in 10th-grade typing. Her cooperating teacher, Ms. Joseph, was an outstanding teacher and a good professional role model.

Salina felt privileged to be student teaching with her. Ms. Joseph's son Kevin was a senior in the same school and had older friends who were also friends of Salina's. Salina was aware of Kevin's increasing involvement in a drug ring within the school; however, she did not want to broach the subject with Ms. Joseph for fear of ruining her student teaching situation. She was aware that in the past Ms. Joseph had refused to believe reports of Kevin's activities in such matters.

1. As a professional person, what is Salina's responsibility in this situation?
2. Should Salina wait until her student teaching is completed and then try to discuss this with Ms. Joseph?
3. Should she discuss the alleged situation with the administration? With the dean?
4. How productive would a conversation with Kevin probably be?
5. How could the university supervisor be instrumental in assisting Salina?

RECOMMENDED READING

Ballast, D. L., & Shoemaker, R. L. (1978). Getting started: An action approach. In *Guidance program development* pp. 8–21. Springfield, IL: Charles C. Thomas. *This material speaks to the special needs that students may have and how students may be served through the guidance office. In the cases in which students have needs that extend beyond the school, it is the guidance office that makes referrals to the community agencies.*

Fennimore, B. S. (1989). *Child advocacy for early childhood educators.* New York: Teachers College Press. *The early childhood student teacher is beginning a career closely related to child advocacy. Through reading Fennimore's work, the student teacher can become more attuned to the possibilities for the need for and location of referral services for students in the classroom.*

Foster, C. R., Fitzgerald, P. W., & Beal, R. M. (1980). Collaboration of teachers and counselors. In *Modern guidance practices in teaching* (pp. 110–131). Springfield, IL: Charles C. Thomas. *The role of the counselor and the potential for collaboration by the counselor and the teacher are stressed. Of special appeal to the student teacher is the list of and the discussion about*

ways in which the counselor can help with student problems in addition to the counselor services to teachers and staff.

Guthrie, L. (1996). *How to coordinate services for students and families.* Alexandria, VA: Association for Supervision and Curriculum Development. *This concise text gives a nine-step plan for working with community and government agencies.*

Maher, C. A., & Zins, J. E. (Eds.). (1987). *Psychoeducational interventions in the schools: Methods and procedures for enhancing student competence.* New York: Pergamon Press. *This material gives an in-depth look at some of the intervention techniques now in use and assists the student teacher in understanding the current alternatives.*

Sandoval, J. (Ed.). (1988). *Crises counseling, intervention, and prevention in the schools.* Hillsdale, NJ: Lawrence Erlbaum Associates. *This book is not to be totally digested by the student teacher because of its in-depth treatment of the subject. However, a review of the kinds of problems that exist aids in recognizing them and discussing referrals with the cooperating teacher. Childhood and adolescence crises that are discussed include maltreatment, illness, death, parenthood, homosexuality, and suicide.*

Observations

Students have been observing in their own classrooms since kindergarten days. Now, in student teaching, classroom observations take on more significance.

In most student teaching situations, the student teacher is required to observe for a time in the teaching assignment as well as in the classrooms of other teachers. It is inappropriate for the student teacher to expect to be ushered into the "best" teacher's classroom to observe; all teachers have some strong points and as many teachers as possible should be observed.

Arrangement can be made by the cooperating teacher for the student teacher to observe in classrooms throughout the school. It is not necessary for student teachers to observe only those subjects they are prepared to teach, and it is advantageous for the student teacher to observe in classrooms of different subjects and different ages in order to maintain an objective assessment of the classroom situation. A physical education student teacher, for example, can profit from observing English, history, or music classes.

An elementary student teacher can easily observe a number of elementary teachers in their classrooms. A secondary student teacher can follow the daily schedule of a single student, noting interpersonal interactions.

The student teacher has two primary things to keep in mind when planning observations. One is the schedule of observations; the student teacher should arrange this with the cooperating teacher. The second is to determine ahead of time what to look for in the individual classrooms.

To make the observation more effective, the cooperating teacher can indicate beforehand strong points of the teacher being observed. Student teachers should be aware of a great deal more that is going on in the classroom than what they may be actually watching.

When initiating observations, the student teacher is encouraged to keep in mind that this is a professional colleague that he or she is observing, to treat the observed teacher with professionalism, and to keep the observation itself confidential. If meeting these teachers for observation purposes causes the student teacher to be nervous, the student teacher may want to role play an introductory conversation and a final conversation with a friend so that he or she will be comfortable when the time comes.

Students sometimes think that teachers have eyes in the back of their heads. This is a trait that teachers must learn. Through peripheral vision or through sound cues learned from various students, teachers can know what is happening in the back of the room even when they are not looking in that direction. Observing other teachers aids in developing this trait.

Other kinds of information that the student teacher wants to glean from observation include the kind of interaction that goes on in the classroom. There are student-student interactions, student-teacher interactions, and probably teacher-other person interactions. If a teacher's aide is in the classroom, there is another set of configurations of interactions. Communication patterns among people in the classroom are also worth noting, although they vary with each teacher.

The student teacher should be aware that these are not just person-to-person interactions but are a different configuration each time. Student teachers should be able to adjust to the intensity of an interaction on the part both of the student and of the teacher (or whoever the involved parties happen to be). Most student teachers are relatively new at dealing directly with students. They dealt with students when they were students, but this assignment is a different relationship.

Another important awareness is the physical logistics of a classroom, such as the management of the physical objects in the room. This refers to such things as the arrangement of the desks, the seating of the students, and the lighting in the room. The student teacher should be aware of such things as the teacher's movement throughout the room. If the teacher stands with his or her back to a window, students have to look into a glare, and all they can see is the silhouette of the teacher. The student teacher should be aware of such things as the following:

1. The location of the pencil sharpener.
2. The order that the teacher has for the students to go to sharpen their pencils. (Is there any order?)
3. The location of the trash basket. (Is it located so that it is in full view for students to pitch toward? Or is it located in some less accessible place so that a student cannot make such a display?)
4. The location of the teacher's desk in relation to the students' desks. The location of the teacher's desk in relation to the doorway.
5. The kind of ventilating system. (Is the room too hot or too cold?)
6. The mechanics of opening and closing the windows. Methods of adjusting the blinds.
7. Adjustment of the lighting.
8. The amount of free movement allowed in the room.

The observer should be intent on finding how these things are regulated. Does the teacher come in first thing in the morning and adjust everything and put it out of mind until the end of the day? What may seem to be minor details are important. Because the students expect routine to remain the same when the student teacher takes over, classroom detail is important to observe and keep in mind. One activity to note is the method used for turning in papers. Does each student take his or her paper up to the teacher's desk so that on the return trip the student has an opportunity to visit other students at their desks? Or are all the papers passed up at one time in an orderly fashion, either directly to the front or directly to the side and then to the front? Is there a pattern? Are there patterns throughout the classroom activity that students know and can depend on, or does it appear to an observer that the students are confused as to which way to turn? In other words, are there established procedures in the classroom?

Another major area in classroom management that the student teacher should be aware of during observations is the emotional climate and styles of rapport in the classroom. How are these managed? How much stress is evident? Are the students hostile toward the teacher? Is the teacher hostile toward the students? Is either irate with the other? Is either frustrated? Do the students seem to help each other in terms of calming each other? Are the students calmed by the teacher? Does the teacher seem to be trusting the students to behave? Is there an air of tranquility or an air of tenseness? How does the teacher calm an upset student? What methods does the teacher use to quiet the class? Presence of a positive emotional climate is evidence of good classroom management, of trust on the part of the students, and frequently of a great deal of faith on the part of the teacher. The cooperating teacher and the student teacher should discuss this in detail.

The student teacher should note the routine maintenance of the room (cleaning of chalkboard, the erasers, the floor). It is important for the novice teacher to realize that students feel a sense of belonging in the room they help maintain, decorate, and care for.

GUIDELINES FOR THE STUDENT TEACHER

- **Observation in the classrooms of other teachers should be planned for maximum benefit to you and minimum concern and bother to your host teachers.**
- **One of the things that most student teachers are concerned with is getting along with students.** As you go from one classroom to another, observe how one teacher gets along with students and mentally compare this with how other teachers get along with students.
- **Try to develop a list of qualities that seem to make one teacher able to appropriately manage the classroom or an individual student.** Notice those qualities that may not be positive. You should mentally file these qualities and never discuss them in terms of personalities.
- **The student teacher should not discuss with the cooperating teacher the fact that Mrs. Z, the next-door teacher, does certain activities that really bomb.** The cooperating teacher may be teaching next door to Mrs. Z for a number of years and such discussions are not appropriate. It is acceptable to discuss particular qualities but do not identify them with any personality.

- **When appropriate, take detailed notes during your observations and record questions.** There may be some activities that you discover while observing that you wish to pursue further, and this is an excellent time to expand your general teaching repertory.
- **Be careful during observations to avoid disturbing those classes you have been allowed to observe.** If you have questions, ask them later, not during the class time of your host teacher. Melt into the classroom environment. Slip into a chair by the door. Avoid moving about if the students are not doing so.
- **For optimal benefit from the observations, a list of objectives of the observation should be discussed with the cooperating teacher, both before and after the observations.**
- **Of major importance in your developing professional reputation is your gratitude.** After the observation, leave the room without disturbing the class but make a point of seeing that teacher before leaving school at the end of the day to thank him or her for allowing you to observe in his or her classroom. Interpersonal relations are very important. You may wish to comment favorably about something you observed.

GUIDELINES FOR THE COOPERATING TEACHER

- **It gives your student teacher self-confidence to see that teachers really have many of the same questions the student teacher has.** At times, student teachers may feel that they alone face classroom problems. They may think, "These are problems only to me. I'm the only person in the world faced with these anxieties. How am I going to get this material across? How will I plan? How will I evaluate? How will I live with all of these people in this classroom?" When student teachers know that all teachers have faced these uncertainties and periodically ask themselves most of these questions again and again throughout their teaching careers, they gain self-confidence. They see how other teachers deal with such questions even if they cannot answer them all.
- **It is the responsibility of the cooperating teacher to establish an observation schedule.** It is wise to plan no more than 1 hour or, in the secondary school, 1 class period at a time. It might be beneficial for the student teacher to observe Mrs. X at one time today and at a different time tomorrow, not two times in the same day.
- **If the student teacher is observing subjects such as English or math, try to develop a schedule that has variety.**
- **If the student teacher is observing in the elementary grades and if there is a junior high or middle school nearby,** it is beneficial if there could be some observation in those levels, not of extended length but enough to know what these students are like after leaving your classes. The student teacher may have observed in such classes during his or her college training.

- **Planning for observations should be done with specific purposes in the minds of both the cooperating teacher and the student teacher.** Arrangements should be made by the cooperating teacher ahead of time so that the student teacher does not appear unannounced in Mrs. X's classroom and say to Mrs. X: "I'm here!" Although Mrs. X and the cooperating teacher may be very good friends, this type of situation is not to be imposed on friendship.

CASE STUDIES

C A S E

6-1   Steve was the new student teacher in Coach Mills' ninth-grade physical education class. Prior to the beginning of the term, Coach Mills had made arrangements for Steve to observe in several classes taught by the other three physical education teachers. The third day of the term, Coach Mills was in his office when in stormed his fellow teacher Mrs. Batley with: "Get that brat out of my class!"

As Coach attempted to calm his colleague, Mrs. Batley explained that as Steve was observing her class just now in basketball exercises, she had her back to the class for a moment and the next thing she knew, Steve was on the court demonstrating trick shots and pretending to be a big-league basketball star. She had requested that Steve get off the court and Steve had responded with: "In just a minute. They need to see this one super shot."

As Mrs. Batley seethed, Coach Mills's mind raced:

1. Had he done the wrong thing accepting a student teacher?
2. Why had the college not warned him about Steve?
3. What could he do?
   a. immediately
   b. during the next several days
4. What other arrangements for observations, if any, should he make for Steve?
5. What specific recommendations should Coach Mills give Steve prior to any future observations?

C A S E

6-2   Rose had been scheduled by her cooperating teacher to observe in one classroom for reading from 8:30 until 9:15 and in another classroom for math from 9:25 until 10:00. The second teacher approached the supervising teacher at lunch and asked about Rose. The cooperating teacher investigated and found that Rose had made the first scheduled observation but had then gone to the teachers' lounge and had become engrossed in conversation and was not aware of the passage of time. At 9:45, Rose had suddenly remembered her second appointment but decided not to go into that teacher's classroom late. She had remained in the lounge until 10:10 and then returned to the classroom of her cooperating teacher, not telling her what had happened. The cooperating teacher felt disappointed and perplexed.

1. How could she explain to the student teacher exactly how she felt?
2. Should she trust the student teacher a second time?
3. How would she know it would be safe to trust her?
4. How should this be explained to the teacher whose observation was missed?
5. What points should the university supervisor make in his discussion with Rose about the importance of keeping professional appointments?

C A S E

6-3   Mary was student teaching with Ms. Ness, the senior English teacher. Mary gave an impression of being very professional and very interested in every teacher she observed. She took notes during her observations and commented to each teacher that she wanted to teach just the same way. She seemed sincere in her compliments but when Mr. Scott and Ms. Jones, two English teachers with methods diametrically opposed, accosted each other in the teachers' lounge with the statement Mary had made during her visit with each of them, both they and the other teachers in the lounge were able to see the artificiality in Mary's compliments. This was called to the attention of the department chairman who in turn talked with Ms. Ness.

1. How could Ms. Ness help Mary to repair her professional reputation in the school?
2. What was Mary's responsibility in resolving the problem?
3. How could the English teachers as a group turn this situation around to help Mary develop as a better teacher and more professional person?
4. Because of the psychological nature of this behavior, how could the college counseling service be of assistance to Mary?
5. On what basis should Mary continue with her scheduled observations?

C A S E

6-4   Bert, the new kindergarten student teacher, was completing his 5th day at school when he was approached by one of the teachers he had observed 2 days prior. Somehow, he knew immediately from the gleam in and squint of her eyes what had happened.

The events of the previous afternoon in the grocery store raced through his mind. Yes, he had run into a friend of his older sister and he had discussed this particular teacher and what, in his opinion, was inappropriate handling of the friend's child. Bert gulped and gathered his courage as the teacher approached.

1. How could Bert have avoided this?
2. What will the content of this conversation likely be?
3. What options does Bert have to regain the respect of this teacher?

4. How would you react if you were Bert's cooperating teacher and had arranged the observation?
5. What is a good rule to keep in mind relative to discussing student problems in public?

6-5   Avra happily anticipated her teaching career and was excited about student teaching. Her cooperating teacher had established an observation schedule in other teachers' classrooms at the beginning of the term. Although Avra was to be working with high school students as a career, she had not gotten over being a shy young woman. Her cooperating teacher recognized this difficulty but had failed to communicate it to those teachers with whom she had set up the observation schedule.

As Avra visited her scheduled observations, she became more and more aware that her host teachers were expecting more reaction from her than she was exhibiting. She was quite embarrassed when one of the teachers asked her a question during his class. Not wanting to speak out, she sat there and just shook her head from side to side. The teacher went on with the class and after a few moments, Avra rose quietly and slipped out of the room.

1. Was it inappropriate for the teacher to ask Avra questions?
2. What do you think Avra did when she returned to her own classroom?
3. In the discussion later between the cooperating teacher and the teacher Avra was visiting, what might have been said?
4. What effect does Avra's shyness have on the students she will be teaching?
5. What positive approach should the cooperating teacher take?

6-6   Middle school home economics students welcomed Jan to observe their class as she began her student teaching assignment in another classroom in their school. Jan's eagerness was almost overwhelming to the teacher whose class was being observed.

During the lecture portion of the period, Jan had furiously taken notes. Later, during the lab time, Jan had proceeded to discuss their projects with several students individually. This hindered the class somewhat, but the teacher had agreed for Jan to observe.

1. Should the teacher allow this procedure to continue?
2. What steps should the teacher take?
3. Should the cooperating teacher be told how disruptive Jan had become in class? How could this be remedied?
4. How could the cooperating teacher assist Jan in becoming more discreet in her data gathering?
5. What steps could the university supervisor take to give Jan positive assistance in this situation?

RECOMMENDED READING

Balch, P. M., & Balch, P. E. (1987). Becoming an effective observer. In *The cooperating teacher: A practical approach for the supervision of student teachers* (pp. 85–106). New York: University Press of America. *Guidelines are given to help the student teacher focus observation activity and recognize effective teaching; checklists are provided. Flanders' Interaction Analysis and a set of questioning skills using Bloom's taxonomy are illustrated.*

Borich, G. D. (1999). *Observing skills for effective teaching* (3rd ed.). Upper Saddle River, NJ: Merrill/Prentice Hall. *Offering competencies in observation for preservice and first-year teachers, this text includes those skills in the areas of learning climate, classroom management, lesson clarity, instructional variety, task orientation, student engagement, student success, and higher thought processes.*

Cohen, L., & Manion, L. (1983). Watching how others make lessons "happen." In *A guide to teaching practice* (pp. 106–112). New York: Methuen & Company. *This brief reading assists the student teacher in learning how to observe effectively. Relating the contents of the classroom and their relationship to the lesson are sometimes overlooked in an observation design. Twelve questions form a good review for observing motivation.*

Duke, D. L. (1990). Making sense of the teacher's world. In *Teaching: An introduction* (pp. 37–61). New York: McGraw-Hill. *This chapter is an important one for the new student teacher in that it assists the student teacher in learning how to identify by observating good teaching practices in the classroom. Hints on conducting an observation, what to look for, how to pinpoint the identification of classroom activity, and potential assistance from theory and research in the other social sciences are included in this material.*

Good, T. L., & Brophy, J. E. (1991). Observing in classrooms. In *Looking in classrooms* (5th ed.) (pp. 47–109). New York: HarperCollins. *The authors present an extensive survey of coding methods for classroom observations. Information is provided on the Brophy-Good Dyadic Interaction System, the Emmer Observation System, the coding vocabulary of Blumenfeld and Miller, and educational ethnography. Although advanced, this material can be introduced to the student teacher by the cooperating teacher at useful times.*

Peters, K., & March, J. K. (1999). *Collaborative observation: Putting classroom instruction at the center of school reform.* Thousand Oaks, CA: Corwin Press. *To improve student performance and assist in the professional development of teachers, the authors propose collaborative observation to serve as a major change catalyst for school improvement.*

Roe, B., & Ross, E. P. (1998). Getting ready. In *Student teaching and field experiences handbook* (4th ed.). (pp. 1–29). Upper Saddle River, NJ: Merrill/Prentice Hall. *In this chapter, the authors offer a succinct set of recommendations for the student teacher to note in observing the classroom teacher, indicating the difference between an onlooker and an observer.*

Wiggins, S. P. (1957). Observing, assisting, and teaching. In *The student teacher in action* (pp. 119–138). Boston: Allyn & Bacon. *Although this material was printed a number of years ago, the content remains important and timely. Wiggins discusses what and how the student teacher should observe; he uses lists and specific steps as the student teacher proceeds through the stages of increasing involvement in the assignment.*

Evaluation of the Student Teacher

Paranoia is sometimes a condition of student teaching that develops when the student teacher feels that everyone is watching. What the student teacher does not realize is that very few of these people watching are in a position to evaluate the student teacher. Students are watching, but they are interested only in what is done to them. Parents of students are watching but they usually cannot evaluate the student teacher; they only hope the student teacher helps their child. Teachers down the hall are watching, but they observe only surface activities. The principal is watching, but the student teacher should be aware that the principal is observing many other teachers and that the relationship with the student teacher is only one of many responsibilities. The department or grade chairperson may also be watching. These people depend on the cooperating teacher for basic information before expressing professional opinions about the student teacher.

Two major participants remain in the student teacher's world: the cooperating teacher and the university supervisor. Both of these individuals should be involved with the student teacher in evaluating progress throughout the term. The student teacher should expect to sit down with the university supervisor and the cooperating teacher at the beginning of the term to review any standard evaluation forms (see Appendix B for a sample evaluation form) and to discuss those criteria for successful completion of student teaching. It is not sufficient for the student teacher to be told, "Just go in there and do a good job. I know you'll do fine!" This is the point in their careers that student teachers can feel lost. Even an effervescent, enthusiastic student teacher is probably hiding a multitude of fears about pending evaluations. Direction at this stage of the professional training is imperative for the student teacher. Responsibilities should be explicitly pointed out.

One method of approaching the initial evaluation conference is for the university supervisor, the cooperating teacher, or both to outline the evaluation materials to be handled during the term by all concerned. Frequently, both the university and the school district require midterm and final evaluation forms completed by the cooperating teacher.

Discussing these point by point aids both the student teacher and the cooperating teacher to bring out related aspects of the student teacher's responsibility that should be considered. Most universities expect the cooperating teacher to submit a midterm evaluation, which can serve as good discussion material, both at the beginning of the term and at the time the evaluation is being completed for turning in to the student teaching office.

The university supervisor has a different sequence of evaluations to complete. In many programs, the university supervisor routinely completes an observation sheet each time visits are made to the student teacher. Arrangements should be made for the cooperating teacher and the student teacher to be given copies of these periodic evaluations. Usually, general topics such as professional manner, classroom management, lesson preparation, and presentation ability are cited on these observation report forms; of course, space is usually provided for any narrative comments of the university supervisor. It is a great advantage to the student teacher to discuss this report with the university supervisor following the observation.

A final evaluation by the university supervisor is expected. This report includes a rating of the student teacher on specific teacher qualities and a comprehensive assessment by the university supervisor of the probability of success of the student teacher as a teacher.

Probably the most important reference for the student teacher is done by the cooperating teacher. This is the main reference that hiring officials want to see before offering employment to a beginning teacher. They know that the cooperating teacher knows the student teacher best of all because he or she has been the main evaluator during the student teaching experience.

It is most important that the student teacher have a positive attitude about evaluation. A few find it very difficult to accept criticism. This is a very immature response. One of the major purposes of student teaching is growth in teaching competencies, and this cannot take place without constructive criticism. Most student teachers want feedback.

One important part of the evaluation of student teachers is their ability to handle the evaluation of the students in their classes. The interest shown and ability to work with grading procedures, student progress folders, and other aspects of student evaluation are true indicators of teaching potential.

The cumulative record for the student teaching experience is the portfolio. A copy of all observation records and all evaluations should be included in the portfolio. Examples of unit and lesson development, tests developed, photographs of bulletin boards, and evaluative and assessment measures that the student teacher has used during the semester should be included. An easy, methodical way to develop this portfolio is to add to it daily, including materials that the student teacher may even doubt should be included. Having too much is better than not having enough. At the end of each week, the student teacher can review what has been added that week and sort through for "keepers." At the end of the semester, the student teacher's portfolio will hold ample evidence of the student teacher's performance in the classroom. An ideal summary for the student teacher's portfolio is a video of her or him teaching a lesson; care must be taken not to include the students in the video, only the teacher.

GUIDELINES FOR THE STUDENT TEACHER

- **You are student teaching to learn how to teach.** Your competence as a teacher is expected to grow as your experience grows.
- **Welcome evaluations from your cooperating teacher as you daily strive to develop appropriate teaching competencies in your classroom.**
- **Spend as much time as possible discussing with your cooperating teacher and university supervisor what they expect of you.** Ask them to be specific; you have sufficient "worry material" during student teaching without their intangible generalizations about evaluation.
- **Feel confident in yourself and in your teaching ability.** Readily develop a style of teaching that is comfortable for you. Seek evaluative comments from your coordinator and supervising teacher and build on them in developing your personal style.
- **Self-evaluation is important during student teaching.** As you begin to openly analyze your objectives during student teaching, you already have begun an important professionalization process. Honest self-appraisal is a real asset to any teacher. Through reflective thinking, you will begin to attain professional growth.

GUIDELINES FOR THE COOPERATING TEACHER

- **Maintain an ongoing evaluation of your student teacher by developing a schedule for such evaluations.** Short, periodic evaluations provide a good record as well as material for conferences with the student teacher.
- **As the university supervisor visits your student teacher, confer with both of them, sharing your records.** Maintain notes of such conferences.
- **Develop an evaluation file on your student teacher.** This file should include samples of the student teacher's work, lesson plans, daily records, anecdotal records, and personal notes. Ask the university supervisor for copies of the periodic observation evaluations for your file.
- **Provide the student teacher with evaluation opportunities and keep a record of them in your file.**
- **Keep in mind the value of positive reinforcement.** Emphasize to your student teacher the high standards you expect.
- **Maintain constant evaluation dialogue with your student teacher throughout the term.**

CASE STUDIES

C   A   S   E

7-1   Greta disagreed with the midterm evaluation that Mr. Smiley, her cooperating teacher, had written about her. Greta called the university supervisor to see what could be done and explained that she had received a low mark on the preparation of lesson plans but that Mr. Smiley had said she could use his lesson plans and need not write her own.

1. What role should the university supervisor play in this situation?
2. Should Greta grin and bear it and begin writing lesson plans no matter what Mr. Smiley said? Discuss.
3. Would it be wise to involve the principal?
4. Is Mr. Smiley doing the right thing to encourage Greta to use his lesson plans? Discuss.
5. What options are available for Greta to adapt Mr. Smiley's lesson plans? Would such plans be effective?
6. Is there a way that Greta can tactfully please both the cooperating teacher and the university supervisor? Explain.

C   A   S   E

7-2   Tim's university supervisor gave Tim a low evaluation mark in instruction and classroom management when, in fact, Tim had precisely copied the method of his cooperating teacher. Unaware of this, the university supervisor gave Tim and the cooperating teacher a copy of the evaluation report, which cited the methods used as "unimaginative, dull, and outdated." The cooperating teacher became agitated and vented her frustration on Tim. Poor Tim!

1. How can the university supervisor help?
2. What actions should Tim take to sooth the situation?
3. Would it be inappropriate for Tim to request permission to use different teaching methods?
4. Does the university supervisor have a right to evaluate the methods of the cooperating teacher? Discuss.
5. What responsibility should the cooperating teacher assume in defending Tim?
6. What valuable lessons for Tim are demonstrated in this situation?

C   A   S   E

7-3   Mindy was a young woman who was excited about being a teacher. Her cooperating teacher, Ms. Stone, was nearly the same age and they became good friends as the student teaching term wore on. In fact, they became such good friends that Ms. Stone realized too late that her suggestions were meaningless to Mindy. The midterm evaluation was soon due and in all professional fairness Ms. Stone was aware that she should give Mindy a below-average rating in some performance areas. Determined to be professional, she attempted a serious conference with Mindy, who at first seemed surprised and then countered with, "But I thought you were my friend!"

1. How could Ms. Stone help Mindy?
2. What chances does Mindy have of succeeding in this classroom?
3. How could the involvement of the grade chairperson or the department chairperson assist Ms. Stone?
4. Does this situation mean that a student teacher and cooperating teacher should not be close friends? Discuss.
5. What psychological preparation could assist Ms. Stone prior to discussing this with Mindy?
6. What guidelines can be useful in avoiding such situations?

C A S E

7-4   Cecil was a 6'5", 210-pound student teacher in physical education. He was getting his teaching degree in the off seasons while playing for a major league football team.

During student teaching, his cooperating teacher felt that Cecil was trying to get by on the waves of his popularity. His classes frequently were "rap" sessions about professional football. Cecil was insulted when the cooperating teacher suggested they preview the evaluation forms.

1. How could the cooperating teacher help instill in Cecil the desire to do as well in teaching as in football?
2. Do you think converting the evaluation forms to score sheets with penalties, completed passes, field goals, and touchdowns would help?
3. Would such a conversion be worth the effort?
4. Do you feel that Cecil has the potential to become a successful teacher of physical education? Discuss.
5. What characteristics of professional athletes might be assets for teachers?
6. What personal qualities should Cecil spend time developing?

C A S E

7-5   Harvey was about midway into his student teaching when he realized that his evaluation at the end of the term would be concerned with many activities he had not planned or experienced. He felt, however, that what he was involved with in his high school music classroom was appropriate for a teacher of music. He and his cooperating teacher agreed that a number of teacher activities required by music teachers were not included on the evaluation form.

1. What other form of evaluation could be used for the student teaching experience in Harvey's case?

2. How should the university supervisor be involved in developing additional evaluation material?
3. How could the cooperating teacher determine the acceptability of any additional evaluation materials?
4. What is the major purpose of a midsemester evaluation?
5. In what other subject areas might there be a need for different evaluative criteria?

C A S E

7-6   Denise was at the end of her student teaching in shorthand class. She had enjoyed the high school students she had worked with and had accomplished quite a bit with them. Her cooperating teacher was very proud of her and insisted that she get an A in student teaching. The university supervisor disagreed and felt that Denise was closer to average and should get no higher than a B.

Because the two individuals had to agree on the grade for the student teaching assignment, a decision had to be made; grades were due to be turned in immediately.

1. What events would contribute to the development of such different opinions?
2. Whose responsibility is it to work out a solution?
3. Should the grade recommended by the cooperating teacher have more weight than the grade given by the university supervisor?
4. How could Denise be involved in this decision?
5. How should a university supervisor and a cooperating teacher avoid the development of such a situation?
6. To avoid this kind of situation, what are colleges and universities doing with grades for student teaching?

RECOMMENDED READING

Association of Teacher Educators. (1988). *Teacher assessment.* Reston, VA: Author. *This monograph is a product of the Association of Teacher Educators' Commission on Teacher Assessment. Purposes of assessment, as well as political, measurement, and legal issues, are included in this discussion.*

Barker, C. L., & Searchwell, C. J. (1998). *Writing meaningful teacher evaluations—right now!: The principal's quick-start reference guide.* Thousand Oaks, CA: Corwin Press. *Although this is written for the administration, it may prove beneficial for the student teacher to review the concepts on which he or she may later be evaluated: curriculum proficiency, preparation and readiness, instructional performance, interaction and climate, and the ability to evaluate student growth.*

Balch, P. M., & Balch, P. E. (1987). Evaluating a student teacher. In *The cooperating teacher: A practical approach for the supervision of student teachers* (pp. 123–141). New York: University Press of America. *Methods of evaluating the student teacher are discussed, including a horizontal evaluation model (intra-individual), a vertical model (skill-based), and a humanistic evaluation model (attitudinal). A comparison of these models is given.*

Heywood, J. (1982). *Pitfalls and planning in student teaching.* New York: Nichols. *This text contains a full range of information for the student teacher; the section on appraisal and self-appraisal is especially recommended. A scheme for self-evaluation for teachers and student teachers is given in addition to an Experimental Pupil Evaluation Form for Teachers and a Student Teaching Evaluation Form.*

Posner, G. J. (1989). What have your learned from your field experience? In *Field experience: Methods of reflective teaching* (2nd ed.) (pp. 141–146). New York: Longman. *Posner offers the student teacher the unusual opportunity to self-evaluate by writing a progress report that includes context, goals, and learnings. Also included is a list of questions to guide future professional planning by the student teacher.*

Stanley, S. J., & Popham, W. J. (1988). *Teacher evaluation: Six prescriptions for success.* Alexandria, VA: Association for Supervision and Curriculum Development. *This book is worthwhile reading for a cooperating teacher who is seeking direction in evaluating a student teacher. Six alternative teacher evaluation approaches are presented, each recommended by different individuals. All six react to the same situation; each approach is followed by a "from-the-field" reaction, typically from a school principal or central office administrator involved in teacher appraisal.*

Stronge, J. H. (Ed.) (1997). *Evaluating teaching: A guide to current thinking and best practice.* Thousand Oaks, CA: Corwin Press. *This text explains how to utilize multiple-source data to assist the teacher in professional growth.*

8

Legal Status

The legal status of the student teacher is a perennial question with both student teachers and cooperating teachers. Although the degree and approved program status of the student teacher are prescribed by state law and interpreted by state board of education rules, the legal responsibility and liability of the student teachers pose questions for both cooperating teachers and student teachers.

Many state legislatures deal with the classroom role of the student teacher in only a general sense. Because this area of school law is developing through the accumulation of case law, student teachers should keep abreast of current cases in their own states.

Most states require the student teacher to comply with local school board rules and regulations and to observe all duties of the classroom teacher. In the application process for student teaching, the candidate signs a statement agreeing to abide by all the laws affecting the state, district, and school in relation to the classroom assignment. Any abridgement of that agreement places the student teacher in jeopardy of losing the student teaching position, and the student teacher will not likely be placed for such an experience in that school district again. School district administrators take very seriously the agreement they enter into with the student teacher and they expect the same attitude from the student teacher.

Under the circumstances agreed on by the district and the student teachers, the student teachers are generally afforded the same legal status as their cooperating teachers when they are in the school. This agreement is usually a part of the student teaching application that the student, the university representative, and the district representative sign.

Although some professionals consider the student teacher to be covered by district liability insurance, every student teacher is encouraged to purchase personal liability insurance to cover the period of student teaching. This liability insurance is available from various organizations of professional educators as well as from independent insurance agencies. Physical education, technical education, and science classes are examples of particular liability coverage needs for the student teacher.

A major source of information relative to the legal status of the student teacher is the appropriate book of state rules for school boards. Most principals have a copy, and the student teacher should borrow the book or spend some time in the administrative office reading the sections pertaining to preservice teachers. These state rules for school boards are the official interpretation of the laws passed by the state legislature and are written in language easily comprehended. If the principal does not have such material, he or she may be able to secure a copy for the student teacher.

It is imperative that the student teacher be aware that the majority of lawsuits in teacher liability cases arise from alleged negligence on the part of the teacher. This deserves special attention from the person preparing to teach.

GUIDELINES FOR THE STUDENT TEACHER

- **Acts of negligence probably give teachers and student teachers more problems than any other law-related situations.** Negligence can be proved only if there is sufficient evidence that the student teacher has failed to warn the classroom students of hazards, either real or potential. Documentation of such warnings is essential and should be kept in a permanent file by the student teacher.
- **Use all available sources to find information concerning your legal status not only as a student teacher but also as a teacher when you have your own classroom.**
- **Discuss your legal status in the teachers' lounge.** Other teachers can provide a wealth of information, most of which will probably be in the form of specific cases.
- **Analyze all that you hear and read.**
- **Find other professionals interested in discussing legal matters with you.** What you learn is more meaningful and will be retained longer by your having discussed and reflected on someone else's ideas.
- **Obtain a copy of the state school board rules from your principal.** Make an effort to read and understand them.
- **Be aware of the responsibilities under which you are working.** You are in a position to be involved in activities with far-reaching effects.
- **Maintain what would be classified as reasonable behavior and you will be relatively safe.**
- **Avoid taking chances, both as a student teacher and as a teacher.** Litigation is expensive, even if you win. Aside from experiencing the legal implications of a lawsuit, you might also experience difficulties with your state teaching certification.
- **Consider purchasing personal liability insurance, available for a minimal fee, for the period of time you are in school as a student teacher.**
- **Because much of the developing law involving your type of position is based on case law, attempt to avoid being party to any such cases.**

GUIDELINES FOR THE COOPERATING TEACHER

- **As the cooperating teacher, you may sometimes find it easy to forget that the novice teacher in your classroom may be unaware of the current legal status of a student teacher.** It is natural to assume that those working with you are as knowledgeable as you are about such professionally related matters as legal status.
- **It is a great help to the student teacher if you share your experiences relating to school law.**
- **With all the matters demanding time on the student teacher's schedule, it may be difficult to find time for additional reading.** If possible, however, share reading materials with the student teacher to extend knowledge of a teacher's legal status.
- **Refer the student teacher to specific individuals on your faculty who are knowledgeable and have practical experience in the area of school law.**
- **Show the student teacher a copy of your teaching contract.**
- **If your local professional organizations dispense materials relative to the legal status and the rights and responsibilities of the teacher,** obtain copies of such materials for your student teacher. Sometimes the student teacher may be too busy or feels awkward pursuing such material on his or her own.
- **Make it as easy as possible for the beginning teacher to learn as much as possible related to school law during the student teaching process.**

CASE STUDIES

C A S E

8-1   Calvin was student teaching in the technology education classroom in a middle school. At the beginning of each unit he carefully outlined safety procedures for the students and watched alertly to ensure that students obeyed safety regulations. The students had learned how to use the equipment and generally were careful to avoid horsing around.

One day, as a student was cutting a piece of wood on the table saw, he asked another student to hold the heavier side of the wood as it passed through the saw. As the wood ran through the saw, the student holding the heavy side moved with the wood up against the wall. The wood caught and injured his hand.

Immediately Calvin saw what was happening and turned off the main power switch. After rescuing the student with the injured hand, Calvin went with him to the office for first aid, leaving the cooperating teacher in charge of the class. As Calvin walked down the corridor with the student, his mind was full of questions. Aside from the safety of the student, he was concerned with his own legal status and what would happen to him.

1. What questions do you think would be on Calvin's mind?
2. In what case would the parents have a legitimate cause for a lawsuit?
3. How would an inquiry into this accident affect Calvin's completing his student teaching?
4. Why would it be important for Calvin to immediately call his university supervisor?
5. With legal issues involving students more and more each day, how would this incident affect Calvin's teaching record?
6. How could Calvin prepare himself to deal with possible accidents in a shop class?

C   A   S   E

8-2   Ginger was thoroughly enjoying the first-grade class in which she was student teaching. With no major problems on the horizon, she was trying to prepare herself professionally as well as possible. She wanted to read the state rules under which the schools and teachers operated, but when she asked the principal whether she might borrow a copy, he shrugged off her request and told her, "You really don't need to read that. We'll tell you everything you need to know here." Ginger was dumbfounded. She had never imagined that an administrator could say such a thing.

1. Should she give up and forget about the rules and their implications for her professional life? Why?
2. Would it be appropriate for her to discuss this with her cooperating teacher? With the university supervisor?
3. Where could Ginger go to find a copy of the state rules?
4. Would it appear that she was trying to make waves if she pursued this matter further?
5. Does she have the right to read the rules? Explain your answer.

C   A   S   E

8-3   During a conference with the parents of one of his sixth-grade students, Johnny realized that the frustration level of the parents was increasing. Johnny had been the student teacher for 2 months. During that time, this student had experienced more difficulty than previously with homework, classwork, and tests. The parents were alleging that the student teacher was not an appropriate teacher for their child.

Johnny had tried several resources but with no success. He and the cooperating teacher realized that the student was beginning to display learning problems that would require more time than they had to give to one student. They were having difficulty getting the parents to understand this.

As the conference wore on, the situation became more disturbing. Finally, the father stood up and stated that it was the responsibility of the school to teach his son and that if they could not do that, he would sue the school, the cooperating teacher, and the student teacher. He intimated that the problem was probably the use of the student teacher in the classroom. As the parents left the conference, Johnny reflected on his future.

1. Did he want to continue in a profession in which he could be sued for doing the best he could for a child?
2. Would he be considered the reason for the child's failure?
3. Would the school take full responsibility for this, or would he have to stand alone?
4. Would the university be involved in any such lawsuit?
5. What interpersonal techniques could Johnny contribute in an effort to salvage this situation before it deteriorates further?

C A S E

8-4   Physical education classes offer many hazards to students. Freddie was aware of the legal hassle that some of the teachers in her field had undergone, and she wanted to plan to avoid any such problems. She considered having the parents of all her students sign a paper absolving her of any responsibility. Before she checked this out with her administrator, she wanted to consider all the ramifications.

1. How would her cooperating teacher consider such a request?
2. Because the student teacher would be in the school only one term, would the cooperating teacher be willing to go along with this?
3. What reaction would parents have?
4. Realistically, what would be the chances of getting such a statement from all the parents?
5. What could be done with the students whose parents refused to sign such a statement?
6. Could Freddie legally absolve herself of the responsibility of these students? Explain.

C A S E

8-5   Laura was student teaching in Mrs. Max's 11th-grade English class. Although much younger than Mrs. Max, Laura was much more traditional in her expectations of students in their dress and conduct. She had expressed her disapproval about the lack of student concern over sloppy clothes and unkempt hair. One day, her reactions reached the boiling point when she asked a student to tie his shoes or leave class. The student refused, saying that he had a right to wear his shoes any way he wanted. As the student and Laura glared at each other, the other students turned to Mrs. Max.

1. What, if anything, should Mrs. Max do in this situation?
2. What options does Laura have?
3. What rights does the student have?

4. What steps could have been taken earlier to prevent this occurrence?
5. In what way could Laura's attitude toward the student be a reflection of what she thought of the cooperating teacher's lax attitude?

C A S E

8-6   Mr. Bannon's new student teacher, Bob, was a seemingly pious young man on his way to the seminary. He was getting his teacher certification to earn his way while he continued his education for the ministry. He felt strongly about having a morning devotion.

Without prior warning, Bob announced one morning to his ninth-grade homeroom that they were to begin having Bible reading and prayer each day and that everyone would participate. There were surprised faces among the group as Bob proceeded to open the Bible to the New Testament and begin reading. A student left his desk and walked out of the room; two others followed. As Bob's face turned red with rage, the group began looking at each other in bewilderment.

1. What immediate action must be taken? By whom?
2. How should the university supervisor be involved?
3. What responsibility does the school administration have in this situation?
4. What rights do the students have?
5. What could the college preparation have done to have helped to avoid such a situation from occurring?
6. Who should respond to the parents' phone calls and visits to the school about this incident? Why?

RECOMMENDED READING

Association for Supervision and Curriculum Development. (1987, August). *Religion in the curriculum.* Alexandria, VA: Author. *This report from the Association for Supervision and Curriculum Development Panel on Religion in the Curriculum examines practices in the schools of today, the basis for these practices, and a baseline for beginning the examination of religion in the public schools. Attitudes affecting textbook publishing and curriculum development are reviewed. This issue, although not a legal one in itself, sometimes causes legal difficulties for the unprepared professional.*

Association of Teacher Educators. (1988). Legal issues. In E. Johnson (Ed.), *Teacher assessment* (pp. 26–32). Reston, VA: Author. *This discussion of legal issues related to teacher assessment includes references to specific course cases. The right of the states to regulate entry into the profession is cited; also included are 10 principles to be applied in considering teacher assessment programs. Student teachers are usually approaching their state professional tests and may have particular interest in this information.*

Bemak, F., & Keys, S. (1999). *Violent and Aggressive Youth.* Thousand Oaks, CA: Corwin Press. *This book will assist both the cooperating teacher and the student teacher to be aware of violence danger zones in schools, how to work with students with innovative interventions, and be aware of how to respond adequately to violent and aggressive youth.*

Clune, W. (1983). Courts and teaching. In L. S. Shulman & G. Sykes (Eds.), *Handbook of teaching and policy* (pp. 449–471). New York: Longman. *This chapter offers the cooperating teacher and the student teacher an overview of the effects that courts have had on educational reform. The authors includes four propositions in their generalizations on the relationship between judicial reform and educational change.*

Essex, N.L. (1999). *School law and the public schools: A practical guide for educational leaders.* Needham Heights, MA: Allyn & Bacon. *This is a paperback text that is written so that not only administrators and classroom teachers but also prospective teachers can easily digest to assist in working in a school and operating within the law. Extensive coverage is given to problems with the law at the school site.*

Fischer, L., Schimmel, D., & Kelly, C. (1999). *Teachers and the law, 5th ed.* New York: Longman. *These authors share information on legal issues that are important to teachers today including their legal rights and responsibilities. Topics include rights of gay teachers and students, sexual harassment, affirmative action, frivolous lawsuits, and gang clothing. This is highly recommended reading for both the cooperating teacher and the student teacher.*

LaMort, M.W. (1999). *School law: Cases and concepts, 6th ed.* Needham Heights, MA: Longwood. *This is a comprehensive book on school law for educators with little background in school law. This text gives legal rational, principles, verbatim court decisions, and references. Special education, student search issues, religion in the schools, compulsory attendance, malpractice, and educator liability are among the many topics covered by these authors.*

Lunenburg, F. C. & Ornstein, A.C. (1991). The state role in education. In *Educational administration: Concepts and practices,* (pp. 278–302). Belmont, CA: Wadsworth Publishing Company. *This chapter deals with good background information for the student teacher on the various levels of state government including the state courts, the state board of education, and the state department of education. Guidelines and strategies for reform and renewal and policy development are included.*

McCarthy, M.M. (1989). Legal rights and responsibilities of public school teachers. In M.C. Reynolds (Ed.), *Knowledge base for the beginning teacher* (pp. 255–266). New York: Pergamon Press. *This chapter covers a review of the law as it pertains to professional educators. The material is comprehensive in terms of topics and general in terms of specific coverage. An extensive bibliography offers additional valuable information. The material is highly recommended for both the cooperating teacher and the student teacher.*

Mitchell, D. E., & Kerchner, C.T. (1983). Labor relations and teacher policy. In L. S. Shulman & G. Sykes (Eds.), *Handbook of teaching and policy* (pp. 215–238). New York: Longman. *Mitchell and Kerchner speak with depth to the policy framework involving labor relations for teachers. This material is recommended for the cooperating teacher to share as appropriate with the student teacher. Diagrams illustrate the support of labor work structures by labor relations.*

Zirkel, P. A. (1988). Teacher evaluation: A legal overview. In J. Sikula (Ed.), *Action in Teacher Education, The Journal of the Association of Teacher Educators, tenth-year anniversary issue, commemorative* edition (pp. 21–29). Reston, VA: Association of Teacher Educators. *The student teacher may not be ready for an article of this nature. However, it is sound information for the cooperating teacher to review and share where appropriate with the student teacher. Federal law, state law, and case law concerning teacher evaluation are reviewed. A reference point for this information should assist the cooperating teacher as well as the student teacher.*

Ethics of the Teaching Profession

A discussion of ethics in teaching early in the semester can serve to guide the student teacher and can allow the cooperating teacher to know much about the professional ideas of the student teacher. Frequently, the cooperating teacher discovers that a review of professional ethics reaffirms a prior personal commitment to teaching. It is important for the student teacher to realize that such a commitment exists. Modeling of professional ethics is one of the most important aspects of cooperating in the student teaching assignment.

Any list of ethical prescriptions should be considered in relation to the particular school involved. When possible, university teacher training programs place students for field experiences in a variety of settings during their preparation. These different exposures help the student teacher identify the implications for professional ethics across a wide spectrum of student populations: social, economic, and cultural.

Terms such as *equal educational opportunity, ethical standards, worthy member of society,* and *professional service* may have different implications for different people. Because of those differences of opinion, the student teacher should investigate widely and think clearly about the need for ethical behavior.

Fairness to the student, the parents, and the school have a high priority. Maintaining confidentiality with respect to grades and other school achievements is extremely important. Trusting students is important to their psychological and emotional development. It is critical to give students an opportunity to accomplish and to achieve at what for them is a doable task, something of which they can be proud.

Ethical behavior for teachers means doing what is good and honorable for the student and avoiding what is bad, painful, or showing lack of honor to the student. It is important for the cooperating teacher to help the student teacher to understand the various cultural groups represented in the classroom so that the definition of honor for each group can be recognized.

An ethical teacher is one who practices equity. Such a teacher makes no differences among students on the basis of sex, race, creed, or handicapping condition. The ethical teacher sees the possibilities for growth, health, and happiness of students and how those possibilities can be enhanced in his or her classroom.

The ethical teacher observes convention; this includes convention of school and community rules. He or she attempts to operate within established policy, though not blindly.

The ethical teacher is compassionate and makes every effort to help students help themselves. Some feel that the ethical teacher strives to put student learning above subject matter content.

According to the Code of Ethics of the Teaching Profession developed by the National Education Association (Kim & Kellough, 1991), the professional educator has two primary commitments: first, to the student, and second, to the profession. Such commitments are taken for granted in many cases. However, it is important for the cooperating teacher and the student teacher to spend time discussing methods of ensuring ethical behavior during the entire professional life of the student teacher. Such behavior tends to bond teachers to each other. The student teacher should be aware that a lack of such behavior tends to exclude him or her from such bonding.

A major test that indicates the level of ethics involved is reflected in the answer to the question, Would I want a teacher to treat me (or my child) in such a manner? If teachers can treat each student in each situation in a way that they would appreciate being treated, the behavior or the treatment passes the test of being ethical.

The National Education Association (1975) adopted the following:

CODE OF ETHICS OF THE EDUCATION PROFESSION

PREAMBLE:

The educator, believing in the worth and dignity of each human being, recognizes the supreme importance of the pursuit of truth, devotion to excellence, and the nurture of the democratic principles. Essential to these goals is the protection of freedom to learn and to teach and the guarantee of equal educational opportunity for all. The educator accepts the responsibility to adhere to the highest ethical standards.

The educator recognizes the magnitude of the responsibility inherent in the teaching process. The desire for the respect and confidence of one's colleagues, of students, of parents, and of the members of the community provides the incentive to attain and maintain the highest possible degree of ethical conduct. The Code of Ethics of the Education Profession indicates the aspiration of all educators and provides standards by which to judge conduct.

The remedies specified by the NEA and/or its affiliates for the violation of any provision of this Code shall be exclusive and no such provision shall be enforceable in any form other than the one specifically designated by the NEA or its affiliates.

PRINCIPLE I: COMMITMENT TO THE STUDENT

The educator strives to help each student realize his or her potential as a worthy and effective member of society. The educator therefore works to stimulate the spirit of inquiry, the acquisition of knowledge and understanding, and the thoughtful formulation of worthy goals.

In fulfillment of the obligation to the student, the educator—

1. Shall not unreasonably restrain the student from independent action in the pursuit of learning.
2. Shall not unreasonably deny the student's access to varying points of view.
3. Shall not deliberately suppress or distort subject matter relevant to the student's progress.
4. Shall make reasonable effort to protect the student from conditions harmful to learning or to health and safety.
5. Shall not intentionally expose the student to embarrassment or disparagement.
6. Shall not on the basis of race, color, creed, sex, national origin, marital status, political or religious beliefs, family, social or cultural background, or sexual orientation, unfairly—
   a. Exclude any student from participation in any program
   b. Deny benefits to any student
   c. Grant any advantage to any student
7. Shall not use professional relationships with students for private advantage.
8. Shall not disclose information about students obtained in the course of professional service unless disclosure serves a compelling professional purpose or is required by law.

PRINCIPLE II: COMMITMENT TO THE PROFESSION

The education profession is vested by the public with a trust and responsibility requiring the highest ideals of professional service.

In the belief that the quality of the services of the education profession directly influences the nation and its citizens, the educator shall exert every effort to raise professional standards to promote a climate that encourages the exercise of professional judgment, to achieve conditions that attract persons worthy of the trust to careers in education, and to assist in preventing the practice of the profession by unqualified persons.

In fulfillment of the obligation to the profession, the educator—

1. Shall not in an application for a professional position deliberately make a false statement or fail to disclose a material fact related to competency and qualifications.
2. Shall not misrepresent his/her professional qualifications.
3. Shall not assist any entry into the profession of a person known to be unqualified in respect to character, education, or other relevant attribute.
4. Shall not knowingly make a false statement concerning the qualifications of a candidate for a professional position.
5. Shall not assist a noneducator in the unauthorized practice of teaching.
6. Shall not disclose information about colleagues obtained in the course of professional service unless disclosure serves a compellng professional purpose or is required by law.
7. Shall not knowingly make false or malicious statements about a colleague.
8. Shall not accept any gratuity, gift, or favor that might impair or appear to influence professional decisions or action.

GUIDELINES FOR THE STUDENT TEACHER

- **Try to strictly obey all the school rules governing your conduct while you are involved in student teaching.**
- **View your student teaching experiences as valuable and use these experiences to develop your teaching career.**
- **Avoid discussing actions or problems that occur in the classroom with unauthorized individuals.**
- **Maintain a sensitive but objective attitude toward your students.**
- **Avoid prejudging a student for any reason—race, sex, or ethnic or economic background.**
- **Be aware that the attitudes of students develop simultaneously with subject mastery.**
- **Respect the rights of the student as required by law (P. L. 94-142).**
- **Keep in mind the dynamic impact that you can have on your students and pursue a positive one.**
- **Be mindful of the example you set for your students. Be fair and honest.**

GUIDELINES FOR THE COOPERATING TEACHER

- **Expose your student teacher to those members on your faculty who exemplify the code of ethics of teachers.** Important lessons on ethics can be learned without having to be formally taught.

- **Be an example in providing daily learning situations in dealing with value-oriented topics for your student teacher.**
- **Use positive approaches rather than criticism when discussing school in particular and education in general.**
- **Help your student teacher see examples of benefits to students when teachers behave in ethical ways.**
- **Explain to your student teacher the benefits of good public relations on the part of the teacher.**

CASE STUDIES

C   A   S   E

9-1   Ingla had always wanted to be a physical education teacher. Working with the cheerleader sponsor as a student teacher added another dimension to her professional preparation. Because it was spring term, Ingla was able to assist with tryouts for the following year by girls who wanted to be cheerleaders. She enjoyed the procedure until something happened that disturbed her.

Although to Ingla it was obvious who the cheerleaders would be for the next year, when they were announced, it appeared that a less talented girl had won out over a very talented minority student. This disturbed Ingla, who attempted to discuss it with her cooperating teacher. Ingla was told that it was none of her affair. Still perplexed, Ingla worried about the injustice committed.

1. Under what ethical constraints was Ingla operating?
2. How would such a discovery affect Ingla's opinion of her cooperating teacher?
3. What would probably happen if Ingla insisted on discussing the situation with the cooperating teacher?
4. In what ways could the university supervisor help Ingla? Should she confide in him?
5. Were any other options open to Ingla? What were they?

C   A   S   E

9-2   Mike was student teaching in Ms. Breen's third-grade classroom and he was delighted when he had received his placement assignment. He knew that a parent of one of Ms. Breen's students was the owner of a local automobile dealership. Early in the term, Mike scheduled a parent conference with the automobile salesman-parent. After briefly discussing the child's progress, Mike changed the subject to automobile sales and discounts to teachers. The parent was really put on the spot. He did not want to say or do anything to this student teacher that would hurt his son.

1. What could the parent do?
2. With whom should the parent discuss the situation?

3. What effect would a case conference on Mike's problem have?
4. Should Mike be withdrawn from student teaching? Should he be allowed to continue?
5. If you were the university supervisor, what would you say to Mike?
6. How could long-range changes occur in Mike's philosophy?

C   A   S   E

9-3   Faye and Barbara were college roommates and had been assigned student teaching placements in different sections of the city. As they compared notes of materials, supplies, and resources available to their students in biology, they became aware of financial discrimination between the schools within the same district. They became enraged about the situation and tried to decide between themselves the best course of action.

1. Who would be interested in listening to these two?
2. If there were other individuals in the school district who were aware of the situation, why do you suppose they had done nothing?
3. How would questioning the practice hurt the women's chances of employment in the district?
4. If you were Faye or Barbara, what would you do?
5. How can such differences be eliminated?

C   A   S   E

9-4   Nelson was a politically active young man prior to his student teaching assignment in junior high civics. Political activity was high because of an upcoming election. Nelson's candidate needed handbills distributed door-to-door throughout the town. Nelson promised an A to every student who would distribute 300 handbills. The next morning, the principal called Nelson to his office and asked him to explain his actions.

1. What gave Nelson the right to reward students in such a manner for political activity?
2. How could he punish those students who did not participate?
3. What conversation probably transpired between the principal and Nelson?
4. What do you think happened when the opponent of Nelson's candidate found out about this episode?
5. In your opinion, what do you think was the final outcome?

C   A   S   E

9-5   Betsy was assigned to student teach in art at the beach high school. Her work in the classroom was barely acceptable. She spent little time planning and preparing her lessons. She had greater problems with her social life. After school on Fridays, the students knew they could find her at the local beach bar, which she usually patronized all weekend. When she began missing school on Mondays, the students explained to the cooperating teacher how Betsy had partied at the bar until early Monday morning. The cooperating teacher knew something must be done.

1. Betsy seems to have a number of problems. Rank them in order of importance to her professional life as a teacher.
2. What action should the cooperating teacher take?
3. Should Betsy's parents be involved?
4. How can the university supervisor facilitate better adjustment for Betsy?
5. Is there any hope for Betsy's future as a teacher?

C A S E

9-6   Randy was a middle school reading student teacher. No one was aware that Randy was gay until one of his students observed him typing material on the subject professing his inclination and sexual preference. Because this did not fit community norms, the school board requested Randy's immediate withdrawal from the classroom in which he was student teaching.

1. Was the college obligated to withdraw Randy from his student teaching placement? Why?
2. What options were open to Randy at this point?
3. Had Randy's rights been violated?
4. How do you think Randy's sexual preference would affect his teaching ability?
5. What could the solution be for Randy?
6. What suggestions would you have given Randy prior to student teaching?

REFERENCES

Kim, E. C., & Kellough, R. D. (1991). *A resource guide for secondary school teaching: Planning for competence* (5th ed.) (pp. 39–41). New York: Macmillan.

National Education Association (1975). Code of Ethics of the Education Profession. http://www.nea.org/info/code.html

RECOMMENDED READING

Broudy, H. S. (1990). Restoring honor: A modest proposal. In M. L. Kysilka (Ed.), *Honor in teaching: Reflections* (pp. 67–73). West Lafayette, IN: Kappa Delta Pi Publications. *Broudy discusses the professional status of teaching due to variations in practice. He points out that until uniformity is established, the label of "professional" will not be awarded and that the more creativity is stressed the less the teachers will be recognized as professionals. He uses the example of whether lawyers or physicians are creative in the practice of their profession.*

Flanders, N. A. (1990). Honor becomes effective teaching. In M. L. Kysilka (Ed.), *Honor in teaching: Reflections* (pp. 83–90). West Lafayette, IN: Kappa Delta Pi Publications. *Flanders questions how teaching could have lost honor during a period when teachers are striving to accomplish more than ever under situations that are worse than before. Restoring honor is related to restoring locus of control of the education environment to the teacher.*

Hostetler, K. D. (1997). *Ethical judgment in teaching.* Boston: Allyn & Bacon. *Using case studies, the author provides information and materials to help teachers think with clarity and knowledgeably discuss ethics in teaching.*

Kellough, R. D., & Kellough, N. G. (1999). *Secondary school teaching: A guide to methods and resources.* Upper Saddle River, NJ: Merrill/Prentice Hall.

Ortman, P. C. (1988). Central ethical issues. In *Not for teachers only: Creating a context of joy for learning and growth* (pp. 38–45). Washington, DC: Author. *This material is presented to help beginning teachers reaffirm their own principles and beliefs. Dilemmas are presented involving the purpose of education, teaching values, punishment, sex education, and the teacher as friend of the student.*

Sergiovanai, T. J. (1992). Moral authority and the regeneration of supervision. In *Supervision in transition: The 1991 ASCD yearbook* (pp. 203–214). Alexandria, VA: Association for Supervision and Curriculum Development. *Sergiovanni suggests that supervision move from the psychological to the professional and moral and that at that time supervision will be from within oneself as a teacher. A valuable chart shows assumptions, strategies, and consequences for the following sources of authority: bureaucratic, psychological, technical rationality, professional, and moral.*

Strike, K. A., & Soltis, J. (1998). *The ethics of teaching* (3rd ed.). New York: Teachers College Press. *This text offers cases that discuss such issues as sexual harassment and child abuse. Topics such as intellectual freedom, equal treatment of students, multiculturalism, religious differences, democracy, teacher burnout, and professional conduct are covered.*

Strom, S. M. (1989). The ethical dimension of teaching. In M. C. Reynolds (Ed.), *Knowledge base for the beginning teacher* (pp. 267–276). New York: Pergamon Press. *The author reviews the knowledge base of teaching as a moral/ethical activity and gives an extensive review of materials promoting ethical sensitivity and moral reasoning. This reading is highly recommended for cooperating teachers and student teachers.*

The People Involved

10

The Student Teacher

During student teaching, the primary people involved are the student teacher, the cooperating teacher in the classroom, the university supervisor, and the students in the student teacher's classroom.

Student teaching is designed to be a rewarding experience for well-prepared student teachers. Each student teacher is placed in a public or private school under the direct and continuous supervision of a teacher who has expressed willingness to participate in the student teaching program. The cooperating teacher, because of experience and background, can assist the student teacher in becoming a competent and caring teacher.

Opportunities are provided in the student teaching program that ensure student teachers an acquaintance with the responsibilities of teaching. These experiences in student teaching provide student teachers with realistic evaluations of their strengths and weaknesses as prospective teachers and help them to develop competencies in classroom management skills. Successful student teachers should progress to the level of expertise needed for independent performance in the classroom as they are in the process of becoming rather than moving toward a finished product.

The student teaching experience consists of three phases:

1. orientation and observation
2. assisting
3. assuming responsibility in the total school program

Student teachers need to observe in their own classroom as well as in other grades and other areas such as physical education, art, music, exceptional child education, and either secondary, middle, or high school subjects.

After observing for at least a week, student teachers should begin assisting students on an individual or small-group basis. Some level of assistance should begin the first day so that the student teacher can feel at ease in the classroom. This period of assisting gives the student teacher the feel for teaching in that particular environment.

After student teachers have progressed through the first two phases, the cooperating teachers should gradually provide opportunities for them to assume greater responsibilities. Student teachers begin by teaching a particular subject, depending on their experience. If they have had several years' experience in a classroom as aides or feel comfortable in the classroom for whatever reason, they may be capable of assuming greater responsibilities sooner. This schedule should be worked out among the student teacher, the cooperating teacher, and the university supervisor.

If student teachers show initiative, enthusiasm, and adequate preparation, they may stay ahead of the schedule suggested by the college. As long as they are showing quality performance in teaching, cooperating teachers may relinquish more and more responsibilities to them. During the latter part of student teaching, student teachers should be in full charge of the classroom.

The prime consideration of the student teacher should be the welfare of the students in the classroom. The cooperating teacher has a master plan to meet the students' needs; the student teacher must learn to operate within the framework of this plan.

One of the first tasks of student teachers is to determine the goals and objectives of their assigned class. Cooperating teachers should explain the goals and objectives that have been completed prior to the arrival of the student teachers, those planned for use during the student teaching assignment, and those that will be realized after the student teachers leave.

Extensive planning in cooperation with the cooperating teacher is essential for a successful student teaching experience. Student teachers soon learn that a high positive correlation exists between effective planning and successful teaching.

Student teachers need to know how to identify best long-range goals for given subject areas as well as how to develop and place in proper sequence the related short-range objectives. The specific format of lesson plans should be agreed on by the cooperating teacher and the student teacher; the student teacher should present lesson plans to the cooperating teacher well in advance so that necessary revisions can be made. This meeting of minds concerning the lesson plans can be a major part of the evaluation process (see Appendixes C through F).

After instructional objectives have been developed, student teachers need to select, adapt, and develop the necessary materials. Not only will the student teachers use materials available in the school and district, but also they may bring in supplemental materials from the college, community, and other sources.

The personal qualities of the student teacher are extremely important; promptness and dependability are qualities that will be observed closely. Maintaining a punctual and regular attendance record is a must. A very important quality is enthusiasm toward teaching because the tenor of student responses and class contributions depends on this enthusiasm.

Student teachers should formulate a standard for student classroom behavior that maintains the classroom atmosphere already developed by the cooperating teacher.

Drastic changes in classroom management tend to add to the students' insecurity. Student teachers should demonstrate skills that help students develop positive self-concepts and respect for the dignity and worth of other ethnic, linguistic, cultural, and economic groups.

Student teachers are responsible for certain forms and reports that must be completed and returned promptly. It has been stated that most teachers dislike keeping records. Even though they consider it a necessary task, they feel that it is an unproductive aspect of accountability (Charles, 1983). Many student teachers report that the whole area of record keeping was not discussed during their university work and they are quite shocked at the variety and amount of paperwork required of a classroom teacher.

Good records are valuable to teachers in many ways. They provide information about academic instructional levels, specific strengths and weaknesses, progress that has occurred in the various subject areas, social behavior, and future plans for individual students. Formats for keeping good records easily include objectives, progress forms, graphs to show progress, work samples, and individual student folders in which to keep the forms and samples (Charles, 1983).

Competency in subject matter should be expected of all student teachers. Knowledge of subject matter is reflected in areas such as effective lesson plans, success of students, and recognition of various levels of abilities among students. Most problems encountered during student teaching, however, have been found to be in the area of interpersonal relations rather than subject matter adequacy.

Student teachers are expected to exhibit skill in using various instructional techniques. Procedures used by the cooperating teacher should be continued but they should be supplemented by the special skill of the student teacher. Student teachers should use methods and materials that are consistent with the philosophy of the school in which they are student teaching.

Last but not least, the student teacher's role includes organizing noninstructional activities for students, such as assembly programs, field trips, and student clubs, and a myriad of record-keeping activities used for both assessment and administration purposes.

GUIDELINES FOR THE STUDENT TEACHER

- **Take your student teaching assignment very seriously.** Expect to do your very best; average work is not acceptable.
- **Look for ways to become involved from the 1st day.** Expect to give more assistance than you receive. Expect and even ask to be allowed to participate in all normal teaching duties, playground, lunchroom, field trips, and clubs.
- **Be a good listener.** You will be learning a great deal about your class during a short period of time. The more you learn about the goals and objectives and your

students, the better you will do when you begin your teaching. Getting to know the students helps you to identify the causes of classroom misbehavior and employ corrective techniques.

- **Carefully observe the organizational patterns and teaching techniques of your cooperating teacher.** Meet with your cooperating teacher and determine objectives for your observations; afterward, discuss your concerns and what you've learned from the observations. Keeping a journal is a big help in preparing for these conferences.
- **When you teach your first lesson, provide your cooperating teacher with a complete lesson plan.** This plan not only shows your cooperating teacher that you are aware of the importance of planning but also provides information for constructive feedback. Discussing the plan provides an excellent opportunity for evaluation and professional growth. After you begin teaching a full schedule, your lesson plans will be shortened, but they should be clear-cut and precise.
- **Operate within the discipline framework in the classroom that has been developed by your cooperating teacher.**
- **Develop a receptive attitude toward suggestions and criticisms.** If errors are to be avoided or need to be corrected, you must be receptive. It is not your task, however, to become a duplicate of your cooperating teacher. This is a unique opportunity to get feedback from a professional teacher concerning your teaching style.
- **Keep in mind that you are another professional in the classroom.** Maintain your enthusiasm for having the opportunity to work with young minds.

GUIDELINES FOR THE COOPERATING TEACHER

- **Be well aware of the purposes of a student teaching program when you agree to participate in it.** Although you feel the responsibility for helping to train future teachers, recognize that your first responsibility will be to your students.
- **Taking time to prepare for the student teacher can produce positive results.** The initial orientation of the student teacher sets the tone of the entire experience. Creating an atmosphere of acceptance of the student teacher in the classroom is most important. The words you use in preparing your students for the student teacher are also critical.
- **Explain your legal status as classroom teacher to your student teacher.** Clarify that you are the main and primary communicator and the one who bears the burden for legal responsibility in the classroom.
- **Guide your student teacher into teaching gradually but steadily.** It is sometimes difficult to give up your class to another teacher, but it is necessary for your student teacher to assume a leadership role. On occasions when you

may be tempted to interrupt the teaching of the student teacher, try to resist doing so unless absolutely necessary.

- **Involve your student teacher as soon as possible.** This not only benefits your program but also helps to free the student teacher from feelings of anxiety. Arrange observations in other classrooms during the early part of student teaching. Guiding the student teacher in determining what to observe and holding post-observation conferences are helpful.
- **Review your total program goals and objectives.** Provide your student teacher with the necessary curriculum guides and teachers' manuals.
- **Introduce the student teacher to classroom routines and instructional procedures.** Acquaint the student teacher with available instructional materials, supplies, and equipment.
- **Make your student teacher aware of your record-keeping responsibilities.** Share pupil personnel records and the manner in which they are kept and used. Let your student teacher assist you in simplifying your records management.
- **Require that your student teacher provide lesson plans prior to teaching.** Assist your student teacher with initial lesson planning and accept no excuse for inadequate planning on the part of the student teacher.
- **Involve your student teacher in the total school program.** Provide opportunities for professional growth through attendance at professional meetings, including staff meetings. Allow as many opportunities as possible to transfer theory into practice in a variety of classroom and extra-class activities.
- **After your objectives have been attained cooperatively, continuously evaluate the student teacher.** Hold frequent conferences, both planned and unplanned. Student teachers are disappointed if they do not receive feedback concerning their successes and failures. Open communication is an important factor.

CASE STUDIES

C   A   S   E

10-1   Susan was a successful student teacher in a high school English class. She had developed an excellent rapport with her students and had been very happy with her own progress.

Everything went well until one of her students yelled out while leaving her class: "Good-bye, Susan!" Susan was shocked but let the matter drop. Word of this spread around the school rapidly. On her way to her car at the close of the school day, Susan was called by her first name at least three times by students.

When Susan arrived home, she was distraught. Things had gone so well until then.

1. What would be the advantages/disadvantages of Susan's ignoring such familiarity?
2. What could Susan do to solve this problem?

3. How could Susan involve her cooperating teacher, principal, or university supervisor in this matter?
4. As Susan's cooperating teacher, what would you do even if Susan did not seek your involvement?
5. How should this be handled with the students?

10-2   Bill had been dependable about turning his lesson plans in early and had undoubtedly spent a great deal of time on them. Today he presented a good introduction to his lesson, gave some valuable information, and assigned his students a worksheet. The problem was that the class was composed of students with varying abilities who finished the worksheet at different times. Students finishing first were not provided anything else to do; therefore, discipline problems resulted. This had happened before, but Bill had not developed any solution.

1. Why is this likely to be a common problem for student teachers?
2. What could Bill have done when this happened?
3. When planning for a similar lesson, what additional plans should be included?
4. What should the coordinating teacher do to help Bill?
5. Why should the university supervisor be informed about the problem?

C A S E

10-3   Todd is successfully completing student teaching in high school history. Everything was going fine until he began dating one of his students in his fifth-period class. The student was a senior who undoubtedly was infatuated with the new student teacher. Several of the students in the fifth-period class began to tease Todd about his extracurricular affairs.

1. Do you feel that it is proper for student teachers to date their students? Why or why not?
2. What attitude should the cooperating teacher have concerning this situation?
3. How could this situation have been avoided in the first place?
4. How do you feel the university supervisor will react to this?
5. What is the role of the principal in a situation such as this?

C A S E

10-4   Mr. Muller's student teacher had designed a dynamic lesson and had motivated the students. While using the blackboard, he misspelled a word. None of the students said anything to the student teacher. However, one of the students privately mentioned it to Mr. Muller.

1. Why should a student teacher be a model for students?
2. What action, if any, should be taken by Mr. Muller?

3. How could this student teacher avoid a recurrence of this mistake?

4. How would you explain this type of spelling error to the students?

5. Do you feel that student teachers should be allowed to make mistakes of this nature? Explain your answer.

C   A   S   E

10-5   Sarah was in her 4th week as a student teacher in a sixth-grade classroom, and her cooperating teacher was very happy with her. Some of the other teachers in the building, however, were critical of Sarah's behavior during lunch period.

Parents were hired by the school district to supervise the lunchroom to give the teachers and students a short break from each other. The teachers ate their lunch together in the workroom and enjoyed chatting. Sarah preferred to eat with her class, and she felt that she could get to know the students better during an informal lunch period. To Sarah, this interaction was more important than joining the other teachers. Some teachers felt that it was rude of Sarah not to join them. One of the teachers, Mrs. Randolph, confronted Sarah in the hallway and told her that her omission at lunch was a sore point with a number of teachers. Sarah tried to explain her position but got a cold response.

1. How could this situation jeopardize Sarah's success in student teaching?

2. Do you think that her cooperating teacher knows about the feelings of these teachers? If so, why did she not mention it to Sarah?

3. In what ways was Sarah's feeling about eating with her class admirable?

4. What could Sarah and her cooperating teacher do to ease this sore point among some of the teachers?

5. In what ways could the university supervisor or principal help in this situation?

C   A   S   E

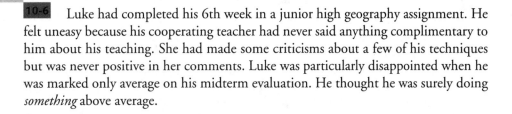

10-6   Luke had completed his 6th week in a junior high geography assignment. He felt uneasy because his cooperating teacher had never said anything complimentary to him about his teaching. She had made some criticisms about a few of his techniques but was never positive in her comments. Luke was particularly disappointed when he was marked only average on his midterm evaluation. He thought he was surely doing *something* above average.

1. What could be some reasons that Luke's cooperating teacher never offered any positive feedback to Luke?

2. Should Luke confront his cooperating teacher about his concerns? If so, how?

3. How could the university supervisor be of help to Luke?

4. What implications would self-evaluation have for Luke in this particular case?

5. How could a three-way conference (Luke, the cooperating teacher, and the university supervisor) on the midterm evaluation be of help?

REFERENCES

Charles, C. M. (1983). *Elementary classroom management: A handbook of excellence in teaching.* New York: Longman.

RECOMMENDED READING

Bey, T. M., & Holmes, C. T. (Eds.). (1990). *Mentoring: Developing successful new teachers.* Reston, VA: Association of Teacher Educators. *Mentoring can be a successful method for the cooperating teacher to bring a student teacher into the profession. The material covered in this monograph is of interest to those who wish to review the research on mentoring in education and to look at the styles of mentoring the new professional.*

Butler, D., Davies, M. A., & Dickinson, T. S. (1991). *On site: Preparing middle level teachers through field experiences.* Columbus, OH: National Middle School Association. *The authors provide innovative models for field experiences and student teaching; shadow studies, interdisciplinary internships, and multiple-site student teaching are showcased as methods of developing change in these programs.*

Calderhead, J. (Ed.). (1988). *Teachers' professional learning.* New York: Falmer Press. *The cooperating teacher may be interested in this entire text for discussion with the student teacher. These chapters are sequenced as development would be in the career of a teacher; the first five chapters deal with the professional development in student teaching relative to theory and practice, reflective teaching, knowledge structures, and planning and post-lesson reflections. Case studies are included.*

Geothals, M. S., & Howard, R. A. (1985). General orientation: Assuming professional responsibility. in *Handbook of skills essential to beginning teachers* (pp. 1–7). New York: University Press of America. *A discussion of the role of the student teacher is given, including diagrams of the functions involved in this role. Responsibilities of the student teacher toward the cooperating teacher, the university supervisor, the rest of the faculty, and the school are listed.*

Grambs, J. D., & Carr, J. C. (1979). Transition: Student teaching and success. in *Modern methods in secondary education* (4th ed.). New York: Holt, Rinehart & Winston. *This material touches on many of the various roles the student teacher is expected to fill. Emphasis is placed on working successfully with both the university supervisor and the cooperating teacher. Characteristics discussed here and considered important for the student teacher to possess are a sense of humor, the ability to maintain professional silence, and the ability to work with students in a humane and professional way.*

Guyton, E., & McIntire, D. J. (1990). Student teaching and school experiences. In W. R. Houston (Ed.), *Handbook of research on teacher education* (pp. 514–534). New York: Macmillan. *The research base for field experiences is documented, including such aspects as curriculum models, structure, organization, and administration of student teaching. A paradigm for field experiences has been developed that fits such ethnographic needs better* than does the paradigm for the methods used by the natural sciences.

Jonson, K. F. (1997). *The new elementary teacher's handbook: (Almost) everything you need to know for your first years of teaching.* Thousand Oaks, CA: Corwin Press. *This book offers the beginning teacher a variety of critical professional solutions, including maintaining your sense of humor and energy level, preparing lesson plans, and preventing discipline problems.*

Kottler, E., Kottler, J., & Kottler, C. (1998). *Secrets for secondary school teachers: How to succeed in your first year.* Thousand Oaks, CA: Corwin Press. *Successful strategies are provided to help deal with stress, workload, and time constraints in the classroom.*

Portner, H. (1998). *Mentoring new teachers.* Thousand Oaks, CA: Corwin Press. *This text is designed to assist effective mentoring; it includes specific activities and exercises.*

Rosenblum-Lowden, R. (1997). *You have to go to school . . . You're the teacher: 200 tips to make your job easier and more fun.* Thousand Oaks, CA: Corwin Press. *The title speaks for this text; it offers wit and wisdom to encourage teachers.*

The Cooperating Teacher

An actual letter from a cooperating teacher to her new student teacher follows:

Dear Student Teacher:

I am so excited and pleased that you will be joining me in my classroom. The children are so lucky to be getting another teacher to help them learn. I'm also a little worried. I'm not worried about your abilities or preparation, but about myself. Will I be able to make you feel welcomed and comfortable? Will I be able to communicate with you in a way that will make you grow confidently into the kind of teacher you want to be? Will I be able to answer all of your questions fully?

Trust and honesty are important qualities in a teacher. I promise to trust you and be honest with you. Will you be honest with me? If you need special help in an area, will you trust me enough to ask? If you are scared, unsure, and worried, will you be honest with yourself and tell me?

I promise to introduce you to the other members of our school team and to make you feel welcomed. I won't leave you out of conversations and make you feel like a fifth wheel. There are times when I might want to be alone with other teachers. I'm not going to talk about you. Remember, you can trust me.

I don't expect you to become me. You will teach differently. I hope you will want to do some things that I do, but then again, you have just completed your college education and should have some new and exciting ideas to share with me. Teach me. Share with me. I will share all my ideas with you. Remember, there is so much that I can share with you.

There is one area that you will have to show me that I can trust you. That's with my children. They are my world to me. Every one of them has become a part of me—an extension of my soul. Through your planning and preparation, your promptness, your interest, your concern for their welfare, your giving that little bit of extra effort, you can show me that they have also become a part of you. I love them and you will grow to love them, too.

Yes, I am called your cooperating teacher, but I hope that I can also be called your friend.

~~~Kathy Brake, Elementary Teacher

The cooperating teacher is the key facilitator in the professional development of any future teacher. Everything that the student teacher learns in college courses fuses during the term of student teaching, and it is the cooperating teacher who assists more than anyone else in fitting all the pieces together to form a complete picture in the novice teacher's professional development.

Before the beginning of the semester of the assignment, the university office of student teaching usually holds orientation meetings with the cooperating teachers and university supervisors to increase their sense of community and the knowledge of the assignment as well as to clear up any questions these teachers may have.

The cooperating teacher is a mentor, an example, a guide, a critical advisor, and a good friend to the student teacher during the student teaching experience. It is only with a great deal of faith and trust that a cooperating teacher is able to turn a class over to a student teacher. Teachers become emotionally involved with their own classes and usually become rather possessive about them. It serves the student teacher well to realize this while working with the students in the cooperating teacher's classroom. The development of a team-teaching partnership from the beginning is one method of dealing with teacher possessiveness.

Initially, the cooperating teacher prepares the students for the arrival of the student teacher. Often such activities as preparing name tags for the elementary students to wear on the first few days the student teacher is there help the students anticipate the arrival of the student teacher. In middle and secondary schools, seating charts are helpful. When the student teacher arrives at school for the first observation, the cooperating teacher should welcome the student teacher to the classroom and introduce the student teacher to the students, to the principal, to some of the other teachers, and to the office staff. A brief tour of the school facility, including such important sites as the cafeteria, the teachers' lounge, and the rest rooms, is beneficial.

To alleviate some initial concerns, the cooperating teacher should give the student teacher copies of all materials the students will be using, including teacher texts and resource lists. Having the materials in hand makes it easier for the student teacher.

Being able to observe the cooperating teacher in actual teaching situations is the second greatest aid to quiet the anxieties of the student teacher. Offering student teachers the opportunity to observe the other classrooms tends to make them feel more at home in the school and see themselves as an integral part of the total school picture.

Planning is critical. The student teacher may not yet be aware that a secret to being a successful teacher is effective planning. The cooperating teacher should explain this point, demonstrating just how important planning really is to the success of the teaching act. Helping with current lesson plans also helps. It is reassuring to the student teacher if the cooperating teacher can, on the very first visit, confer and make tentative written plans for the entire term. Such plans do not have to be detailed, but they can give some closure that would make the student teacher feel more comfortable. Occasionally, cooperating teachers carry their plans around in their head, but this is not a good example to set. Planning is extremely important, and the cooperating teacher and the student teacher should spend time on it during the term. It is better to overplan than for the students to have time on their hands and develop behavior problems.

The cooperating teacher should have the student teacher work into the teaching situation gradually by assigning work with individuals who need help, with small groups, with portions of the day's lesson with the entire class, and then with the entire class for the entire period or lesson.

The cooperating teacher should plan specific times for uninterrupted conferences with the student teacher. Frequency is more desirable than length. From the very beginning, there should be an air of friendly criticism, with the cooperating teacher using positive reinforcement whenever possible. If a specific point that may seem rather harsh needs to be made to the student teacher, the cooperating teacher should use the "sandwich" technique: sandwiching the criticism between two compliments. Tactfully done, this can be effective professional development for the student teacher.

During conferences, the cooperating teacher should help the student teacher look back as well as forward. In discussing those classes already taught, relate feelings and ideas so that in planning for the future the student teacher can capitalize on successful techniques. Maintaining a journal (see Appendix G for sample journal format) assists both the student teacher and the cooperating teacher.

It is the responsibility of the cooperating teacher to keep a watchful eye on all that is happening in the classroom. Being accessible at all times is also important. After the student teacher takes over the teaching responsibility, it may be appropriate for the cooperating teacher to stay out of the classroom as much as he or she remains in it, gauging his or her decision on the ability of the student teacher. Some student teachers follow cooperating teachers when they leave the room but others blossom when cooperating teachers are out of the room. Some classes of students cannot divide the cooperating teacher's authority to include the student teacher; in such cases, the students will not see the student teacher as their teacher until such leadership in the classroom is established. Deciding when to intervene in a situation is one of the most difficult decisions for the cooperating teacher to make.

The cooperating teacher should evaluate continuously and maintain a folder of notes relative to the student teacher. Some cooperating teachers keep a steno pad record, using one page per day with one side of the page for the student teacher and the other side for the cooperating teacher. Both teachers can jot down ideas and questions that come to them during the day so that when conference time comes, they have much to discuss. This serves well as a reminder when the time arrives for the cooperating teacher to evaluate the student teacher. Also, the student teacher is more able to self-evaluate by having collected sufficient notes throughout the term (see Appendix J for format).

Most colleges ask the cooperating teacher to formally evaluate the student teacher during the middle of the term and again at the end of the term. Although some colleges use only grades of "pass" or "fail," other colleges request that the cooperating teacher assign a letter grade. Usually all grades are derived in conjunction with the university supervisor to maintain continuity between the student teacher's college work and the work in the cooperating teacher's classroom.

GUIDELINES FOR THE STUDENT TEACHER

- **Your cooperating teacher is probably devoted to the profession and would like to help another see the rewards of teaching.** Do not add to your cooperating teacher's burden; lighten it.
- **Do not wait to be told what to do.** If you see something that needs to be done, do it after clearing it with your cooperating teacher.
- **Think ahead.** Anticipate your responsibilities. Plan for ways in which you can best fit into the classroom.
- **Naturally, you will be anxious about your own performance in the classroom.** When you begin to work with the students who need you, you will gradually begin to lose yourself. By helping them, you will become more self-confident and more skilled in teaching and dealing with students.
- **Try to make life as easy for the cooperating teacher as possible.** Be professional. Avoid having to be reminded of deadlines.
- **Learn as much as you can from your cooperating teacher, both in classroom management techniques and in content delivery.** You will find that your student teaching will be a profitable experience.

GUIDELINES FOR THE COOPERATING TEACHER

- **Be aware that you have accepted a tremendous responsibility in agreeing to work with a student teacher.** Know that your university supervisor will be there to assist you.
- **Know that some student teachers arrive at the cooperating teacher's door well prepared and ready to teach and conduct themselves in a professional manner.** Some are not so well prepared as others, although they may have had the same college courses and teachers. The university supervisor can help you determine the level of readiness of your student teacher.
- **You should know that as a cooperating teacher you have the right at any time to request that the student teacher be withdrawn from your classroom.** Discuss this with the university supervisor.
- **Be aware that most student teachers have areas of weaknesses and areas that need much development.** If you can picture the student teacher as a diamond in the rough that needs some polishing and see yourself as the jeweler, the task may be less difficult.
- **The cooperating teacher should never complain to peers about a student teacher.** It would be appropriate, however, to boast if the occasion arose. Problems can be discussed with the university supervisor.

- **Most student teachers do not know exactly where to start.** Usually they are somewhat overwhelmed by the reality of the profession they have chosen for themselves. The cooperating teacher should work with the university supervisor to guide explicitly and carefully until it is obvious that the student teacher can maneuver alone.
- **Avoid the loss of precious time at the beginning of the term as you wait for the student teacher to act.** Not knowing what to do, the student teacher may be waiting for directions from you or from the university supervisor. Too often the cooperating teacher feels that the student teacher is lazy when it really is a case of the student's not knowing what to do.
- **Be patient with your student teacher. Be firm in conjunction with the university supervisor in demanding professional standards in performance.** Understand the stress under which the student teacher works.
- **Be helpful when help is requested.** Keep in mind that the objective of student teaching is to help the student teacher learn to stand alone. With the university supervisor, encourage the development of those qualities that will make the student teacher independent, not more dependent.

CASE STUDIES

C A S E

11-1   Bert, the new student teacher in Mrs. Lambert's journalism class, arrived at school on time and hurried past the office to the classroom. When he arrived, Mrs. Lambert was in conversation with some other teachers. Bert approached the group, and with a large smile and a loud "Hello, folks," he proceeded to slap one of the male teachers on the shoulder and peer directly into the eyes of the pretty young female teacher talking to Mrs. Lambert. Both teachers, never having met Bert, were somewhat appalled and backed away.

1. What do you think causes Bert to be overly friendly?
2. How should Mrs. Lambert react?
3. What impressions has Bert made on the other teachers?
4. How can Bert make up for such a beginning?
5. What responsibility does Mrs. Lambert have concerning Bert's actions?

C A S E

11-2   Since the initial visit, the cooperating teacher, Mrs. Strong, had suggested to her student teacher that she preferred that he develop his lesson plans in detail at least a week before he planned to implement them. As the time approached for the student teacher to take over his first class, Mrs. Strong repeatedly asked to see his plans so that they could discuss them. The student teacher always put her off with remarks to the effect that he was not yet happy with the plans and had not finished working with them.

The day before he was to begin teaching, the student teacher still refused to allow Mrs. Strong to see the plans or to discuss them with her. Mrs. Strong told him that she would be at school 45 minutes early the next day for the specific purpose of reviewing his plans with him before he taught. She would not allow him to take over her classroom without the plans. The next morning, she arrived at school early but the student teacher came at his usual time. When she asked him about his plans for teaching the class that day, he shrugged his shoulders and said, "I know what I'm going to do; I have it all in my head."

1. How do you think Mrs. Strong reacted?
2. What would have been the best action to have taken in this situation? Why?
3. How should the cooperating teacher report the student teacher's actions to the university supervisor?
4. What kind of attitude changes should the student teacher make for this to be a successful experience?
5. How could the cooperating teacher build on the planning strategies the student teacher had developed in college methodology courses?

C A S E

11-3   Mr. Stein, a biology teacher, had agreed to serve as cooperating teacher for a student teacher, Rob. Rob was unaware that Mr. Stein had routinely accepted student teachers in the past and was a good friend of Dr. Flowers, his university supervisor.

Rob was not overly ambitious; he told Mr. Stein that he wanted to get his teaching certificate so that he could teach just in case other job opportunities fell through. During discussions while on his initial visits at the school, Rob told his cooperating teacher who the university supervisor would be and, unaware that Mr. Stein and Dr. Flowers were good friends, began discussing Dr. Flowers in an unfavorable light.

Back on the college campus, as Rob was preparing to student teach, he asked Dr. Flowers whether he could discuss with him some possible problems. He then related some inappropriate details about Mr. Stein to Dr. Flowers, who realized that the student teacher was deceiving only himself in establishing the triangle.

1. Whose responsibility is it to discuss the truth with the student teacher?
2. Why should the student teacher not be allowed to play his game further?
3. As cooperating teacher, what approach would you have taken?
4. Why is it wise for student teachers to avoid criticizing their cooperating teacher or their university supervisor?
5. How would a change of cooperating teacher affect the situation?

C   A   S   E

11-4   Mr. Lyons, a fifth-grade teacher, had made arrangements for Nyasha, his new student teacher, to observe in several teachers' classes during her first 2 weeks in the new assignment. The observations went well until one of the observed teachers reported to Mr. Lyons that Nyasha had wanted to discuss with her what she referred to as different attitudes and methods of approach of the teacher previously observed.

1. How should Mr. Lyons approach the student teacher without indicating where he obtained his information?
2. What should he say to her?
3. How could he verify with other teachers whether this pattern of behavior existed elsewhere?
4. How could he keep this type of behavior from occurring in the future?
5. Why would it be important for evaluation sessions to be restricted to the cooperating teacher and the university supervisor?

C   A   S   E

11-5   Maria, the new student teacher in Miss Elbert's fourth-grade classroom, really wanted to be a good teacher. She was enthusiastic about her future as a teacher; she was also enthusiastic about her wedding that was scheduled for the week following the end of the term. At the beginning of the term, Maria explained that she was spending a great deal of time in the evenings getting things organized for the wedding but that she would soon be finished with that and be able to spend plenty of time on lesson preparation.

As the weeks wore on, Maria seemed less and less prepared with materials. Miss Elbert habitually arrived at school early and organized materials for the day. Maria had become lax and frequently arrived at the last minute with her arms full of papers. Often, she would ask Miss Elbert to watch the class while she went to the teachers' workroom to prepare materials; then while the students were working on those, Maria would prepare the next materials. This hurt Miss Elbert, who feared for her students' achievement. Until this point, Miss Elbert had not told the university supervisor of her concern, because she had hoped Maria would improve.

As things got worse instead of better, Miss Elbert confronted Maria with the problem. Maria explained that she just did not know any way to improve, that she could not get everything done that she was responsible for, and that she felt that she should withdraw from student teaching.

1. What alternatives should Miss Elbert offer Maria?
2. Should Miss Elbert take over any of Maria's responsibilities in the classroom?
3. What assistance could the university supervisor offer?
4. What should be the limit of the principal's involvement in this case?
5. In what ways would a student teacher's attention to personal affairs affect professionalism?

C   A   S   E

11-6   Eric was assigned to student teach with a young female coach. Although his major was physical education, he resented being placed to student teach with a female.

During his initial observations and early visits with his cooperating teacher, Eric expressed to her the possibility of his being placed with another teacher, since it just did not seem appropriate for him to be placed with a female.

As the term wore on, week after week, his remarks and hints became less subtle. The cooperating teacher, exasperated, decided she had had all she could take of Eric's attitude.

1. What procedure should the cooperating teacher follow?
2. What alternatives are available to the cooperating teacher? To the student teacher?
3. Under what conditions should the cooperating teacher be expected to allow the student teacher to complete the term?
4. In what ways would Eric's attitude affect his professional relationships with females?
5. How could the attitude have been identified earlier?

RECOMMENDED READING

Balch, P. M., & Balch, P. E. (1987). The responsibilities of a cooperating teacher. In *The cooperating teacher: A practical approach for the supervision of student teachers* (pp. 29–47). New York: University Press of America. *The variety of roles and responsibilities of the supervising teacher are explained. Helpful, practical suggestions are given for supervisory style and time management.*

Good, T. L., & Brophy, J. E. (1991). Instruction. In *Looking in classrooms* (5th ed.) (pp. 439–520). New York: HarperCollins. *This chapter on instruction is excellent reading and reference for both the cooperating teacher and the student teacher. Research on instructional methods, on teacher behavior related to learning, and on higher-order thinking and problem-solving strategies is a valuable resource for establishing competence in teaching.*

Gottesman, B. L., & Jennings, J. O. (1995). Peer Coaching for Educators Lancaster, PA: Technomic Publishing Company. *Coaching is a valuable tool for the cooperating teacher to use in assisting the student teacher, and this text gives clear procedures and reproducible checklists and questionnaires.*

Kottler, J. A. (1997). *What's really said in the teachers' lounge: Provocative ideas about cultures and classrooms.* Thousand Oaks, CA: Corwin Press. *The author gives ways in which beliefs and biases affect teaching and learning and offers effective strategies to deal with this problem.*

Posner, G. J. (1989). What is the situation with the cooperating teacher and the classroom? In *Field experiences: Methods of reflective teaching* (2nd ed.) (pp. 47–59). New York: Longman. *Posner shows the student teacher how to see the cooperating teacher and the classroom from the perspective of a teacher instead of from that of a student. Taking a fresh look at the teacher, the room itself, the students, and the activities enhances the readiness of the student teacher.*

Reiman, A., & Thies-Sprinthall, L. (1998). *Mentoring and supervision for teacher development.* New York: Longman. *This is an extensive text that deals with dimensions of teacher development, cy-*

cles of assistance, guided reflection, ethics, and professional revitalization.

Rohrkemper, M. M. (1982). Teacher self-assessment. In Daniel L. Duke (Ed.), *Helping teachers manage classrooms* (pp. 77–96). Alexandria, VA: Association for Supervision and Curriculum Development. *As cooperating teachers begin to assess the classroom activities of the student teacher, they begin to review their own assessment more critically. This chapter assists cooperating teachers to be more aware of the relationships between their intentions and the student behaviors.*

Rottier, J. (1996). *Implementing and improving teaming: A handbook. for middle level leaders.* Columbus, OH: National Middle School Association.

The author provides practical advice for team leaders, including team designs, scheduling for teaming, and roles of the team leader.

Ryan, K. (1982). The cooperating teacher: Who? what? why? when? how? and whither? In G. A. Griffin & S. Edwards (Eds.), *Student teaching: Problems and promising practices* (pp. 57–68). Austin: Research and Development Center for Teacher Education, University of Texas at Austin. *The author discusses the role of the cooperating teacher and two possible scenarios related to involvement in student teaching assignments. A number of questions are considered, and the author concludes by recommending that the current orthodoxies of student teaching be questioned.*

12

The University Supervisor

The university supervisor serves as the liaison between the school where student teaching is taking place and the college or university that is sponsoring the experience. Furthermore, the university supervisor is ultimately responsible for recommending the student teacher for certification. University supervisors serve as public relations agents and may be the only people from the university to work directly with the schools. Often they are asked to explain specific services of their institution.

An additional responsibility of the university supervisor is to provide interpretation of the university program to student teachers. This involves visiting the student teacher in the school, conducting seminars, and conferring with principals and cooperating teachers. Seminars in which groups of student teachers gather for discussion with the university supervisor provide a high level of comfort to the student teacher and offer the group an excellent opportunity to exchange useful ideas and materials.

University supervisors guide student teachers through the development and use of teaching skills. The one-to-one relationship between university supervisor and student teacher should present an ideal teaching atmosphere; the unique problems faced by each student teacher can be considered and suitable courses of action prescribed. Education majors seldom experience this one-to-one assistance prior to student teaching. Working closely with both a cooperating teacher and a university supervisor during the last term can enhance this type of individualization. The university supervisor should be considered a friend and helper who is accessible.

A university supervisor is primarily an evaluator during the supervisory visits. It is unrealistic to think that a university supervisor can size up the total teaching-learning situation during the typical four or five visits. The cooperating teacher must also be a major evaluator. The university supervisor, relying heavily on the coordinating teacher, is, however, usually responsible for the final evaluation of the student teacher.

The troubleshooting role of university supervisors is evident. Supervisors serve as intermediaries in situations that may arise between student teachers and cooperating teachers. Because many student teachers face difficulties, they should feel free to confide in the university supervisor who, by virtue of their position, must keep confidences.

Student teachers and cooperating teachers may not have had previous contact with their assigned university supervisor. The university supervisor should represent expertise in certain academic areas and should be recognized and used as a professional resource during student teaching both in and outside of class. One of the most important tasks of a university supervisor is to ensure close communication, getting all involved persons to give their best efforts in providing a successful learning experience for the student teacher.

GUIDELINES FOR THE STUDENT TEACHER

- **Communicate openly with your university supervisor.** One purpose of student teaching is to meet and resolve problems. A successful student teaching experience cannot be void of conflicts; it is a strength to be able to recognize problems and to discuss them with your college supervisor. You should also have many joys and successes to relate.
- **Meet with your university supervisor very early in the student teaching experience.** University supervisors usually visit schools during the 1st or 2nd week. There is a good possibility that a group meeting with your university supervisor and other student teachers will be scheduled on campus before you report to the school.
- **Consider your university supervisor to be a friend and helper.** An effective supervisor is well aware of the emotional aspects of teaching with its highs and lows and is always ready to listen.
- **Make your university supervisor feel welcomed when first visiting your classroom.** Introduce your supervisor to your coordinating teacher and your students, if feasible. An acceptable time to present your supervisor to the students is immediately before the first observation. If your prefer not to make a formal introduction, be sure to explain to your students the purpose of the supervisor's visit.
- **Keep your lesson plans and other information in a folder or notebook for review by your university supervisor.** Allow for a discussion of your teaching tasks. An effective supervisor helps you learn to evaluate your performance and can be invaluable in the development of instructional techniques.
- **Be yourself when your university supervisor visits.** Supervisors can easily recognize a dramatic presentation; they want to see a normal classroom situation. Be at your best for your students and yourself.
- **Appreciate and encourage the two- and three-way conferences with your university supervisor and your cooperating teacher.** Tremendous professional growth can take place during these conferences. Although in the future you will experience teaching without supervision, during student teaching you will know that you have at least two people who are deeply interested in your teaching skills
- **Your university supervisor will probably hold seminars during student teaching.** This would be a good opportunity to compare notes with other student teachers.

Morale is improved when you discover that others are struggling and working hard to accomplish the same goals.

GUIDELINES FOR THE COOPERATING TEACHER

- **Facilitate open communication with your student teacher and university supervisor.** Do not protect your student teacher from the life experiences of teaching.
- **Student teachers should have the opportunity to try out their ideas during student teaching and experience failures as well as successes.** Discuss openly the strengths and weaknesses of your student teacher with the university supervisor.
- **Use the strengths of the university supervisor who could possibly provide some alternative plans of action to enrich your classroom.** However, the university supervisor will not present suggestions for change unless specifically asked and is not there to evaluate a cooperating teacher's methods.
- **Make arrangements for a three-way conference (cooperating teacher, student teacher, university supervisor) immediately following the initial observation by the university supervisor, if possible.** University supervisors usually prefer three-way conferences, particularly at the beginning of student teaching; this will enhance communication. If such a conference cannot be arranged, provide time and a place for suitable two-way conferences between you and the university supervisor and between the student teacher and the university supervisor. (See Appendixes H and I.)
- **Be helpful by convincing the student teacher that the university supervisor is there to assist.** It enriches the student teaching program to involve as many professionals as practical.
- **Call your university supervisor if major concerns develop.** University supervisors expect cooperating teachers to communicate with them and seek help when necessary. Although university supervisors normally visit each student teacher four or five times, they could be available more frequently if necessary.

CASE STUDIES

C A S E

12-1   Juan was assigned as one of Dr. Jones's student teachers; Dr. Jones was the university supervisor. At their meeting on the 1st day of the semester, Dr. Jones explained that he would drop in unannounced during student teaching. He felt that he would see a more normal situation if student teachers and cooperating teachers did not know when he would visit. Juan expressed his displeasure over this arrangement and stated that it would be more fair if the student teachers were informed, at least for the first two or three visits.

1. Why should the student teacher be informed of the time of the university supervisor's first observation?
2. Why is the university supervisor's first observation a big deal in the mind of a student teacher?
3. What is the primary role of a university supervisor?
4. What are the advantages/disadvantages of the student teachers' knowing when the visits will take place?
5. How important are the evaluations of a university supervisor?

C   A   S   E

12-2   During his first observation of Shondra, her university supervisor, Dr. Brown, made some comments on his observation report that disturbed the cooperating teacher. Dr. Brown wondered why the third grades were not grouped for reading instruction to provide for the wide range of reading levels.

Shondra is quite concerned because she was only following her cooperating teacher's guidelines. She feels that she is caught between two different theories and cannot possibly come out a winner.

The cooperating teacher is distressed and threatens to discontinue working with her student teacher.

1. Why was Dr. Brown wrong about raising the question about the teaching of reading?
2. How should the cooperating teacher confront Dr. Brown concerning her displeasure?
3. How could Dr. Brown raise the question without upsetting the cooperating teacher?
4. What could be done to prevent Shondra's situation from becoming unbearable?
5. What measures should Dr. Brown take to reduce the tension?

C   A   S   E

12-3   Phong, a technology education student teacher, was in his 2nd week of student teaching. His university supervisor, Dr. Randolph, arrived on the scene to discover that the cooperating teacher was spending very little time in the classroom because he had explained to Phong that he wanted him to get the feel of complete control of the situation.

Dr. Randolph was quite concerned. He felt that this student teacher was not ready to take over the class. In fact, Phong was hardly familiar with the safety precautions in the lab. Dr. Randolph also wondered how effective supervision could be with the cooperating teacher gone most of the day.

1. Is there ever a valid reason for the cooperating teacher to stay out of the classroom for long periods of time during the beginning of student teaching?
2. How could Phong accomplish his goals during student teaching with his cooperating teacher out of the room most of the time?

3. Why is it important for a cooperating teacher to leave the student teacher periodically?
4. How should Phong's problem be resolved?
5. What role should the principal or Dr. Randolph take in this situation?

C A S E

12-4   Jamie was not pleased when Dr. Jacobson was assigned as her university supervisor. Jamie had received poor grades in two of his classes; she felt that he was most unfair in his evaluations.

   After his first observation of Jamie, Dr. Jacobson wrote up a very negative observation report. Jamie was quite upset because she thought she had taught an excellent science lesson with her third graders that day. Jamie believed that Dr. Jacobson had given her a negative report because of preconceived notions of her abilities. Jamie discussed the matter with her cooperating teacher after Dr. Jacobson left the school.

1. How should the cooperating teacher handle this matter?
2. Why do you think Jamie did not discuss this matter with Dr. Jacobson during their conference?
3. Is there any way that Jamie could win the approval of Dr. Jacobson? How?
4. Because Dr. Jacobson will be responsible for Jamie's final grade, should Jamie drop out of student teaching and hope for a different university supervisor next time? Why?
5. What situations could require that the university supervisor be changed during a student teaching assignment?

C A S E

12-5   Jen was assigned as a student teacher in a second-grade classroom. On arriving at school the 1st day, Jen was informed by her cooperating teacher that she felt that Jen was too immature to work with her low math group. Since the cooperating teacher did not want Jen to experience failure, she planned to send her to another classroom to work with an above-average math group during the first part of the morning.

   Jen, a top-notch teacher candidate, was distraught. She felt that her cooperating teacher had little faith in her abilities and had already labeled her a failure. She wanted the experience of working with the low math group and wondered how she could be fairly evaluated while working in another classroom.

   Feeling that she had no chance to succeed, she called her university supervisor to explain the situation. She requested a change of assignment. The university supervisor made plans to visit Jen the next day.

1. Were Jen's objections justified?
2. Was the cooperating teacher unfair in assigning Jen to another classroom for math?
3. How could communication have been improved in this situation?

4. Why would it be advantageous to work out the problem rather than change Jen's assignment?
5. What could the university supervisor do to resolve this conflict?

C A S E

12-6   Bradford had not passed his first student teaching assignment but was given another chance in an eighth-grade English class. It was the opinion of Bradford's first coordinating teacher that Bradford had potential as a teacher but had not been able to get his act together.

Bradford's newly assigned coordinating teacher observed one of Bradford's classes during the 3rd week of this second assignment. The coordinating teacher felt that Bradford's teaching was satisfactory but noticed some definite idiosyncracies in his behavior that bothered her considerably. She felt too embarrassed to discuss the matter with Bradford and decided to videotape his next lesson. Bradford was quite distraught at the idea of being videotaped and wondered why he had been singled out.

1. Is it unrealistic for Bradford's cooperating teacher not to discuss the matter with Bradford?
2. What kind of idiosyncracies could cause this much confusion?
3. Why did the cooperating teacher feel that a videotape would be helpful?
4. Should student teachers be given a second chance to student teach? If so, under what conditions?
5. What would be the advantages and disadvantages of giving Bradford the same cooperating teacher and university supervisor he had during the first assignment?

RECOMMENDED READING

Acheson, K. A., & Gall, M. D. (1997). *Techniques in the clinical supervision of teachers: Preservice and inservice applications* (4th ed.). New York: Longman. *The authors speak to effective clinical supervision, observation techniques, teacher roles, direct and indirection supervision, and peer consultation.*

Balch, P. M., & Balch, P. E. (1987). Establishing professional relationships. In *The cooperating teacher: A practical approach for the supervision of student teachers* (pp. 143–157). New York: University Press of America. *This chapter includes a discussion on the relationship between* the college supervisor and the cooperating teacher. *Of special note is the discussion of collaboration necessary for this team.*

Colton, A. B., & Lander, G. S. (1992). Restructuring student teaching experiences. In C. D. Glickman (Ed.), *Supervision in transition: 1992 yearbook of the Association for Supervision and Curriculum Development* (pp. 155–168). Alexandria, VA: Association for Supervision and Curriculum Development. *This article proposes to help to develop thoughtful and self-directed educational professionals, including student teachers, by initially structuring the basis of the perception of the student teaching experience. The second step is to train cooperating teachers and university supervisors who can use these restructured experiences. This model was developed through work with the Ann Arbor (Michigan) public school teachers and the faculty of Eastern Michigan University.*

Hevener, F., Jr. (1981). Relating to the college student teaching counselor. In *Successful student teaching: A handbook for elementary and secondary student teachers* (pp. 54–61). Palo Alto, CA: R.&E. Research Associates. *Hevener refers to the university student teaching supervisor as the college student teaching counselor. The roles of the supervisor are explored. Student teachers are encouraged to expect three-way conferences, conferences between the coordinator and the supervising teacher, and post-lesson conferences to evaluate their teaching skills.*

Machado, J. M., & Meyer, H. C. (1984). Common problems of student teachers. In *Early childhood practicum guide: A sourcebook for beginning teachers of young children* (pp. 98–106). Albany, NY: Delmar Publishers. *Areas of conflict that may occur involving the university su-*

pervisor, the cooperating teacher, and the student teacher are considered in this chapter. Suggested activities are listed and reassurances are provided for the student teacher.

McNeeley, S. (1997). *Observing students and teachers through objectives strategies.* Boston: Allyn & Bacon. *Both the preservice and novice teacher can learn to look at classroom behavior reflectively and develop an improved conceptual basis for decision making.*

Slick, S. K. (September–October 1998). A university supervisor negotiates territory and status. *Journal of Teacher Education 49*(4), 306–315. The author discusses some of the tensions and problems of being the university supervisor.

Sorenson, V., & Veele, M. (1978). The student teaching team. In *The student teacher's handbook* (pp. 7–14). Holmes Beach, FL: Learning Publications. *This brief chapter contains suggestions for the student teaching team: the university supervisor, the cooperating teacher, the school administrator, and the student teacher. These responsibilities are listed in an effort to improve communication among the entire team.*

The Students
in the Classroom

The focal point of any educational program is the student in the classroom. A successful student teacher assumes a partnership in meeting the educational needs of a given group of students.

Knowledge of pupils can benefit a student teacher enormously; therefore, student teachers who begin this assignment at the beginning of the year learn along with the cooperating teachers the needs of the students, their capabilities, and their learning levels. Student teachers who begin at midyear are at a disadvantage in knowing the level at which the students have been working. It is then more difficult for the student teacher to communicate with the students and to understand the structure of the classroom setting. It is up to the cooperating teacher to fill these gaps.

One of the major concerns of the student teacher is classroom control. It is a shock for most student teachers to realize that they will soon be in charge of the discipline for an entire class. Often the student teacher cannot distinguish between teaching the students and "making friends" with the students and many times does not have the knack of handling the entire group. Until the student teacher gains self-confidence and more knowledge about the group, it is necessary to begin by working with individual students and small groups. Most student teachers by this stage of their college work have had several practical experiences in other classrooms and will soon be able to prepare for entire-class teaching.

During student teaching, ample opportunity to study and further develop skills and competencies that had been introduced earlier in the teacher education training program become available. The following are some personal and professional qualities that the student teacher should attempt to refine during these weeks in the classroom:

1. A desire for fairness to all students.
2. A respect for all students regardless of ethnic, cultural, and socioeconomic background or state of health.
3. The desire to be a good role model for the students and to help them in developing their own positive self-image.

More and more, schools are becoming involved with children who may suffer from a health problem or a physical impairment. Each of these students deserves the very best in the way of emotional support and teaching skills. Frequently, instructional patterns must be altered to accommodate these students, and the student teacher should make every effort to serve these students well. Through cooperative learning strategies, the student teacher can demonstrate to the other students the joys of assisting those who may have physical problems and cannot participate as others do in the learning situations. Students often try to become personally involved with the student teacher. This is true at the secondary level as well as the elementary level. Everyone becomes involved to a degree, but the student teacher should avoid becoming too personally involved.

Younger students like to touch or pat their teacher on the arm or shoulder. There is a time and a place for this, but it is not during class. The cooperating teacher can be helpful in guiding such situations.

GUIDELINES FOR THE STUDENT TEACHER

- **Think through a philosophy for working with students.** Such a philosophy may include the following:
    a. Give students some freedom of choice and self-expression.
    b. Treat each student as an individual and give the student an opportunity to express ideas.
    c. Give opportunities for students to think for themselves.
    d. Try to avoid doing for the students what they can do for themselves.
    e. Try to have a positive approach, using a kind firmness.
    f. Make suggestions more frequently than issuing commands.
    g. Follow through when you have asked for a response. If you ask a question, give the students time to think about it. Do not keep on talking.
    h. Try to give the students reasons for doing certain things required of them. Lead them to think through the reasons themselves.
    i. Be consistent in your approach so that the students know what is expected of them.
    j. Lead the students to finish the projects they begin.
    k. Talk in the language of the age group with which you are working. Avoid talking down to the students.
    l. Avoid having favorites.
    m. Plan ways students can accept responsibilities; help them to follow through.
    n. Be alert to changing conditions and new needs.
    o. Remember that one does not have to be constantly talking to students for them to learn.
    p. Listen when students talk to you. Be alert to their ideas.
    q. Use questioning techniques to help students think through problems on their own.

    r. Study each student to learn the directions in which he or she needs to grow. Be aware of all students who do not participate.

- **Learn the names of students quickly.** This can be done by making a seating chart. Try to get to know the students individually. Your cooperating teacher is your best resource in this respect.
- **Get to know your students through observation, conferences, test scores, and school records.** During observations you may ask the following questions:
  a. How are the responsibility and initiative of the student promoted?
  b. How are student and student-teacher planning encouraged and implemented?
  c. What is the evidence of student personality factors such as excessive shyness, extremely critical attitudes, extreme sensitivity, daydreaming?
  d. What are the work habits of the students, such as the ability to work independently or cooperatively with other students and the willingness to ask for and use help from others?
- **Do your very best in working with the students.** Regardless of age, students are quick to notice lack of preparation, uncertainty, and insincerity. They will try you at times, but they will want you to succeed if they feel you are sincerely interested in them.
- **Avoid the following common errors in working with students:**
  a. Calling on the better students too often.
  b. Failing to explain material at the level of the students.
  c. Taking for granted that students know certain facts.
  d. Punishing the entire class for misbehavior of one or two people.
  e. Punishing individual students before the entire class.
- **Student teachers are not to touch or paddle a student in disciplinary action.** Under no circumstances is the student teacher to inflict corporal punishment.
- **If you become aware of students administering medications to themselves or to others on the school site, report this immediately to your cooperating teacher.** Self-administered medications may be illicit drugs. This is a serious responsibility.
- **Keep in mind that your students are learners and are the center of the enterprise we call education.** They are the reason for your being there.
- **Keep in mind that as a teacher, you are a public servant.** This is sometimes difficult but it is imperative. Discuss with your cooperating teacher and university supervisor how this will affect your professionalism.

GUIDELINES FOR THE COOPERATING TEACHER

- **Prepare your students for the student teacher.** Convince them that the student teacher is there to assume the role of the teacher.
- **Encourage the students to cooperate with the new person.** The attitude of the students depends a great deal on your attitude.

- **Placing name tags on the desks of the students when the student teacher arrives is a good practice in the elementary schools.** This will be appreciated by the student teacher who is usually eager to learn names. In middle and high schools, the student teacher should be given a seating chart for each class.
- **Review the class rules with the students in the presence of the student teacher.** Beginning student teachers are concerned about the status of their authority in the classroom; reviewing the rules should avoid misunderstandings at a later date.
- **Provide the student teacher with an opportunity to learn about the students who are in your classes.** Cumulative records, individual conferences, open-ended questionnaires, or small-group activities provide sources for this purpose.
- **Some cooperating teachers prefer to avoid pointing out which pupils have discipline problems.** Student teachers thus would have no preconceived ideas about pupils. Students often respond differently to student teachers. At times, student teachers see a side of the pupil overlooked by the cooperating teacher, and the cooperating teacher gets a new perspective on the child.
- **Assist student teachers in setting realistic standards of performance for themselves and the students.** Encourage creative thinking and planning by students and by the student teacher. This means permitting the classroom routines to vary to provide for the special needs and abilities of the student teacher.
- **Update your student teacher on any real or threatened drug problem at your school.** Caution the student teacher to be aware of certain areas and problem students. Review the current laws relating to drug use at school.

CASE STUDIES

C   A   S   E

13-1   Sharon is a student teacher in a fifth-grade classroom. She has progressed satisfactorily but has been a bit ill at ease about the behavior of two or three of the boys. There were no major problems until today when one of her students, Don, refused to go to the office at her request. Don was larger than the student teacher, and the cooperating teacher was in the workroom. Sharon decided to ignore the situation.

Shortly afterward Sharon asked one of her other problem boys to quit bothering his neighbor. He yelled out: "I don't have to! You aren't my teacher!"

1. Was there a better way of handling Don after he refused to go to the office?
2. How should the cooperating teacher deal with this situation?
3. How should Sharon respond to the second situation?
4. What prior preventive measures could have been taken to avoid the development of such a situation?
5. How will these two incidents affect the confidence of the student teacher?

C   A   S   E

13-2   Teresa is a student in the biology class of Anthony, a new student teacher. She is very much attracted to Anthony, who has been the star quarterback at the nearby university.

Anthony asked Teresa to sit down during a lesson, and Teresa proceeded to run out of the classroom. Teresa's parents were contacted, and the situation was explained to them during a conference. Teresa was counseled by the guidance counselor and she explained her deep attraction for Anthony. She felt that he was also interested in her and was crushed when he asked her to sit down.

1. What parties should have been included in the conference with the parents?
2. Was Anthony at fault in this situation? Explain your answer.
3. How would a good background in human growth and development help Anthony in understanding what was happening to Teresa?
4. How could Anthony avoid any indication that he was encouraging Teresa in her fantasy?
5. How will Teresa fit into Anthony's class after this?

C   A   S   E

13-3   Randy is a student teacher in an eighth-grade science class. He has taken over three classes and appears to be doing a good job. Today Randy presented an activity project and became quite upset at the end of the lesson when his students went to the cooperating teacher rather than to him for assistance on the worksheet. The cooperating teacher noticed Randy's reaction and asked the students to go to Randy with their problems. The students continued to go to the cooperating teacher.

1. Why do you feel that the students would not seek out the student teacher?
2. What would be the best way for Randy to solve this problem?
3. Could the cooperating teacher be of assistance in this matter? In what ways?
4. What steps could Randy take to analyze the day's lesson to determine what went wrong?
5. How should Randy approach the next activity lesson? Under what conditions?

C   A   S   E

13-4   Elisabeth is in her 2nd week as a student teacher in a second-grade classroom. Her cooperating teacher runs a very relaxed classroom, which is a concern to Elisabeth. As a student teacher, Elisabeth is afraid that when she begins teaching she will not have control at all. The few times the cooperating teacher has left the room, the students have gotten completely out of hand. Elisabeth feels she has become overly friendly with two or three of the students and fears that this works against her. In fact, one of the students mentioned that he could hardly wait until she began teaching because he was "tired of working."

1. Do you feel that Elisabeth's fears are justified?
2. Should Elisabeth attempt to structure her classroom control according to the framework already set up by the cooperating teacher? Explain.
3. What can be done by the cooperating teacher to resolve this situation?
4. How should Elisabeth prepare her university supervisor for the initial observation?
5. What could Elisabeth have done differently from the very beginning?

C A S E

13-5   Jack has completed his 5th week in a seventh-grade English student teaching assignment. His cooperating teacher is concerned about his passive attitude toward the seventh graders. Jack worked hard in preparing his lessons but never talked to the students individually or seemed interested in their affairs. He was primarily concerned with his lectures and treated his students as a group rather than as individuals.

1. Why is it necessary for an effective teacher to be interested in students as individuals?
2. What approach should Jack's cooperating teacher take concerning this matter?
3. Should Jack be allowed to pass student teaching if he uses only the lecture approach to teaching?
4. In what way could the university supervisor be of assistance to Jack?
5. What problems usually arise if the student teacher is more interested in the subject matter than in the students?

C A S E

13-6   Marta was assigned to a senior high school to student teach. During the 3rd week, she discovered she was pregnant. Up until that time, Marta had shown little enthusiasm; from then on the situation got even worse. Marta seldom got out of her seat, which was located in the front of the room. During tests the students began to copy from each other because there was so little supervision. Word got to the cooperating teacher, who became furious. Cheating had not previously been a problem.

1. Should Marta be discouraged from student teaching because she is pregnant? Why or why not?
2. How could the cheating situation have been avoided?
3. In what way were the students at fault?
4. Can one teach effectively while sitting in front of the room most of the time? Explain?
5. How does the development of this situation present opportunities for teaching values?

RECOMMENDED READING

Duggan, M. A. (1998). *Notes home: 115 letters and forms on CD-ROM for busy teachers.* Thousand Oaks, CA: Corwin Press. *Compatible for Mac and Windows, this CD-ROM provides letters and forms to parents that you can use as is or customize for your own classes. A real time saver!*

Garcia, C. L. (1998). *Too scared to learn: Overcoming academic anxiety.* Thousand Oaks, CA: Corwin Press. *This text guides the teacher to help students overcome their fear of solving problems, making speeches, or writing papers so that they can become more successful in their learning.*

George, P. S., Stevenson, C., Thomason, J., & Beane, J. (1992). Teachers and students: Relationships and results. In *The middle school and beyond* (pp. 15–31). Alexandria, VA: Association for Supervision and Curriculum Development. *These authors emphasize the needs and wants of both teachers and students in classroom relationships. Healthy traits and desirable qualities are discussed.*

Gilbert, R. N., & Robins, M. (1998). *Welcome to our world: Realities of high school students.* Thousand Oaks, CA: Corwin Press. *This text encourages teachers to be more sensitive to the universe of pressures, such as social, academic, sports, jobs, and family, that high school students face.*

Good, T. L., & Brophy, J. E. (1991). Classroom complexity and teacher awareness. In *Looking in classrooms* (5th ed.) (pp. 23–46). New York: Harper Collins. *This chapter is a good review for the cooperating teacher and a good introduction for the student teacher to the complexities of the classroom. Factors presented in this chapter include problems caused by a lack of teacher awareness of space, gender, time, and interaction difficulties.*

Good, T. L., & Brophy, J. E. (1991). Classroom life. In *Looking in classrooms* (5th ed.) (pp. 15–22). New York: HarperCollins. *Good and Brophy give the prospective student teacher a glimpse of the classroom. This chapter includes classroom narratives for both the elementary and the secondary schools.*

Krovetz, M. (1998). *Fostering resiliency: Expecting all students to use their minds and hearts well.* Thousand Oaks, CA: Corwin Press. *The author provides a method for developing a resilient learning community.*

Meehan, A. M., & Astor-Stetson, E. (1998). *Annual editions: Adolescent psychology 98/99* (2nd ed.). New York: McGraw-Hill. *This book of readings covers articles that have previously appeared in press on the spectrum of adolescent development. The articles are brief and to the point and offer excellent food for professional discussions.*

Scheidecker, D., & Freeman, W. (1998). *Bringing out the best in students: How legendary teachers motivate kids.* Thousand Oaks, Calif: Corwin Press. *These authors illustrate how setting an example for your students and helping them develop so they want to come to school will assist in their viewing your classroom as meaningful.*

Sorenson, V. M., & Veele, M. L. (1978). You and your students. In *The student teacher's handbook* (pp. 23–29). Holmes Beach, FL: Learning Publications. *Sorenson and Veele stress the importance of beginning the student teaching experience with the right relationship with your students. They give pointers in developing skills for initiating and maintaining those relationships.*

Tauber, R. T. (1997). *Self-fulfilling prophecy: A practical guide to its use in education.* Westport, CT: Praeger. *As the title implies, this book indicates to teachers that students will do about what we expect of them and stresses that teachers' expectations of student achievement are very important.*

Taylor, B. J. (1991). Guidance techniques for teachers and parents. In *A child goes forth* (pp. 263–276). New York: Macmillan. *Taylor gives valuable realistic suggestions for working successfully with the young child. Although this chapter focuses on the preschool child, the information can be adapted for older children.*

Diversity

14

Multicultural Students

If student teachers can visualize a matrix of potential psychological characteristics among the students in any given class and see the diversity of such psychological characteristics, it is much easier for them to see a similar matrix of the characteristics possessed by the students from culturally diverse backgrounds in the assigned classes. Such a matrix could look something like a honeycomb with the same labels across the horizontal axis as across the vertical axis. These characteristics include such things as sex, race, country of family origin, disability, age, language preference, and economic status.

At a minimum, student teachers in most schools have students of both sexes from various economic levels. Some of these students also have disabilities. Most schools have a population variety from several races, ethnic groups, and countries of family origin. A picture of most classrooms shows a rich cross section of different skin tones, different hair and facial characteristics, and different styles of clothing, just as classrooms have always exhibited a wide variety of psychological characteristics.

Although some teachers feel they must learn a great deal more to function effectively with different kinds of individuals, it is important to keep in mind that the most essential element and the key to success with each student is to relate to each one individually. All other differences matter little if a real desire to work together for the benefit of the student is expressed by the student teacher to each individual student. This expression takes the form of patience, body language, use of the eyes in communicating, and facial expressions. A teacher's smile can go a long way when languages are incompatible. It is important to keep in mind the purpose of the school and the student teacher's relationship to that purpose: to help educate children, to take them where they are and move them forward in the skills of living, working, studying, and getting along with others in order to make their lives better according to their own definitions of what is better.

Many times teachers are frustrated because students from culturally diverse backgrounds are not making the same progress as other students. In fact, those students may be making far more progress because of their point of beginning, the amount of translation they must use, and the kinds of feelings they must deal with as they work on their school assignments.

It is important for the cooperating teacher and the student teacher to discuss characteristics of students in the classroom from culturally diverse backgrounds. What assists them in learning? What different instructional techniques can be used to help them succeed? It is very helpful for the student teacher to observe in as many classrooms as possible in which there are students from culturally diverse backgrounds to note how teachers and how other students successfully relate to these students.

Most contemporary schools have a good mix of students. If a third-grade Asian child is having difficulty, one source of assistance is a successful fifth-grade Asian student. Most often, students do not have the problems relating to other students that adults anticipate. Peer acceptance and involvement are very important, however, prior to successful classroom achievement. Occasionally, the teacher can assist peer acceptance through purposefully directing classroom activity combining specific students in small-group work. Most classrooms have students who want to help others with their work; teachers should use these students to assist with students from culturally diverse backgrounds.

Some disabilities among students are temporary; such conditions can be truly educational. Once the student is out of the wheelchair or off the crutches, he or she is more understanding and tolerant of other students who may have similar problems adjusting to the classroom.

A concept that should receive major emphasis during student teaching is that of the likenesses of students. Emphasizing the ways in which all students are alike, for example, enjoying play activities, enjoying food, liking friends, needing rest and sleep, helps students to understand that people have more likenesses than differences.

Differences among students can be used as instructional enhancement. The music, art, customs, foods, dances, styles of clothing, and folklore of the different cultures within a class can generate many approaches to learning. When information about these exciting differences is used, the subjects in the curriculum can be more exciting for all the students. Language arts is a natural subject for examining cultures: Writing, storytelling, listening, reading, library research, and even spelling can be involved in studying different cultures. Any subject in the curriculum can be related in this way; all it requires is creativity and appreciation of differences.

The differences of cultures tend to stimulate students into their own research, whether that takes the form of interviewing older people or spending time in the library or on the Internet looking up specific topics. These differences are a vast resource of rich, available educational activity. With the help of the cooperating teacher, the student teacher can enlist the parents and other family members of students from culturally diverse backgrounds to come to the school for presentations, interviews, and cultural reviews.

GUIDELINES FOR THE STUDENT TEACHER

- **Put on your adventurer's hat and be ready for some exciting study.** By using the information represented by the various cultures in your student teaching classroom, your students have exciting topics to study and learn about firsthand. Their living data are more exciting to them and probably more accurate than your library and cyber research, although such research is necessary. This is a part of your student teaching that can be fun and can be a learning experience for both you and the students in your classroom.
- **Practice deliberately smiling and caring.** Frequently, students from different cultures tend to isolate themselves either alone or within small groups. Break through these walls; let them know that you are there to help them learn and that being comfortable in their classroom is a prerequisite for such learning.
- **Read everything you can find in the university library; have your students do research in the school library.** Develop a game of verifying information about cultures represented in your class. Assign students to library projects on what writers think customs of those groups are and compare those with the reality of the customs of the children in your classroom. This is live, exciting research for the students.
- **Emphasize the foods of different cultures.** Where possible, prepare some of these foods in your classroom so that students know the ingredients and flavors for themselves. Research on why certain ingredients are used by some cultures and not by others helps students understand more of our physical world and its flora and fauna.
- **Plan for students to write and act in their own drama depicting certain cultural customs.** Students enjoy this and remember these lessons.
- **Use the music and art of the various cultures as subjects through which to study history as well as contemporary society.** Some music and art are quite different from what you or the children have been previously exposed to. Students can learn to appreciate them or even just to accept them as being representative of another culture's efforts toward entertainment and personal expression.
- **You may wish to plan your multicultural studies around a "Culture of the Month" organization.** Plan an initial outline of activities and research and use it as a template for each month so that each culture receives equal treatment and support.
- **Visualize each different student in your classroom as an opportunity for you to learn.** Your culturally diverse learning under the direction of the cooperating teacher is priceless. Observe how other teachers in the school celebrate cultural diversity. Take notes. Keep records of all ideas. Such materials and ideas will enrich your own teaching for your professional life.

- **You will find that as you accept students of other cultures, they learn from you to a similar degree.** Care for each student; let the students know that you have a real concern for their learning experiences to be successful and that you are working toward that objective. Keep in mind that to the student of another culture, you are from a different culture yourself!

GUIDELINES FOR THE COOPERATING TEACHER

- **Give your student teacher optimum exposure to students from as many cultures as possible.** This is a time for the student teacher to learn to interact with students of all kinds.
- **Set the role model of patience and caring** in helping students from culturally diverse backgrounds find their niche in your classroom.
- **Encourage your student teacher to find and read as much material as possible about the nature of cultures other than his or her own.** This is excellent discussion material for the two of you; you will find that this research on the part of the student teacher benefits your own learning.
- **It is possible that you and your student teacher are of different cultures, sexes, or economic strata.** Learning to work together benefits both of you and helps your student teacher to more readily adapt to other cultures.
- **Help your student teacher to understand that whatever traditions and customs other cultures have is really just their way of coping with the processes of life.** These processes may be very different from culture to culture, but the purpose is the same: to maintain life and improve it. This kind of understanding assists the student teacher in realizing that likenesses among different cultures are much greater than their differences.
- **As your student teacher prepares special materials on various cultures, request that two sets of everything be produced.** This will allow the student teacher to take a set with him or her when he or she completes student teaching, and it means that you will have a set to keep for permanent use. These can be time-consuming to develop and keeping copies is important.
- **A notebook with a section for each culture represented in your classroom is a gold mine for your student teacher to use.** Depending on their ages, your students could produce the entries for such a notebook that include food, dress, customs, music, dance, drama, history, and geography. Such a collection could eventually become a cardboard file drawer with appropriate culturally diverse artwork decorating it.
- **People love exciting things. Be aware that student teachers are no different** from your classroom students in this regard. They enjoy studying the various cultures in the class as much as the students do.
- **Demonstrate the effects of positive body language and smiles.** This may be the initial opportunity for the student teacher to see such measures demonstrated effectively.

CASE STUDIES

C   A   S   E

14-1   Ichiro was a new Asian student who had just transferred into the eighth-grade class where Ester was student teaching. He seemed to be a loner, was quiet, and did not mix with the others. Although initially he had done very well on the mathematics work and tests, he had recently just barely passed. The cooperating teacher encouraged Ester to have a talk with Ichiro as soon as possible without having a scheduled conference (which could cause Ichiro anxiety). Ester found the right moment for a brief talk with Ichiro and discovered that some of the larger boys in the class had taunted him for his good grades in mathematics. So that they would not continue to bother him, Ichiro had decided the mathematics grades were not worth it and deliberately did poorly on his papers.

1. What kinds of emotions do you think Ichiro was experiencing?
2. How could Ester cause better acceptance of Ichiro's mathematics ability by using cooperative learning within the group?
3. What would be the outcome if Ester openly scolded the larger boys for threatening Ichiro?
4. What would happen if Ester and her cooperating teacher left the matter alone and did nothing?
5. What would be the ideal resolution of this problem?

C   A   S   E

14-2   In developing a research project in seventh-grade social studies, the student teacher assigned the students to talk with their parents and grandparents and develop a family tree that they could bring to class as a way of illustrating to the class the wide variety of cultural backgrounds within the group. The project had been cleared earlier with the cooperating teacher.

The next morning when the student teacher arrived at school, a parent of one of her students was waiting for her in the classroom. The cooperating teacher had not yet arrived. As the student teacher walked into the room, she was greeted with a hostile "What in this world do you mean, nosing into my family background? You and your students have no business whatsoever knowing anything about my family. That was a crazy assignment you gave my son yesterday, and I have told him that he doesn't have to do it!"

1. What do you think was the immediate reaction of the student teacher? How would you have responded?
2. What are some of the statements the student teacher may have made to the angry parent?

3. What kinds of alternate assignments could the student teacher have suggested?
4. How do you feel the student teacher treated this person's son after this meeting?
5. What kinds of psychological preparation should student teachers make prior to their student teaching in order to survive such a meeting?

C A S E

14-3   Sammy Runningbear enjoyed being at his new school. The family had just moved to town and his sixth-grade class had accepted him because he had helped them win the baseball game against the other sixth-grade class. As sixth-grade peer groups will, the boys became buddies with each other.

The student teacher in Sammy's classroom was about to initiate a short unit on rhythm in dance, music, and poetry. When she discovered that Mr. Runningbear was an accomplished Native American drummer, she invited him to perform with his drums for the class. Mr. Runningbear accepted the invitation; he visited the class, played his drums, and explained some of his Native American customs.

The visit appeared to be a success until the following day when the boys in class began drumming on their desks, singing "I am Runningbear; I am Runningbear." Sammy was very embarrassed and ashamed.

1. What immediate action should the student teacher and the cooperating teacher take?
2. What steps could have been taken prior to Mr. Runningbear's visit to have avoided such a demonstration?
3. What is happening to sixth graders physiologically and psychologically to make them particularly susceptible to this type of behavior?
4. How could Sammy's embarrassment and shame be turned to pride in his ancestry? Is there need for this? Why?
5. How could the student teacher involve the parents of the demonstrating students to discuss their cultural heritage with the class?

C A S E

14-4   Hannah was student teaching in the 11th-grade history class and received a request for a conference from the mother of one of her students. The conference time was set and the mother appeared. It seems that she objected to Hannah's use of terms such as *forefathers, the common man,* and *founding fathers.* The mother suggested that she use, instead, such words as *ancestors, the average person,* and *founders.*

1. How should Hannah respond to the student's mother?
2. Which terms are more appropriate? Why?
3. If there was a problem with the terms Hannah was using, why had they been used in her classes at the university?

4. What other terms would be considered sexist language and should be avoided by teachers?
5. Why had no one ever told Hannah before that such terms cause problems for some people?

C A S E

14-5   Cecelia was an African American student teacher in Mr. Piner's senior class in English literature. She enjoyed her students and the professional association with the faculty at the high school. Cecelia was very proud of her African American heritage, including the fabric art prints that had been made into beautiful clothing. She liked to wear such clothing to her student teaching assignment, and the students appeared to appreciate the relief from the rather conservative clothing that most of the other teachers wore. Mr. Piner had a personal dislike for such clothing and told Cecelia that she should not wear it to school again. The clothing represented a part of Cecelia's heritage, and Cecelia was hurt by Mr. Piner's order.

1. How could Mr. Piner say such a thing? Did he have the right to do so?
2. What feelings would have prompted him to forbid her to wear such clothes?
3. How could the university supervisor convince Mr. Piner that his decision was very narrow?
4. If you had been Cecelia, what would you have done?
5. In what ways should the opinions of the students be considered?
6. What options were available to Cecelia?

RECOMMENDED READING

Adler, M., & McKenzie, F. D. (1985). *Must all students be given the same kind of schooling?* In J. W. Noll (Ed.), *Taking sides: Clashing views on controversial educational issues* (pp. 150–163). Guilford, CN: Dushkin. *Mortimer Adler and Floretta Dukes McKenzie debate the nature of current reform in education. This very interesting discussion gives a basis for thought-provoking professional conversations.*

Amodeo, L., & Martin, J. (1988). A neglected educational issue: Rural, minority women. In J. Sikula (Ed.), *Action in teacher education, the journal of the Association of Teacher Educators, 10th-year anniversary issue, commemorative edition* (pp. 99–102). Reston, VA: Association of Teacher Educators. *Rural, minority women seem to have compounded problems in employment, education, and other job-related factors. Eight recommendations are given indicating areas of priority for improving conditions for these women.*

Baptiste, H. P., Jr., Waxman, H. C., deFelix, J. W. & Anderson, J. E. (Eds.). (1990). *Leadership, equity, and school effectiveness.* Newbury Park, CA: Sage. *This book contains material on equity in schooling written by 22 outstanding educational professionals. Of particular interest to the supervising teacher are "Teacher Effectiveness Research and Equity Issues" by Jane Stallings and Jane McCarthy and "Teacher Education That Enhances Equity" by James B. Boyer.*

Cushner, K., McClelland, A., & Stafford, P. (1995). *Human diversity in education: An integrative approach* (2nd ed.). New York: McGraw-Hill. *This text is excellent background for teachers in working with the various forms of diversity found in today's schools.*

Dunn, R., & Griggs, S. A. (1995). *Multiculturalism and learning style: Teaching and counseling adolescents.* Westport, CT: Praeger. *Provides information about learning style characteristics, including multicultural learning style characteristics.*

Franklin, J. H. (1990). The desperate need for Black teachers. In M. L. Kysilka (Ed.), *Honor in teaching: Reflections* (pp. 95–97). West Lafayette, IN: Kappa Delta Pi. *The author briefly describes the need for African American teachers in America, particularly for the role models children need. A suggestion offered is the redevelopment of education as a profession that is again attractive to young African American students.*

Pai, Y. & Adler, S. A. (1997). *Cultural foundations of education.* Upper Saddle River, NJ: Merrill/Prentice Hall. *This book examines education as a cultural phenomenon and considers the process of teaching, learning, and counseling within such a perspective. Case studies are included that involve African American, Asian American, Hispanic American, Native American, and White American groups.*

Whitehurst, W., Witty, E., & Wiggins, S. (1988). Racial equity: Teaching excellence. In J. Sikula (Ed.), *Action in teacher education, The Journal of the Association of Teacher Educators, 10th-year anniversary issue, commemorative edition* (pp. 159–167). Reston, VA: Association of Teacher Educators. *This article discusses the shortage of minority teachers in the workforce and two major efforts to improve this situation. One effort is a predominately African American institution that is trying to maintain its teacher education program, and the other effort is a Virginia school district of over 25,000 students.*

15

Special-Needs Students

Mainstreaming students with special learning needs into the regular classrooms is a present-day common occurrence. When the trend changed from placing special-needs children in special classrooms to mainstreaming them, there were numerous anxieties among classroom teachers who were not familiar with the problems and joys of working with special-needs students. Today, most student teachers have had some training in how to assist such students. Teacher education programs require an introductory course in exceptional education in many NCATE and state programs. This assists the beginning teacher to recognize and work with special-needs students, often obtaining assistance from more highly specialized personnel at the school.

Lewis and Doorlag (1999) state that for these special-needs students to learn successfully, they require instructional adaptations. The authors classify the variety of special students into four groups: handicapped, gifted and talented, culturally diverse, and at-risk for school failure. The divisions within categories generally are as follows:

1. Students with disabilities: learning disabilities, mental retardation, behavior disorders, speech and language disorders (including speech and hearing impairments and autism), vision and hearing disabilities, physical and health disabilities.
2a. Gifted students: unusually bright, creatively gifted.
2b. Gifted in special areas: art, music, drama, leadership.
3. Culturally diverse students: home culture at variance with school, difference from peers in language, most typically members of minority cultures (Asian Americans, African Americans (largest minority group), Hispanic Americans (second largest cultural group and largest bilingual groups), Native Americans.
4. Students at risk: threatened by complex societal problems (poverty, homelessness, child abuse, alcohol and other drug abuse, potential dropouts, potential and actual delinquents, runaways, teenage parents, suicide risks.

In many cases, the problems of the students are confounded by their exhibiting indications of more than one of the above-listed characteristics. A cross-categorical approach (Hardman, Drew, Egan & Wolf, 1993) will help teachers in training to understand a combination of the characteristics of the categories listed above. The Americans with Disabilities Act (PL 101-336) was implemented "to end discrimination against individuals with disabilities in private-sector employment, all public services, and public accommodations, transportation and telecommunications" (Hardman et al., 1993, p. 16). It is critical that student teachers understand the implications of providing equal service to all students to meet the letter of the law, but more important to meet the intent of the law. Students must be prepared to maximize their skills for their own and society's benefit; they must be given the skills, attitudes, and knowledge to move them forward in their social and work life, no matter what their disability is.

Many student teachers will experience classroom responsibilities with students who have been diagnosed with attention-deficit disorder (ADD). According to Hardman et al., attention-deficit disorder is subdivided into attention-deficit hyperactivity disorder (ADHD) and undifferentiated attention-deficit disorder (UADD). A primary difficulty for children diagnosed with ADD is the inability to concentrate. The student teacher should avoid making judgements about children's inability to concentrate; sometimes the condition is normal, considering what is going on in the child's life at the time. Prolonged inability to concentrate by a student would have already attracted the attention of the cooperating teacher, and referrals would already have been made to benefit the student. It is mentioned here so that such characteristics are not a surprise to the beginning student teacher.

Regular classroom teachers are usually given assistance by exceptional student educators who help in planning the educational programs of these mainstreamed students, providing suggestions for modification of regular classroom activities, and helping to supply specific materials and equipment.

Student teachers should become familiar with the educational plan devised by the mainstreaming team, which includes the cooperating teacher. This individual education plan (IEP) is required before exceptional students can receive special assistance. Some exceptional students remain in the regular classroom at all times; most of them can succeed in the mainstream. Others are released for part of the day to work with the exceptional education teachers. Placement outside of the regular class occurs only when deemed appropriate by the mainstreaming teacher, the exceptional student educator, and the administration.

Some student teachers have the opportunity during student teaching to work with exceptional education students who present a wealth of experiences that should be valuable for these future teachers.

Experienced teachers may tell student teachers that the special-needs students are most likely to cause confusion and concern if provisions are not made for them. If student teachers feel some anxiety about their knowledge in the area, the resources listed at the end of this chapter should be helpful. The more the student teacher knows about such students, the better job of teaching can be done.

The attitude of the teachers who are working with special-needs students is most important. Most of the students' needs are the same as those of all children and youth. The best strategy is to be flexible and make modifications for these exceptional students. The arrival of a student teacher should make additional time and attention available to work with them. If the cooperating teacher and student teacher consider *each* student in the class as a unique individual who could become a worthy citizen, all should go well.

GUIDELINES FOR THE STUDENT TEACHER

- **Keep in mind that all students can learn.**
- **Depend on your cooperating teacher for advice in working with special-needs students.** This person is a master teacher and probably has worked previously with a large number of special-needs students. You may be involved with other members of the mainstreaming team.
- **If you can incorporate ethnic studies into the curriculum, it would give a big boost to the self-concept of the ethnically diverse students.** Of course, this would have to meet the approval of your cooperating teacher.
- **Be a good listener when working with special-needs students.** Whether the students are gifted, mildly retarded, physically disabled, or otherwise, they can sense whether you are truly interested in them as worthwhile persons.
- **Make sure you are familiar with Public Law 94-142.** The needs of children and youth with disabilities are addressed by this law, which is called the Individuals with Disabilities Education Act. This law guarantees educational services to all students with disabilities, including the development of individual educational programs (IEPs) for each child and education in the least restrictive environment.
- **Do not expect students to perform beyond their capacities.** Students cannot be expected to perform tasks just because they are bright. Some quite intelligent individuals have specific learning problems (Patton, Blackbourn, & Fad, 1996).
- **Keep in mind that individuals with mental retardation are people who are much more like than unlike the rest of us.** It is important to treat them, as well as persons with physical impairment or health problems, in ways that are as normal as possible. Do not underestimate their abilities (Patton et al., 1996).
- **Be conscious of appropriate seating arrangements of your special-needs students.** For example, seat persons with hearing impairments near the speaker or interpreter.
- **Respect the worth of every student in your class, especially all of the special-needs students.** If you do not understand the background and needs of special-needs students, do additional research.

GUIDELINES FOR THE COOPERATING TEACHER

- **Orient your student teacher appropriately concerning the learning-disabled students in your classroom.** You have undoubtedly identified the learning-disabled students in your classroom. Their difficulty in processing information might be quite perplexing to the student teacher. Unless properly oriented concerning these students and their needs, the student teacher might be at a loss as to how to plan for their achievement.
- **Point out to the student teacher any gifted and talented students you might have in the classroom.** Your student teacher may be helpful in assisting with their special learning projects and assignments. Gifted students can work on and accomplish amazing projects if given a chance to "beat their own drum."
- **Get the student teacher involved early with assisting the culturally diverse students.** This gives the student teacher an opportunity to develop a respect for each culture represented in your classroom.
- **At-risk students will probably make themselves known to the student teacher in a short time.** It is most important to discuss these unique students prior to the time the student teacher begins teaching. There is a good chance that student teachers have had little experience in working with such students; they need much guidance. Students who use or abuse alcohol or other drugs, are victims of child or substance abuse or neglect, and are delinquents who are potential dropouts are particularly challenging for the student teacher.
- **Acquaint your student teacher with the various exceptional education teachers who assist you with the special-needs students, letting him or her spend some time with them if possible.**
- **You and your student teacher should have some challenging conference sessions working out plans to best use your time and activities to meet the needs of these special-needs students.** Your student teacher will have valuable experiences as a result of your efforts.

CASE STUDIES

C   A   S   E

15-1   William, a gifted 10th-grade student, is in Mrs. Yamamoto's homeroom class. He has become a special concern of Mrs. Yamamoto's new student teacher, Ronda. William has a knack of stirring up trouble in the classroom. His bluntness has a tendency to irritate his classmates as well as several of his teachers.

Today Ronda tried to encourage William to attend the upcoming career fair where she told him he might gain some insights concerning various careers. He was very huffy to Ronda, telling her that he intended to become a medical doctor and did not want to consider any other careers. Ronda was trying to be helpful to William and felt very bad about his response.

1. Why do you think William was so blunt?
2. How could attendance at a career fair benefit a student like William?
3. What could Ronda and Mrs. Yamamoto do that might help William become better accepted by his classmates?
4. Is bluntness a characteristic of gifted students? What characteristics do they usually exhibit?
5. Many gifted students drop out of school. How could this talent loss be prevented?

C   A   S   E

15-2   Part of Fred's student teaching assignment was hall duty every Monday and Wednesday. As a new student teacher, he was very eager to do a good job. All went very well the 1st week of duty. Then Ramon, a senior student with muscular dystrophy who was confined to a wheelchair, entered the picture. Ramon was disgruntled because of his condition and his outlook for the future. He barrelled through the halls with his motorized wheelchair at top speed. Fred did not want to hurt his feelings but finally reprimanded Ramon for his dangerous maneuvers. Ramon was quite disrespectful to Fred and told him to "bug off!"

1. Why was Fred justified in attempting to discipline Ramon?
2. What measures should be taken with Ramon because he was disrespectful to Fred?
3. How should Fred have reacted to Ramon's discourteous response?
4. What should Fred's cooperating teacher do about this matter?
5. Why is it important for student teachers to be assigned to duties typically given to classroom teachers?

C   A   S   E

15-3   Gordon has been assigned to student teach with Mrs. Bontrager, a 10th-and 11th-grade social studies teacher. Amy, a deaf student who is relatively new to the school, is in the 5th period history class. Amy has an interpreter assigned to her but seldom looks at him during lessons. Gordon is in his 6th week and is teaching three of his five assigned classes, including fifth period. He asks Amy, through the interpreter, why she ignores help. Amy indicates that she has little interest in social studies. Gordon is in a quandary!

1. Why should this matter be taken to the teacher of the hearing impaired?
2. How should Gordon respond to Amy's noted lack of interest in social studies?
3. What can Mrs. Bontrager do to assist Gordon?

4. How could Amy's attitude affect the other students in her class?
5. If Amy does not change her attitude, should she be allowed to continue to be mainstreamed? Explain your answer.

C A S E

15-4 Charles' student teaching assignment is a fourth-grade classroom with Mrs. Delgado as cooperating teacher. Charles is in his 7th week of student teaching and has thoroughly enjoyed the experience.

On Wednesday, as he was having lunch in the cafeteria, Charles was a bit startled at what he saw. Keith, one of the boys in his class, appeared to have a small gun in his pocket. Charles, thinking it was a water gun, confronted Keith and asked for the gun. To his surprise, Keith handed him a loaded pistol. Charles was in shock!

1. Should Charles have been more cautious in approaching Keith? Explain your answer.
2. What measures should be taken by Charles and Mrs. Delgado now that the gun has been found?
3. How should this be handled with Keith's classmates?
4. What can an elementary school do to avoid such happenings?
5. How should the parents of the other students in Charles' class be informed of this occurrence?

C A S E

15-5 Janey was shocked at how fast her student teaching assignment was flying by. She was already in her 5th week and was presently teaching half of her seventh-grade classes.

Janey felt that for the most part she had been successful in her teaching. As she took over her third class, however, she was confronted by her first major problem: Rebecca. Rebecca had serious problems that, according to the cooperating teacher, were reflected in temper tantrums, imitations of animal noises, and complete rejection of the people around her.

Janey felt her first lesson was a disaster. Rebecca paid no attention whatsoever and delighted in periodically neighing like a horse. Janey ignored her and completed her lesson; however, she was completely drained of energy. She wondered whether Rebecca was going to keep her from becoming a teacher.

1. Should Janey have ignored Rebecca's misbehavior? Explain your answer.
2. How could the cooperating teacher have prepared Janey better for this class?
3. Why is it important to let students such as Rebecca know what is expected of them?
4. Why would a student like Rebecca be mainstreamed into a regular classroom?
5. Janey had observed Rebecca for more than 4 weeks. Why do you think she was shocked at her behavior?

REFERENCES

Hardman, M. L., Drew, C., Egan, M. W. & Wolf, B. (1993). *Society, school, and family*. Needham Heights, MA: Allyn & Bacon.

Lewis, R. B., & Doorlag, D. H. (1999). *Teaching special students in general education classrooms* (5th ed.) (pp. 6–7). Upper Saddle River, NJ: Merrill/Prentice Hall.

Patton, J. R., Blackbourn, J. M., & Fad, K. (1996). *Exceptional individuals in focus* (6th ed.) (p. 43). Upper Saddle River, NJ: Merrill/Prentice Hall.

RECOMMENDED READING

Castles, E. (1996). *We're people first: The social and emotional lives of individuals with mental retardation*. Westport, CT: Praeger. *Castles deals with the affective side of mental retardation, a side generally ignored by cognitive specialists.*

Evans, W. H., Evans, S. S., Gable, R. A., & Schmid, R. E. (1991). *Instructional management: For detecting and correcting special problems*. Boston: Allyn & Bacon. *This book focuses on the classroom needs of special students. A comprehensive analysis of instructional environments is provided. Practical examples of instructional problems in the form of vignettes may be of particular interest to the student teacher.*

Garcia, R. (1991). *Teaching in a pluralistic society: Concepts, models, strategies*. New York: Harper-Collins. *This book contains much useful information that the cooperating teacher may be able to share with the student teacher. The author includes material relative to teaching and learning in a pluralistic society in addition to instructional models and strategies for successful educational practices in such a society.*

Hall, E. T. (Fall 1989). Unstated features of the cultural context of learning. *The Educational Forum, 54,* 21–34. *This professor emeritus of Northwestern University gives an anthropological perspective on learning. Differences among cultures and assumptions related to context, information, and meaning are clearly explained.*

Keeves, J. P. (1988). Sex differences in ability and achievement. In J. P. Keeves (Ed.), *Educational research methodology and measurement: An international handbook* (pp. 482–487). New York: Pergamon Press. *Keeves gives a historical overview of the research in sex differences in ability and achievement, including a reference indicating that differences between sexes are not large when compared with differences within sexes. Developments in this area of research are included.*

Kottler, E. (1994). *Children with limited English: Teaching strategies for the regular classroom*. Thousand Oaks, CA: Corwin Press. *Practical techniques are offered to assist in working with language-limited students.*

Lewis, R. B., & Doorlag, D. H. (1999). *Teaching special students in general education classrooms* (5th ed.). Upper Saddle River, NJ: Merrill/Prentice Hall. *The practical strategies in this book suggested to meet the needs of mainstreamed students are particularly good. Specific information about students with special needs is informative and clear-cut. The tips for the teacher sections presented in each chapter are helpful.*

Nielsen, L. B. (1997). *The exceptional child in the regular classroom: An educator's guide.* Thousand Oaks, CA: Corwin Press. *This text explains legal requirements, reviews the major disabilities, and offers suggestions for success for all students.*

Office of Educational Research and Improvement, Urban Superintendents Network. (1987). *Dealing with dropouts: The urban superintendents' call to action.* Washington, DC: Author. *One of the categories of special-needs students is the at-risk students who may be on a collision course with further schooling. This monograph is a collective request for concerted community effort to save these students and keep them in school.*

Ovando, C. & Collier, V. P. (1998). *Bilingual and ESL classrooms: Teaching in multicultural contexts* (2nd ed.). New York: McGraw-Hill. *This text integrates theory and practice in teaching bilingual, ESL, and multicultural children. Cooperative learning, interdisciplinary, and multisensory lessons are covered.*

Patton, J. R., Blackbourn, J. M., & Fad, K. (1996). *Exceptional individuals in focus* (6th ed.). Upper Saddle River, NJ: Merrill/Prentice Hall. *These authors present a very practical easy-to-read book that is quite effective in describing exceptional children. Particularly helpful are the suggestions for working with children with special needs.*

Reynolds, M. C. (1989). Students with special needs. In *Knowledge base for the beginning teacher* (pp. 129–142). New York: Pergamon Press. *Reynolds gives a succinct review of various groups labeled special-needs (SN) students. His review of some strategies for instructing SN students includes the recommendation that we should put our greatest teaching strengths with these children and youth.*

Robinson, P. C., & Huene, G. V. (1982). Meeting students' special needs. In *Helping teachers manage classrooms* (pp. 70–76). Alexandria, VA: Association for Supervision and Curriculum Development. *This chapter focuses on the services becoming more and more available to special-needs students. Understanding teachers and community resources combine to help these students stay in school and succeed.*

Shepard, L. A. (1989). Identification of mild handicaps. In R. L. Linn (Ed.), *Educational measurement* (3rd ed.) (pp. 445–472). New York: Macmillan. *This article contains a variety of issues relating to the schooling of individuals with mild disabilities, including the bias of assessment and issues related to early identification. The definition, assessment, and school placement of mild mental retardation, learning disabilities, and emotional disturbance are discussed fully.*

Tallent-Runnels, M. K. & Candler-Lotven, A. C. (1995). *Academic competitions for gifted students: A resource book for teachers and parents.* Thousand Oaks, CA: Corwin Press. *This text helps the teacher prepare gifted students for the pressures of competing and for achieving their best in competition.*

Westling, D. L., & Koorland, M. A. (1988). *The special educator's handbook.* Boston: Allyn & Bacon. *This book contains helpful information for student teachers in exceptional student education and with other special-needs students. The Suggestion Boxes make the material immediately useful.*

Zeichner, K. M. (Spring 1989). Preparing teachers for democratic schools. *Action in teacher education, 11*(1), 5–10. *Zeichner looks at the demand for reform and crisis in inequality in schools as well as the need for beginning teachers to experience community-based teacher education. He indicates the need to broaden school empowerment to include parents. This contains good reference material for the supervising teacher.*

P A R T

4

Student Learning

16

Helping Students Learn

What is the objective of school? Why, learning, of course, and learning is separate from but related to teaching. If it were not, a teacher could report to an empty classroom and teach all day and the kids could stay home. Excellent teaching can take place without any learning at all occurring, and learning can occur without any deliberate teaching taking place. It is more important to study learning than to study teaching, unless you understand that teaching is the facilitation of learning. That is why a focus on learning is included in this text for student teachers. Ask any secondary school teacher what she teaches, and you will most likely get the answer, "English" or "Math" or "Social Studies." Ask any elementary school teacher what he teaches, and most likely he will say, "Kids."

Much social learning is accomplished by example and imitation. Academic learning, on the other hand, is not as easily accomplished. A wider variety and greater depth of skills and information exist for the student in academic studies. Thus, educators calculate the extension and depth of any subject to be covered by their classroom students in specific levels; this curricula is apportioned by the grade level or subject teacher. After the initial benchmarks are established—sometimes by state departments of education and sometimes by school district—learning themes, annual plans, and semester, unit, and lesson plans are prepared and adapted for particular classes or grade levels. This chapter deals not so much with what to teach but with how children learn what they are given and expected to learn.

Some stages of learning that students go through in your classroom will include attraction, interest, motivation, and possession. Students are initially attracted; this attraction causes some interest to develop; this interest causes motivation, and if the motivation is strong enough, the student will work to possess the knowledge or skill. Your most difficult work as a student teacher will be the first two stages: attraction and interest. If these are sufficiently strong, the student's motivation grows, and the student will be driven to possess the knowledge and make it his or hers. During the third and fourth segments of this process, the teacher is more and more a facilitator and less didactic.

Students sometimes succeed even though one or more of the four stages have been missed. Since the motivation may come from negative factors such as fear (of punishment, of not receiving awards, of shame), the first two stages may be skipped entirely. As the momentum of motivation grows, students will strive to "own" the learning—to make it theirs, to store that knowledge or skill in their memory.

Of these four stages of teaching, the first two are easily accomplished with imagination and flair. It is during the third stage that each student requires individual work, and his or her movement into and through the fourth stage requires intense knowledge and guidance. The knowledge of the subject matter is necessary, but a knowledge of how the individual child learns is more important and comes into play at this juncture. The entire class can be attracted to and interested in a new topic; this can be a total class or a group activity, but the movement from interest into motivation is accomplished at the individual student's pace and within the parameters of the student's personal learning needs.

The motivation stage can be divided into two segments: initial and prolonged. It is to the teacher's advantage to have sufficient materials, exercises, and procedures for the child to maintain the initial motivation and lock in the prolonged stage. This is the point at which variations in learning readiness and learning styles are most obvious.

GUIDELINES FOR THE STUDENT TEACHER

- **Be aware that your every move in the classroom is being watched by the students.** This is not because they want to catch you at something; it is because they are interested in how you behave, how you act in certain situations, how you relate to others, how you handle yourself. You are a new professional in their lives and they want to know more about you.
- **Guard carefully your negative attitudes.** Being in the limelight, you may indicate to students who are observing you that you may think less of this or that; this may color their impressions and attitudes. Let your observable attitudes be positive in all things; you owe your students that.
- **Think through your lessons and presentations around the idea of attraction, interest, motivation, and possession.** Keep in mind that the greatest service you can be to your students is to help them be attracted to knowledge so that it becomes theirs for reflection and use for a lifetime.
- **Recall how you were when you were going to school.** Think of the teachers you learned most with, not necessarily the ones you liked best. Reflect on what those teachers did to cause you to learn more with them. Also, reflect on those teachers with whom you don't recall learning much. Why was that? These ideas will be indicators for characteristics you may want to develop in yourself and for characteristics you want to avoid developing.
- **Be aware of the impression you make on our students.** Try to be positive, clear, and understandable. Keep to a minimum personal mannerisms that might inhibit student learning: Avoid rattling change in your pockets, playing with a keyring, twisting your hair, etc. Be a neutral element in the classroom.

- **Wear conservative clothing.** Conservative clothing may seem a little dull, but it has two major points in its favor: It will not get in the way of student learning, as would flashy clothing and jewelry, and it costs less to purchase and maintain a well-planned, conservative wardrobe.
- **Make your classroom warm, cheerful and inviting but not loud, demanding, and distracting.** You have probably observed in classrooms that seemed to distract you with too many "pieces" (bulletin boards, pictures, calendars, notices, student work samples) around the room. You have probably also been in rooms that appeared well-ordered with some artwork, a bulletin board, and maybe a space for notices; the feeling of those rooms was stimulating but not exciting. This "room essence" can contribute to the students' successful learning experiences. You want to aim for stimulating student learning, not for exciting the student.
- **Keep in mind that you want your classroom to be a learning center, not an entertainment center.** Some feel that teachers must be entertainers; beware of that notion. Students must be attracted to learning, and learning is an active state; entertainment is a passive state. If your students are learning, they will prefer that to being entertained. This means that you must get them involved in the learning process, which does not include listening to a lecture, doing rote work, or completing worksheets. Such activities can be managed by a person off the street. You are a trained professional! Use higher level activities.

GUIDELINES FOR THE COOPERATING TEACHER

- **Reassess what you are modeling for the student teacher.** Review your patterns of behavior and organization in the classroom, your interactions with students and with other faculty members, and your methods of handling classroom activities. Are you going to be proud of your student teacher if he or she learns to do things the way you do them?
- **In conversation, point out to your student teacher characteristics of other teachers that seem to enhance student learning.** Using discretion, mention those qualities that some teachers possess that just naturally lead students to commit themselves to learning. Also, point out habits that teachers (though not those at your school) have that seem to inhibit learning and cause students to be too excited to concentrate.
- **Model through your own teaching the steps of attraction to, interest in, motivation for, and possession of knowledge so that the student teacher's learning task is easier.** The vast amount of learning that has to go on in the student teacher's mind can be helped through your using the model of teaching that you expect the student teacher to use to result in student learning. Keep in mind that your student teacher is currently in the possession stage of the learning curve and is trying out that knowledge. The student teacher's success to a great degree depends on the way you pave the road for him or her.

- **Give your student teacher a copy of all benchmark materials, state requirements, professional association literature, and school district requirements for your subject.** Some of this will be new to the student teacher, and although it may seem overwhelming initially, it will be an excellent foundation for the student teacher to build upon. Explain how each component is used in both the learning scheme of things and the accountability scheme of things. It is hoped that these two would dovetail; in reviewing with the student teacher, your own knowledge and application will be reinforced.

- **Point out to the student teacher the variety of stages of intellectual development occurring simultaneously in your classroom.** This is usually a revelation to the student teacher. As he or she studied the ages and stages of children's psychological growth and development, it seemed that all students moved forward in sync. The opposite is true, and the earlier the student teacher discovers this fact, the earlier he or she will understand the need for a variety of teaching techniques and materials.

- **Help your student teacher to organize for the variety of learning abilities in your classroom.** By giving him or her a variety of plans that include learning challenges and opportunities for every individual in the class, the student teacher will be able to cluster abilities and provide interesting learning experiences for all the abilities in the class.

- **Emphasize the need to have a variety of individual tasks ready for the students immediately upon their arrival at the classroom.** This allows students to become involved in the learning process right away and to continue throughout their time in the classroom if they finish their other work early. Of the many things that student teachers have to keep in mind, a few slip through the cracks. It is important that they remember to organize early and thoroughly for all levels of learning that will be going on in the classroom. This can seem a forbidding task; help your student teacher to plan and organize this well. This will give him or her an excellent brick in the foundation of his or her professional career.

- **Keep in mind that being the cooperating teacher is an active not a passive process.** You have taken one more learner into your classroom. Use gentle professional firmness in expressing what your student teacher needs to learn, know, and demonstrate to you and to the university supervisor.

CASE STUDIES

C A S E

16-1   Shaq, a student teacher on his first assignment, enjoyed watching the students work. He was troubled, however, by Amanda, who always sat at her desk and appeared to be studying hard, whether the cooperating teacher's assignment was reading, writing an essay, or answering questions. He had noticed that she was very quiet and never spoke up in class.

After school when Shaq had a chance to review the papers, he noted that Amanda's paper made no sense; Amanda had written a page of words that meant nothing. Shaq showed the sheet to Mr. Judd in bewilderment.

1. Do you think Amanda was testing Shaq?
2. What do you think was the answer Mr. Judd gave Shaq?
3. Why would Mr. Judd not warn a student teacher beforehand about the behavior of such a student? Is this fair to the student teacher?
4. How can Shaq work with Amanda to find acceptable ways that she can participate?
5. Why is this conforming behavior on the part of students important to identify and remedy?

C A S E

16-2   Wesley was assigned to student teach in Mr. Gabriel's fourth grade. In the excitement of getting started to work with the children, Wesley took it upon himself to show a new learning technique to a student who was having trouble learning. What he was not aware of was that the student, in addition to having a learning difficulty, had shown indications of emotional problems. The new technique did not work; it caused the child to be even more confused about the concept he was trying to learn.

The student went home and told his mother, who returned to the school with him the next morning and demanded an explanation of Mr. Gabriel.

1. Was this situation a responsibility of Wesley or of Mr. Gabriel?
2. What lesson did Wesley learn from this experience?
3. What right did the mother have getting involved in this situation?
4. How does a student teacher know when to try something new and when to avoid trying something new?
5. What responsibility does the university supervisor have in such a situation?

C A S E

16-3   Natalia had been student teaching in sixth grade for 3 weeks when the cooperating teacher pointed out to her that one of the girls in the class seemed to be changing her handwriting style. As Natalia showed writing samples over the 3 weeks she had been in the classroom to the cooperating teacher, Mr. Henry, they both puzzled over why the child would be trying to make such changes in her handwriting. Mr. Henry suggested that Natalia hold a private conversation with the student and see whether she could determine the reason.

Natalia met with the student the next day, and they had a chance to talk. The student explained that she admired Natalia's handwriting and was trying to change hers so it would look like Natalia's. Natalia was surprised.

1. Why would the student try to imitate the student teacher's handwriting?
2. How can Natalia make the student proud of her original handwriting?

3. How do you think Natalia reflected on how other students were trying to copy her in other ways?

4. Would this affect the way that Natalia behaved in front of the students, how she spoke, and the clothes she wore? Why?

5. Can you remember an incident from your school days when you tried to model your behavior or characteristics after one of your teachers? Explain.

C A S E

16-4   Tyrone was excited about his student teaching assignment in Miss Barry's 10th-grade math class. He realized that he must follow through the loop of attraction, interest, motivation, and possession. It seemed that with mathematics, some students would try, but since they were not attracted, they were starting off on the second step. Their interest and motivation were usually that the course was required for something else they wanted to study; Tyrone realized that was a weak link. Most of the students did not have any possession of concepts; they just brushed through to get by. Even if they received a high grade, they didn't seem interested in the content, just in getting the high grade.

1. What would you recommend to Tyrone?
2. Why does this condition exist in schools? Who is responsible?
3. Should Tyrone expect this to be the nature of students throughout his teaching career?
4. How could discussion with other teachers help Tyrone to understand?
5. Is this type of student reaction discussed in the university classes prior to student teaching? How? What solutions are usually offered?

C A S E

16-5   Ben was very excited about finally getting to teach. In his student teaching assignment in fifth grade, he felt privileged to have as his cooperating teacher Mrs. Osnack, who had the reputation of being an excellent teacher with most children. He was determined to learn everything about teaching he possibly could from her.

During his observations with other teachers in the school, Ben noticed that many of them had fewer visuals around the room, and he discussed the question of the amount of visuals (bulletin boards, calendars, pictures, student work, printed materials, and special holiday effects) with his university supervisor. He felt that Mrs. Osnack's room was much too busy for some of the students to learn efficiently; his university supervisor agreed with him. Ben wondered whether those students who had difficulty in Mrs. Osnack's classroom were students whose learning was affected by too much visual stimulation in the room.

1. What could Ben do to investigate his theory? What data could he collect? How?
2. What could happen if he made waves and Mrs. Osnack was offended?
3. Who would suffer if Ben just said nothing and decided he would be out of there in a semester, letting the matter drop?
4. How could Ben delicately show Mrs. Osnack that less is sometimes better in visuals for some children's learning styles?

5. How have you felt in classrooms that appear to be cluttered? Did you have any classmates for whom this was a problem?

RECOMMENDED READING

Bissel J., Manring, A., & Rowland, V. (1999). *Cybereducation: The Internet and World Wide Web for K–12 education.* New York: McGraw-Hill. *This text is a guide to the use of the World Wide Web for K–12 teachers and includes Internet sites for teachers to utilize for lesson planning, collaboration, and references. These sites can be passed along to students for their research on the web.*

Heide, A, & Stilborne, L. (1999). *The teacher' complete and easy guide to the Internet* (2nd ed.). *This text includes instructions on how to use streaming audio, off-line browsers, browser plug-ins, FTP, basic telnet, and a PC-compatible CD ROM with web sources for new ideas.*

Jensen, E. (1998). *Teaching with the brain in mind.* Alexandria, VA: Association for Supervision and Curriculum Development. *Written in an easily readable and understandable format, this text offers the latest research on learning and the brain, including emotions, movement, motivations, threats, and enriched environments and their relationship to the brain and learning.*

Joyce, B., & Weil, M. (1996). *Models of teaching* (5th ed.) Boston: Allyn & Bacon. *Joyce and Weil offer a comprehensive coverage of the models of teaching, including how each particular model can serve particular students well and can serve particular classroom teaching needs. This is the textbook that makes all the information you learned in methods fit together; if you can read only one book, read this one. The models are divided into various families because of likenesses among models, and this process enables the beginning teacher to have a much greater command of teaching theory and knowing how to help students learn.*

Lambert N. M., & McCombs, B. L. (Eds.). (1998). *How students learn: Reforming schools through learner-centered education.* Washington, DC: American Psychological Association. *Lambert and McCombs have collected works from leading educators and psychologists on the needs of learners and the learning process. This material reflects the psychological knowledge base necessary for being able to help children learn in a methodical, organized, and scientific manner.*

Walker, D. E. (1998). *Strategies for teaching differently: On the block or not.* Thousand Oaks, CA: Corwin Press. *This is a how-to book that will add variety to your teaching skills, particularly in the area of students' constructing knowledge and demonstrating understanding. Walker has included excellent blackline masters on a variety of helpful techniques such as mind-mapping, thinking at right angles, using a Venn diagram to show comparison and contrast, what-so-what-now-what, and 14 others.*

Wiggins, G., & McTighe, J. (1998). *Understanding by design.* Alexandria, VA: Association for Supervision and Curriculum Development. *These two assessment experts have written with effective diagrams and matrices about what we mean by understanding in classrooms, how we can get students to do it, and how we can measure it.*

Vatalaro, M. (Spring 1999). Enhancing learning and interpersonal relationships. *Kappa Delta Pi Record, 35*(3), 115–126. *This author explains how students exposed to programs in conflict resolution and peer mediation learn skills to communicate more effectively, thus enhancing classroom learning for students with conflict or need-for-power problems.*

17

Some Current Theories

Accredited teacher education programs include a course in psychological foundations of education that primarily relate to learning theories. Although it may have been only a few months since these were last reviewed, it is always a good idea for the student teacher to further review the theories and their applications prior to actually working with students, as in student teaching. Coming into student teaching with the enthusiasm and self-confidence that knowledge about the task ahead of you can give you will make your task more exciting. You will likely have more energy, and you may be a positive motivator for your cooperating teacher.

A good idea is to review class notes and your textbook from the psychological foundations class. As you review, you may find a number of theorists whom you should study further. Some of them—and the major aspects of their theories on learning—are discussed in the following paragraphs.

Of major importance in the field of learning theory is the work of Piaget's Cognitive Development Theory, in which Piaget labeled knowledge as a process of the individual child's interacting with what is around the child. Piaget (1972, p. 5, as cited in Thomas, 1996, p. 234) expressed this as, "All knowledge is continually in a course of development and of passing from a state of lesser knowledge to one which is more complete and effective." Piaget cited the development from infancy through early and middle childhood and to adolescence in egocentrism versus objectivity, object permanence (conservation), symbolic functioning, and classes and relationships.

Piaget's levels and stages of development (Thomas, 1996) have now become famous throughout educational circles. They include four stages: Sensorimotor (birth to 2 years), Preoperational Thought (about 2 to 7), Concrete Operations (about 7 to 11), and Formal Operations (about 11 to 15). Student teachers should remember that these are approximations but are valuable in determining how to relate to children, what methods and materials are appropriate, and what kinds of thinking to expect of the children in their classrooms.

The behaviorism theory of B. F. Skinner is utilized by many teachers in the reinforcement of learned behaviors. In contrast to Piaget, Skinner did not see the development of children as a series of stages but instead as a "continous, incremental sequence of specific conditioned acts" (Thomas, 1996, p. 180). The use of Skinner's stimulus response theory has evolved for some teachers into the current behavior modification practices. Some educators prefer to utilize Skinner's theory as a supplemental training technique within a broader scope of teaching and learning.

Social learning theorist Albert Bandura (Thomas, 1996) brought to educators the concepts of self-efficacy and modeling. Self-efficacy is basically the ability an individual has to cope with his or her environment and to have the power to manage it successfully. Modeling is just that: imitating. Most children and youth model adult behavior and that frequently causes problems. However, it is the wise student teacher who is aware that he or she is being observed by students who will probably model the behavior and attitudes they pick up from the student teacher, particularly if they admire her or him.

The Russian psychologist Vygotsky, although from an earlier period, has contributed instrumental theories on the development of thought and language in a child. One of his primary concepts is the Zone of Proximal Development (Thomas, 1996). This zone identifies the space between the actual development of the child and the potential immediate next development that can be enhanced by another's guidance. "Vygotsky saw the language environment—the culture—in which a child is raised as being crucial in determining the direction and extent of the individual" intellectual growth (Thomas, 1996, p.287)

Another theorist who should receive attention from the student teacher is Urie Bronfenbrenner (Thomas, 1996), who produced an ecological theory of learning. Bronfenbrenner believes that a child's microsystems of home, school, and peer group influence the progressive development of the child. As a developmental psychologist, Bronfenbrenner completed cross-cultural research around the world and concluded that the environment influences the development not only of children but also of all plants and animals. A student teacher who follows Bronfenbrenner's theory would find that specific changes, possibly in the school environment, could bring about success where there previously had been only failure.

Humanistic theories of learning include those such as Maslow's Theory of Hierarchy of Needs, in which those more pressing physiological and safety needs must be fulfilled prior to much academic learning. Self-actualization (Thomas, 1996) represents the highest level of development, according to Maslow.

GUIDELINES FOR THE STUDENT TEACHER

- **Reread your psychological foundations textbook and review your notes from class.** College is a busy time and students lead busy lives. You especially need a thorough review of the theories you studied in your psychological foundations class.

- **Take the psychological theories one step further: Apply them.** Such application should not be done large scale at the beginning; keep in mind that you are a novice teacher.
- **Learning to teach is not like taking a vitamin pill or an antibiotic.** You can't swallow enough at one time. We must learn how to teach in small doses. These small increments, if properly arranged, will build an excellent foundation and you will feel secure in your knowledge of theory and application.
- **As you begin teaching, you will realize the importance of theory; such theory is more than just someone's idea of what may work.** Theory based on research is what has already worked and what has passed the test of research criteria.
- **You must bridge the distance between you and theory.** You must make the effort to understand what the theorists were saying, and you must apply it to your own situations. In your efforts, you become more possessive of the use of the theories, which are stored in your repertory and will be available for you when you need them. You must make the effort.
- **You will probably become eclectic in your use of theories.** Keep in mind that each theorist was not arguing against other theorists; he was indicating what he saw as a true way of student behavior and learning. You will find that one theory works best for one student while another theory seems to fit another student better. It's acceptable to choose components of different theories to fit your students' needs.
- **Avoid using one theory exclusively.** As important as both Piaget and Vygotsky are in our current theories of learning, their theories don't agree in some ways. Each student requires that you assess his or her learning abilities and choose what fits him or her best.
- **Don't put off until tomorrow becoming familiar with a set of basic minimum theorists and their theories.** Sooner or later, if you stay in education, you will need to know them well. If you leave education, you may still work with people and this knowledge will help in your work with people. If you remain in education, you will need this knowledge more and more. Learn it now.

GUIDELINES FOR THE COOPERATING TEACHER

- **Review with your student teacher some of the theories of learning that you use most in your class.** Because of your teaching experience, you may feel that the greatest value is in the pragmatic approach of "what works." However, that is based on your original application of theories during the years you have taught. Such a review may be good memory reinforcers for you.
- **Show your student teacher how to apply the theories that seem most appropriate with the students in your class.** Your student teacher is looking to

you for leadership and will follow through with a higher degree of comfort and confidence. This will be good practice for you.

- **Involve other teachers around you in your study and application of current learning theories.** If there are other student teachers in the school, it would benefit everyone for them to work together on such a project.
- **Ask your librarian or media specialist to obtain videotapes for you and the student teacher to watch together.** Watching and discussing incidents that have been programmed for study will enhance the knowledge that both of you have about current learning theories.
- **Do not mind saying that you do not know when your student teacher asks about applying a particular theory.** Use this as a positive learning experience for both of you. Suggest that the student teacher get additional information from the university that would enhance his or her application of the theory.
- **Be patient with the student teacher as he or she tries out new techniques that reflect specific learning theories.** The student teacher has to get a feel for the techniques and methods that are most comfortable for him or her as well as for what seems to fit the student needs most.
- **Help your student teacher to understand that some lessons will best be taught in terms of the child's stage according to Piaget while other lessons can best be taught using an approach advocated by Skinner.** Based on the topic and the kind of information to be learned, student teachers have a choice. If they are training the student in a skill development, Skinner's behaviorism may be the best method. However, if they are working with creativity, they should keep in mind Piaget's concrete operations stage for the 7- to 11-year-old child.
- **Explain to your student teacher how important his or her classroom behavior is in terms of the student modeling his or her behavior.** Bandura felt that many children learn best by imitating behaviors. In a sense, that is what the student teacher is doing with you: modeling your behavior. Model professionalism.

CASE STUDIES

C   A   S   E

17-1   Monica loved English literature and was pleased that she had been assigned to teach 12th-grade English; it would give her the opportunity to teach what she loved! Monica had been working on a series of class-long lectures and would have enough lectures prepared before the term began to cover the entire term. After all, with only 4 1/2 months of class, that amounted to about 18 weeks. Counting time off for tests and other activities, she would have 70+ days to lecture.

When Monica visited her student teaching assignment, she was disappointed to find that her cooperating teacher did not use lectures but seemed to be using a variety of teaching techniques. Monica was not prepared; she felt that English literature was straightforward, and that was how she wanted to teach it.

1. What advice would you give Monica?
2. Have you known anyone who loved her subject so much she ignored the students she was responsible for teaching?
3. How can the cooperating teacher best help Monica?
4. Where do you think Monica missed the boat in her training program?
5. What responsibility does the university supervisor have in this? How can he or she assist the cooperating teacher in bringing Monica around to reality?

C   A   S   E

17-2   Nellie was student teaching in Mrs. Peters music class. As an observer, she had been having fun experiencing all the different classes that came in throughout the week. As she had opportunity to get used to the students and get to know them more, she realized that Mrs. Peters had students who covered the range from much interest to absolutely no interest in music.

After discussing this with Mrs. Peters and getting her permission to talk privately with some of the students, Nellie pulled a few students out of chorus and talked with them about how they felt about learning music. Some of the responses included: "I hate this class." "Man, I can't wait til I get out of this class." "I just can't understand that teacher. I like music, but I don't know what she's talking about most of the time."

1. Nellie seems to have stumbled onto some information. What should she do with it?
2. How would Mrs. Peters feel if she knew that some of her students felt this way?
3. How could a student's learning style in a particular subject not be observable to a trained professional such as Mrs. Peters?
4. With no other music teachers in the school, how could Mrs. Peters observe others?
5. Is such a concern for students worth the effort?

C   A   S   E

17-3   Richard was making progress in his student teaching assignment in Mr. Burgess's middle school mathematics classes. All the classes were run by the book, and Mr. Burgess was very organized with his plans, classwork, homework, tests, and entire grading system. When Richard began teaching small groups, he noticed that some of the students could not readily comprehend some kinds of math problems. This did not seem to be a problem to Mr. Burgess; the students seemed to like him and to learn well under him.

When Richard approached Mr. Burgess about the student learning problems, Mr. Burgess suggested that he restudy the Concrete and Formal Operations stages of

Piaget and come back to him with ways of applying this theory in the middle school mathematics classroom.

1. What could be the connection between the middle school mathematics students' difficulty in learning and Piaget's theory?
2. How could this account for the success Mr. Burgess had with students?
3. What do you think Richard reported back to Mr. Burgess?
4. What effect could this have on Richard's own thinking?
5. How could this apply in other teaching levels and subjects?

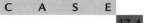

17-4   Coach Hunter enjoyed his reputation as a tough physical education teacher, and Arnie was excited to be working in his classroom. Coach's motto was "Do as I say, not as I do." Arnie could recall from his psychological foundations course the material on Albert Bandura's modeling, and it did not fit together well for him to see the coach, hear his motto, and know Bandura's theory.

1. What kind of professional dilemma was Arnie undergoing?
2. Could he make any changes in a teacher like Coach Hunter?
3. How could he make the coach aware of Bandura's theory?
4. No students in particular seemed to be hurt by the coach's attitude. Was it worth the effort to try to get the coach to understand?
5. Have you known parents with the same attitude that the coach had? How can teachers help them to understand before their children turn out like them?

C   A   S   E

17-5   Lori was from a middle-class, suburban family and was assigned to student teach in an urban, low-income school. She and her parents had always resisted the idea of tax money going for school breakfasts and lunches for low-income children. As a student teacher in third grade, Lori had the opportunity to observe the differences between children who appeared to have and those who might not have sufficient nourishment. After several days of seeing what a difference the food made to the children and how the rate and quantity of the children's learning increased after having food, she changed her mind. She began bringing food from home for the class and helped the students learn to cook simple dishes in the classroom that they might be able to make at home with supervision by an adult.

1. What was the major lesson that Lori learned?
2. Do you think she shared this lesson with her family and friends? Why?
3. How do you think that student teaching will change Lori's life?
4. Have you had any such experiences in your work with students?
5. In foundations of education classes, such needs are often discussed. Why had Lori not taken those needs seriously when they were discussed in class?

REFERENCE

Thomas, R. M. (1996). *Comparing theories of child development* (4th ed.). Boston: Brooks/Cole.

RECOMMENDED READING

Caine, G., & Caine, R. N. (1999). *Teaching and the human brain*, Vol. 3 in *Windows to the mind*. Bloomington, IN: Phi Delta Kappa. *This is one in a series of four excellent video programs that deal with learning and the brain. This particular videotape is an introduction to new theories of teaching and learning and how they are changing education today. Seeing this video will help both the student teacher and the cooperating teacher learn more about functioning in a transformational learning process. This is a 60-minute video with a companion discussion guide. Additional information on this and other Phi Delta Kappa publications is available at the PDK website at www.pdkintl.org and you may find other pertinent materials at this location.*

Campbell, L. (1996). *Teaching and learning through multiple intelligences* (2nd ed.). Boston: Allyn & Bacon. *This text provides a thorough explanation of Howard Gardner's Multiple Intelligences Theory. One chapter is devoted to each of the eight intelligences and recommendations for application in the classroom are made for a variety of instructional approaches, including team teaching.*

Fishman, S. M., & McCarthy, L. (1998). *John Dewey and the challenge of classroom practice.* New York: Teachers College Press. *The authors discuss Dewey's educational theory and review his concepts of student-curriculum integration, interest and effort, and continuity and interaction.*

Klein, S. (1996). *Learning: Principles and applications* (3rd ed.). New York: McGraw-Hill. *This text offers a review of the basic principles of learning and their application in the classroom. Critical-thinking questions are included that the student teacher could work through with the cooperating teacher.*

Miller, P. H. (1993). *Theories of psychological development* (3rd ed.). New York: Freeman. *Miller analyzes several of the major theorists in developmental psychology in a methodical, easy-to-follow manner so that comparisons are easily made by the reader. This is a scholarly work that can be applied in the classroom to enhance the teaching/learning time and effort.*

Phye, G. D. (Ed.)., (1996). *Handbook of academic learning: Construction of knowledge.* Boston: Academic Press. *Phye has compiled an extensive set of materials from scholars in the field of learning theory in the major categories of academic learning, teaching how to learn, learning to learn, and assessment of classroom learning. He has included a section by Spandell on portfolios which is an excellent guide.*

Sylvester, R. (1995). *A celebration of neurons: An educator's guide to the human brain.* Alexandria, VA: Association for Supervision and Curriculum Development. *This book describes how traditional classroom practices are giving way to thematic curricula, project-based learning, and other brain-compatible approaches to learning.*

Thomas, R. M. (1996). *Comparing theories of child development* (4th ed.). New York: Brooks/Cole. *Thomas presents a comprehensive volume on theories of child development and the implications of learning that are important to teachers and parents. He provides information on each theory and offers an assessment in a standard format for ease in comparability.*

18

Learning Styles

One of the greatest surprises that student teachers discover when they begin working with students in their assigned classrooms is that they can teach the identical content using the same materials to a classroom of students and some of the students will understand and some of them will miss it completely. The rest of the class is somewhere in between. As these teachers mentally review their lessons to find what may have gone wrong, they find that a new world is opened to them in terms of why some students learn and some do not seem to learn.

Hungry kids do not learn; sleepy kids do not learn. In considering these points, the student teacher may want to review Maslow's Hierachy of Needs Theory. School free breakfast and lunch programs have been established in the belief that students need the nutrition unavailable elsewhere for the healthy development of both their bodies and their minds. In dealing with a sleepy child, the student teacher should first discuss the situation with the cooperating teacher and make a referral to the counselor or telephone the parents based on school policy. All calls to parents about student problems should first be discussed with the cooperating teacher. It may be that the cooperating teacher already has discussed the problem with the parents and another call may not be appropriate at the time. It is possible that a remedy is in the works and the cooperating teacher is aware of the impending solution.

People learn differently. Because we process information differently, some students will immediately understand the student teacher's lesson, some will puzzle over it for a while and then "see the light," and some will not understand it and will become bored and more difficult to interest in the next lesson.

Some educators see a relationship between the theory of multiple intelligences and the variety of learning style preferences. The student teacher may want to consider the multiple intelligences theory as the basic machinery the child is working with and the theories of learning as that child's method of accessing those intelligences.

According to Armstrong (1994), Howard Gardner's multiple intelligences theory maintains that we have not just one kind of intelligence but several kinds, and that finding the predominate kind of intelligence a child uses will help in determining the appropriate teaching mechanisms to fit the child's learning style. Gardner has researched the following kinds of intelligences: linguistic, logical-mathematical, spatial, bodily-kinesthetic, music, interpersonal, intrapersonal, and his most recent, the naturalistic. Armstrong indicates that a teacher can, based on Gardner's theory, determine to some extent by a child's misbehavior where the child's intelligences lie.

In the area of learning theory, teachers and researchers are aware that students may have a preferred way of learning but can utilize a method that is not first preference. According to Drake (1998), learning styles are based in personality and can be primarily auditory, visual, or kinesthetic. One student may require material to be sequential while another student can easily make intuitive leaps, just as one student can think best in a singular linear fashion and another can see the gestalt and can understand immediately.

A mistake student teachers sometimes make is to assume that all individuals learn as they themselves do. Traditionally, we teach as we have been taught. Using that model, it is easy to see that over a series of teachers, those who learn differently will have effectively been excluded from school altogether. One may want to look at the students who are dropping out of school to determine whether one of the reasons contributing to the students' dropping out was that the predominate learning style was not one that those students could assimilate. Sometimes it is difficult for student teachers to identify methods of teaching that are different from their own, but their success in doing so will probably mean success with more students. No one style is the correct one. A combination of styles, using them with students as appropriate, will serve the student teacher better. This will require some trial and error with teaching methods on the part of the student teacher, but it is well worth it in the long run. Current methods of teaching across the curriculum include the spectrum of also teaching across learning styles.

Drake (1998) recommends techniques that will appeal to a variety of learning styles and allow across-the-curriculum content to be covered. These techniques include storytelling, graphic organizers, metaphors, reflection, questioning, researching, intuitive thinking, and the impact of emotions on learning as well as the impact of learning on the emotions.

Armstrong (1998) offers the student teacher an unexpected challenge in that he believes that every child is a genius and that the classroom is the place for awakening and nurturing that genius. The 12 qualities of genius that he believes all kids have include curiosity, playfulness, imagination, creativity, wonder, wisdom, inventiveness, vitality, sensitivity, flexibility, humor, and joy. Although he does not equate these qualities with Gardner's multiple intelligences theory, he does indicate that relationships exist among the qualities and gives research in anthropoloogy, developmental psychology, and the neurosciences to support his theory.

Jenson (1998) cites the importance of memory and recall in the learning process. If the student has learned the material that the student teacher has taught but he can not recall it, the student teacher will be puzzled even more. Jenson indicates that contrary to previous opinion, the brain does not "videotape" life into memory but rather feels that the kinds of memories determine where they are stored. It is important to keep in mind that memory is a process that is still not well understood. Jenson believes that the complex experience of school can be better accomplished if we think in terms of "what kind of memory and how it can be retrieved" (p. 104). The inability of a student to retrieve information will cause a sense of failure and loss of self-image and self-confidence. It is critical that the student teacher identify such a sequence early to provide students better learning opportunities.

GUIDELINES FOR THE STUDENT TEACHER

- **Be aware that we tend to teach as we have been taught.** This practice causes a proliferation of teachers with the same teaching style which may not be the preferred learning style of many students.
- **As you observe in other teachers' classrooms, notice how some students seem to understand exactly what the teacher is working with and others seem to be on another planet.** Find the teachers who seem to be successful with those students who other teachers consider hard to teach. Note what learning styles are incorporated into their teaching.
- **Adopt a repertory of teaching styles to accommodate a variety of learning styles.**
- **This is your time to try out new ideas and teaching techniques for different learning styles.** Now, while you have the safety net of your cooperating teacher, be willing to risk and try new techniques.
- **Make careful note of which learning styles seem to be preferred by different students.** Chances are that when you have your own classroom of students next year, you will have some of the same types of students who prefer a variety of learning styles.
- **Develop a portfolio on learning styles and the accommodating teaching techniques.** This will serve you well throughout your profession. It will take some effort to put together, but start on a small scale and add to your collection at every opportunity.
- **Become your own expert on learning styles.** Other student teachers will begin to come to you with their problems with students who have difficulty learning. Then the teachers will come for advice, and in a couple of years, you will be expert enough to be giving inservice workshops on learning styles. It all starts now, today.
- **Keep in mind Maslow's hierarchy of needs.** The student who is hungry or sleepy or who has problems at home will not learn much no matter how much professional expertise you show in teaching to his or her learning style. Get the student some help with his or her problems; then you can help the student learn.

GUIDELINES FOR THE COOPERATING TEACHER

- **Help your student teacher analyze his or her own learning style.** This can be fun and interesting for the student teacher and will give you both an opportunity to converse in a relaxed atmosphere. Discuss differences in your learning styles and your student teacher's, how differences in learning style occur across the classroom, and how significant these differences are to your individual learning styles.

- **Give your student teacher any information about a student's personal life that would help her or him understand learning differences.** Although it is not a learning style, a dysfunctional family life can impact a student's ability to concentrate and learn.

- **Establish some times for reflective conversation with the student teacher about the students.** It probably is not convenient for you and the student teacher to have long conversations each day, but plan into your schedule at least once each week a time for extended conversation that can allow reflection on additional learning possibilities for the students in your classroom.

- **Indicate to your student teacher how she or he can learn about students' learning styles from other students.** The other students in the classroom generally know a lot about each other. When they help each other with learning activities, they generally know how to approach another student with a technique that will increase the speed and effort with which the student can learn. Help your student teacher to be aware of such opportunities to learn.

- **Be a role model for your student teacher in utilizing a variety of techniques that reach across the span of learning styles.** Using the same content, vary the delivery so that the student teacher can understand and observe the range of student learning styles.

- **Suggest that the student teacher have one student teach another student some content or skill.** Watching the student doing the teaching will be an indication of how that student learns; we tend to teach to someone else as if the person has the same learning style as our own.

- **Remind the student teacher that most students can learn something from any approach, but there may be a special approach that best fits the student's learning style and will render more learning to particular students.** Although the student teacher may be teaching to the learning style of student X, student Y will learn some from that but probably not as much as if his or her own learning style were being utilized.

- **Allow the student teacher to use games in the classroom for discovering learning styles.** By allowing the students to play a game, their own learning style may be determined. As other students chime in on the directions, the student teacher can observe the differences in understanding the initial directions that at least one student thought was clear.

CASE STUDIES

C   A   S   E

18-1   Cliff was assigned to student teach in computer classes at the high school. He was generally known among his fellow students at the university as a techie, and he was proud of his skill with computers, particularly with the software. He believed that most students would be interested in his classes because most young people he knew had access to computers and many of them were going into jobs that required computer knowledge.

As the student teaching semester began, Cliff was excited with his classes. By the time the 4th week rolled around, he was very aware that several of the students were not turning in their work. He always moved through class periodically to note that everyone was working on his or her keyboard. Later in the week, he discovered that some of the students were working on the keyboard but were not doing the work they were supposed to. He stopped the entire class from their work and said, "All right, now. I want to know why six of you are not working on your assignment." A young girl at the back of the room began to cry. A second student said, "I can't understand your directions on how to do the work."

Cliff was puzzled. He had been careful to explain what he wanted the students to do for classwork. He sought out his cooperating teacher.

1. What are some of the possible problems here?
2. What learning styles may be different from Cliff's in this classroom?
3. Should Cliff have to go to the trouble of teaching the material several ways? Why?
4. How is learning computers in a linear style difficult for someone who needs to see the big picture first?
5. How could Cliff bring those unproductive students up to speed?

C   A   S   E

18-2   Gretchen was delighted with her student teaching assignment with Mrs. Chinn's third-grade class. She kept the students in constant involvement, moving from one activity to another so that they would not be bored. Mrs. Chinn was concerned about the constant activity but was hesitant to curb Gretchen's excitement with her work with the children; it was so nice to have the extra help. Two more hands could get so much more done with the children.

Mrs. Chinn received a phone call from one of the parents who said that her child had become very anxious lately about school and she was trying to track down anything that had changed in the classroom. As they talked, Mrs. Chinn realized that the constant activity was wearing on some of the children, some of whom needed a slower pace with down time.

1. How should Mrs. Chinn explain this to Gretchen? In what steps?
2. How will Gretchen react?
3. Gretchen was trying so hard to do well in her assignment. How do you think this will affect her attitude toward her student teaching?
4. How would this situation have played out if the parent had not called?
5. In what way could Mrs. Chinn involve the university supervisor to help Gretchen?
6. How could the university supervisor work with the methods teachers back on campus to better prepare the elementary student teachers?

C A S E

18-3   Gary was a health and physical education student teacher in middle school and had experienced a successful unit on health practices. Now it was time for tennis training, his first experience teaching tennis other than to a few of his friends. He save the class several pointers on how to hold the racquet. On a chalkboard diagram he showed the students where to stand and moves to make toward the net. He explained to them the way to serve and reviewed rules of tennis with them. He then sent them to the tennis courts and told them to go out and practice.

As he followed the students to the courts, he noticed that some of them walked over and sat on the grass although there were courts for everyone. He walked over to the seated group and asked why they were not practicing. One of the girls looked up and explained, "I didn't understand a thing you said, and I can't even hold a tennis racquet."

1. What physiological step did Gary skip in his lesson?
2. Is it reasonable to assume that students could take a verbal explanation and apply that to a physical activity without some hands-on experience?
3. Have you or has someone you know had such a learning experience? What helped you or the other person most?
4. Do you think middle school students would speak up and indicate they don't understand? Why?
5. What influence does their stage of physical development at this age have on middle school students in this kind of activity?

C A S E

18-4   Mari was assigned to student teach with Mr. Frederick's sixth grade. She was especially excited because she could utilize her knowledge of sign language with one of the students in the room who was hearing impaired.

Mari successfully communicated with the hearing-impaired student and asked Mr. Frederick's permission to teach the entire class sign language so that they could more fully communicate with their classmate. Most of the students learned the alphabet quickly and took pleasure in spelling their own names and other words to each other. However, Carissa came crying to Mr. Frederick because she just could not remember the hand signals.

1. What could Mr. Frederick do?
2. This was a special "fun" learning project that Mari had been so excited about, and the hearing-impaired student was enjoying it immensely. What could have been the problem with Carissa?
3. Could a student with otherwise normal learning ability have a problem interpreting and remembering the visual signals?
4. With what other kinds of related learning styles could Carissa be having an undiagnosed problem?
5. What other techniques could Mari use to help Carissa learn sign language?

C A S E

18-5   Terry was assigned to student teach in English 10 with Mrs. Alvez, and the term was progressing nicely. Terry was enjoying her hard work and she felt that the students—most of them, at least—were learning. During her planning period one day, a student named Jonas dropped by to see her. She realized that he was supposed to be in class and reminded him of that. He replied that it really didn't matter, that he was going to drop out of school anyway.

Shocked, Terry asked him what he meant. Jonas explained that he had to work too hard to learn, it wasn't interesting to him, and he saw no point in punishing himself anymore; he would just drop out of school and get a job.

1. Should Terry tell Jonas that he would have to learn how to perform a job and that may be difficult for him to learn also? Why?
2. How could the guidance counselor assist in this situation?
3. Should Terry try to convince Jonas to stay in school and "tough it out"?
4. What alternatives could exist to make school more meaningful and attractive for Jonas?
5. If Jonas were your son, what would you want the school to do?

REFERENCES

Armstrong, T. (1994). *Multiple intelligences in the classroom.* Alexandria, VA: Association for Supervision and Curriculum Development.

Armstrong, T. (1998). *Awakening genius in the classroom.* Alexandria, VA: Association for Supervision and Curriculum Development.

Drake, S. (1998). *Creating integrated curriculum: Proven ways to increase student learning.* Thousand Oaks, CA: Corwin Press.

Jenson, E. (1998). *Teaching with the brain in mind.* Alexandria, VA: Association for Supervision and Curriculum Development.

RECOMMENDED READING

Armstrong, T. (1998). *Awakening genius in the classroom.* Alexandria, VA: Association for Supervision and Curriculum Development. *The author's thesis is that every student is a genius and that teachers can help children overcome dysfunctional systems outside the school and develop their true genius in a classroom that offers freedom and withholds judgement. The author also offers extensive suggestions for the teacher to create self-genius.*

Harmin, M. (1994). *Inspiring active learning: A handbook for teachers.* Alexandria, VA: Association for Supervision and Curriculum Development. *This handbook offers easily read and understood effective instructional strategies for involving all students in the classroom, including motivating, classroom activities, homework, testing, and grading.*

Johnson, D., & Johnson, R. T. (1999). *Learning together and alone: Cooperative, competitive, and individualistic learning* (5th ed.). Boston: Allyn & Bacon. *This classic should be on every student teacher's reading list. Descriptions of these three types of learning are included with guidelines on how and when to implement each type in the classroom. The techniques can also work with at-risk, gifted, and multicultural students.*

Keirsey, D., & Bates, M. (1984). *Please understand me: Character and temperament types.* Del Mar, CA: Prometheus Nemesis Book Company. *This book deals with the 16 temperament types based on the research of Carl Jung and developed by the Myers-Briggs team. Although this does not apply to younger children, the student teacher may wish to analyze her or his own temperament style and thereby become more aware of differences in others.*

Lazear, D. (1999). *Eight ways of teaching: The artistry of teaching with multiple intelligences.* Tucson: Zephyr Press. *This book is for teachers of grades K–12; it includes the naturalist intelligence and offers teachers many ways to expand their classroom experiences and afford students new ways to process information successfully.*

Leaver, B. L. (1997). *Teaching the whole class.* Thousand Oaks, CA: Corwin Press. *Leaver gives practical approaches to teachers to include all the students' learning styles in the classroom activities to increase learning for all. The student teacher can immediately apply these approaches.*

Mamchur, C. (1996). *A teacher's guide to cognitive type theory and learning style.* Alexandria, VA: Association for Supervision and Curriculum Development. *Sixteen types of learners are given in this text, with instructional approaches for each type of learner. Curricula ideas for each learning type are included.*

Thomlinson, C. A. (1999). *The differentiated classroom: Responding to the needs of all learners.* Alexandria, VA: Association for Supervision and Curriculum Development. *Thomlinson explains the use of the differentiated classroom, including instructional strategies for such classrooms and appropriate learning environments. The differentiated classroom is one in which instruction and assessment are adjusted to meet the needs of individual students.*

19

What Seems to Work

Trial and error in the classroom works fine if the student teacher is successful. If the result is failure, both time and effort have been wasted, and the student teacher may become discouraged. In addition, the students may exhibit doubt. This never helps the student teacher's self-confidence. One of the best forms of insurance against such an occurrence is to review what seems to work in other classrooms. The best source of this information is the cooperating teacher, the teachers down the hall, and the university supervisor. An additional good source of information on what seems to work in the instructional process is a review of current research.

As the student teacher, you are going into a classroom in which a culture has already developed. Don't try to change that. It is probably a good learning environment, and as you work with the students day by day, you will become more aware of it as the culture of your classroom. After you have been there for a while and feel comfortable, you may want to add dimensions to that culture. One dimension necessary in a successful classroom is the culture of thinking (Tishman, Perkins, & Jay, 1995). This refers to the totality of the classroom environment reflecting a valuing of thinking in all its dimensions.

As a student teacher, you may feel compelled to cover a great amount of material that you feel is important. In discussion with your cooperating teacher, you may find that less is better and that although it may seem important to you, the truth of the matter is that the likelihood of student learning will increase if the quantity of information is decreased. A basic state of idealism common to beginning student teachers reflects a need to teach more content without being aware of the understanding by the student. Wiggins and McTighe (1998) indicate that teaching involves the decision of what *not* to teach and that generally we want to teach more and are making a sacrifice to teach less.

As you move into full-time teaching, you will have the opportunity to work with individual students throughout the classroom so that when the time comes for you to group students, you will have an understanding about which students to group together for the best learning results. This experience will also assist in the selection of students for grouping for like learning styles.

GUIDELINES FOR THE STUDENT TEACHER

- **Accept the classroom climate that your cooperating teacher has developed.** Keep in mind that she or he has been working with the students previously and knows them and their needs better than you do.
- **Listen to what your cooperating teacher does not say as well as to what he or she does say.** Avoid being in such a rush to help students that you do not hear what your cooperating teacher is saying (and not saying) about your new suggested method. Cooperating teachers do not want to hurt your feelings, but neither will they allow you to place one of their students in a precarious learning situation.
- **Use those techniques that your cooperating teacher has already tried with his or her students.** You will build your own self-confidence and go farther with the students' learning if you use a method that already works. You may later be able to enhance the method with changes.
- **Keep in mind that child's mind is nothing to gamble; every learning minute counts.** Keep in mind the importance of your work with students and the responsibility you have to make every minute of school be a worthwhile learning experience for every child.
- **Avoid being tempted to group students by their own preferences.** In a learning situation, every student in class should learn to help every other student learn.
- **As you develop groups for learning activities, have your group criteria clearly in mind before you begin grouping.** Such criteria will assure that your groups are balanced and hold learning opportunities for the mix of students.
- **If a learning technique is working with a child, be careful about introducing another technique to any great extent.** You may know of a better way, but if you change the child's learning strategies, you may confuse the child more than help him or her. Be very careful introducing new strategies.
- **Compile a folder on those techniques that work with students.** Keep a record of students' characteristics and the techniques that seem to work best with the students. In another classroom next year, this folder of information will be invaluable to you.

GUIDELINES FOR THE COOPERATING TEACHER

- **Ask your student teacher to give you any ideas that he or she has learned recently at the university about effective instruction based on research.** Current research continues to add to what we know about effective instruction; this is an efficient way for you to stay up-to-date in this area.
- **Share your professional journals with the student teacher.** As you find appropriate materials in journals, suggest that your student teacher read them; this is a good basis for an extended professional conversation.

- **Be firm with the student teacher regarding the use of activities and techniques that you know work with students.** The student teaching program is a time for student teachers to learn from you what works best in helping students learn.
- **Utilize your colleagues down the hall.** Anytime during the term when the student teacher seems to need more observation, it is appropriate to request observations with those you are assured will be demonstrating techniques that help students learn better.
- **Help your student teacher form a network for professional advice on teaching techniques and learning styles.** In most schools, there are teachers who use a variety of teaching techniques for improved student learning. Suggest that your student teacher discuss with all these teachers their suggestions for increased student learning. Most teachers are delighted to share professional tried-and-true methods with a new teacher.
- **Insist that your student teacher keep good notes on what he or she learns from other teachers as well as from you.** Frequently, student teachers are so busy that they do not stop to take notes, thinking that they will remember. Those of us with a few years of experience know that even the most important items get forgotten sometimes. Maintaining a notebook or file is a must.
- **Help your student teacher to understand that her or his planning should revolve around the individual student and not around the teacher's text.** This is a secret to successful teaching that is difficult for student teachers to discover on their own; however, when they try it under the protection of your cooperating teacher umbrella, they will believe!
- **Help your student teacher to have a positive regard for the hearts and feelings as well as the mental activity of the students.** This will help the student teacher teach the whole student, not just the student's head. For many of our students in today's world, this concept is more critical than ever before.

CASE STUDIES

C A S E

19-1   Henry grew up in the Boy Scouts and was used to instructing others in how to do things, whether it was earning a merit badge or setting up a campsite. He was a natural teacher. Kids flocked to him and learned from him. As a student teacher in physics, although the subject was very different, his manner with students was the same; he also used some "homemade" techniques. Mr. Mercer, the cooperating teacher, would watch as Henry would take the students who had trouble learning off into a small group and work with them; they came back to the class with understanding. One day, he approached Henry and asked what kind of magic he performed on those students.

Henry explained that he just tried several ways of teaching them and saw what worked best for each student. He took notes and repeated the use of the same technique the next time the student had trouble with a concept or skill. He explained to Mr. Mercer that it was not difficult to do in a small group; it was how he had always worked with people.

1. Would you like to be a student in Henry's class? Why?
2. Although called a natural teacher, Henry really had good basic teaching skills. How would you describe them?
3. When someone learns from a teacher such as Henry and is in a position to teach someone else, what method do you think she or he will use?
4. What changes in his teaching habits do you think Mr. Mercer made?
5. Have you ever known a natural teacher like Henry? Describe.

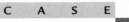

19-2   Mamie was student teaching in home economic and her cooperating teacher had been assigned some of the more difficult learning cases in the high school. Some of the students just did not seem to be able to learn at all. Mamie began working with the students one by one on just a few problems at a time; she had developed a method that seemed to work and several of the students began to show interest in school and in learning.

When her cooperating teacher asked her what her secret was to get the students to understand the problems and to have a renewed motivation for school, Mamie responded that the renewed interest in school came about when the students found learning possible. She told the cooperating teacher that the way she helped the students learn was to carefully walk through a problem with them at their speed and then have them walk through the same problem with her, repeating exactly what was to be learned or done. This seemed to work because the students could express their learning in their own words.

1. What part does decoding a message have in the thinking of a student who is learning?
2. Do we as teachers stop to remember that it is necessary for the student to understand (by decoding) and then to express again (by encoding) the lesson we want them to learn? Why?
3. Why do we consider speed so important in learning? Important to whom?
4. As all of us have learned, do we analyze how we have learned easiest and try to apply that for others' learning?
5. Where do you think Mamie learned her teaching technique?

C A S E

19-3   Susie came in to her student teaching classroom bursting with enthusiasm following her senior seminar at the university. The university supervisor had brought to class the previous night several papers reflecting current research on learning problems and immediately Susie identified students in her cooperating teacher's classroom with each of the theories. Ready to offer assistance to all the students at once, she related some of the information to Mr. Lee and explained how she wanted to get right to work with the students, involving them in some of these new techniques.

Mr. Lee knew he had a problem although Susie was really trying to help.

1. How could Mr. Lee get Susie to calm down and reflect on how such changes would affect the students?
2. Would you recommend that Susie try one method with one student for starters? Why?
3. Enthusiasm is so valuable. How could Mr. Lee not hurt Susie's enthusiasm and yet keep what's best for the students uppermost in his actions?
4. What kind of conversation do you think Mr. Lee and the university supervisor had later? What suggestions would have been in order?
5. Have you known someone like Susie who got really enthusiastic about new projects on a large scale? How did things turn out?

C A S E

19-4   Mr. Singh's new student teacher, Tonya, was happy in her student teaching and particularly enjoyed observing in other teachers' classrooms. When planning the observations, Mr. Singh had instructed Tonya to take written notes following each observation to keep her memory fresh about those practices and techniques that she wanted to add to her own repertory. As time went on, Tonya did not seem to be keeping such notes. Mr. Singh asked her about them and she replied that it took too much time. Mr. Singh also noticed that Tonya did not take notes, as he did, during their meetings. He expected her to keep notes and explained that to her.

Mr. Singh found it necessary to talk with Tonya about keeping her file on observations, on their meetings, and on new approaches that she learned from him.

1. In Mr. Singh's talk with Tonya about her keeping notes, what would he say?
2. Does everyone really need to keep a file on such things?
3. Do you think that Tonya would sit down following the semester of student teaching and make notes on all that she had learned?
4. How could such notes be of profit to Tonya next year in her first professional teaching job?
5. Could someone just develop a form that student teachers such as Tonya could fill out during the semester so that they did not have to keep notes on everything? Why?

C A S E

19-5   Mr. Kokavich wanted his student teacher, Bryan, to network with the other teachers in the building; they were a group of excellent teachers and had many good ideas, techniques, and skills that Bryan could borrow. Bryan, however, was a little shy and wanted to stay in the classroom with Mr. Kokavich, indicating that he needed to learn from him first and then maybe he would get to know the other teachers better.

After Bryan had completed the initial required observations in the school, Mr. Kokavich still could not get him out of his room to spend any time with the other teachers. His suggestions were repeatedly resisted.

1. If you were Mr. Kokavich, what would you do?
2. What possibilities exist for bringing some of the teachers into Mr. Kokavich's classroom to work with Bryan?
3. Do you think Bryan's attitude is a personality characteristic or a feeling of fear and inadequacy?
4. How could the university supervisor help with this problem? Should he assign Bryan some work with the other teachers? Would Mr. Kokavich be the appropriate person to do this?
5. Since this may be a problem that developed over a long time, what kind of plan would you suggest to overcome it?

REFERENCES

Tishman, S., Perkins, D. N., & Jay, E. (1995). *The thinking classroom: Learning and teaching in a culture of thinking.* Boston: Allyn & Bacon.

Wiggins, G., & McTighe, S. (1998). *Understanding by design.* Alexandria, VA: Association for Supervision and Curriculum Development.

RECOMMENDED READING

Freiberg, H. J. (1999). *Perceiving, behaving, becoming: Lessons learned.* Alexandria, VA: Association for Supervision and Curriculum Development. *This text provides a humanistic view of how important it is for students to feel good about themselves in the learning process and how important it is to educate the whole student.*

Greenwood, G., & Fillmer, H. T. (1999). *Educational psychology cases for teacher decision-making.* Upper Saddle River, NJ: Merrill/Prentice Hall. *This set of case studies on development, learning, instruction, and assessment will assist the student teacher in examining possibilities of learning behavior in the classroom and seek possible solutions patterned after the text. This is excellent material to discuss with the cooperating teacher.*

Johnson, D. W., Johnson, R. T., & Holubec, E. J. (1994). *Cooperative learning in the classroom.* Alexandria, VA: Association for Supervision and Curriculum Development. *This text offers student teachers and cooperating teachers the classic cooperative learning methods to use for arranging the classroom, assigning students to groups, and encouraging students to think.*

Johnston, C. A. (1996). *Unlocking the will to learn.* Thousand Oaks, CA: Corwin Press. *Johnston offers practical advice on finding the patterns in students' learning. Checklists and examples show differences in the sequential processors, precise processors, technical processors, and confluent processors and how to enhance the facilitation of their learning.*

Keirns, J. L. (1999). *Designs for self-instruction: Principles, processes, and issues in developing self-directed learning.* Boston: Allyn & Bacon. *Using self-instruction in the wide range from print media to hypermedia on the Web, this text can assist the teacher in moving more mature students into a self-instruction mode.*

Roe, B., & Ross, E. (1998). Language, thinking, and learning across the curriculum. In *Student teaching and field experiences handbook* (4th ed.) (pp. 174–201). Upper Saddle River, NJ: Merrill/Prentice Hall. *This chapter includes a framework for higher order thinking skills and a synopsis of study skills, including metacognitive skills and study habits.*

Sousa, D. (1998). *How the brain learns and Learning manual for How the brain learns.* Thousand Oaks, CA: Corwin Press. *This text and manual offer suggestions to the teacher to incorporate "brain-friendly" methods of dealing with each child's needs in age level and learning style.*

USA Education Briefs (September 7, 1998). *Federal resources for educational excellence.* Http://www.ed.gov/free. *This Internet site offers access to many free teaching and learning resources from the U.S. government. It offers information on organizations, how to develop Internet-based learning resources, and Internet-based learning communities.*

P A R T

5

Planning for Success

Chapter 20   *Planning*

20

Planning

Successful teaching is a result of effective planning. Planning enables one to predict the future course of events. Although planning involves a knowledge of many elements of the educational picture, for example, scope and sequence and taxonomies of development and learning, many candidates for student teaching identify planning with the immediate activity. It is important for the beginning teacher to realize that effective planning for a particular class is rooted in a realistic plan for the total school year. Without long-range planning, short-range planning is ineffective, inefficient, and frequently a waste of time.

A review of materials from professional organizations will help anchor the student teacher in the planning process and assist in confidence building. Many of these organizations have free materials to send to educators, and most have journals that are periodically published with the latest research in the field. Students teachers are urged to subscribe to these journals and join the organizations as a student member prior to graduating because the fees for student membership are usually significantly lower than for those already graduated. With the help of these journals and materials from the professional societies, the student teacher can more effectively plan with the latest research from the field. The following list includes some of the professional societies the student teacher may wish to contact (Armstrong, Henson, & Savage, 1997):

American Alliance for Health, Physical Education, Recreation, and Dance
1900 Association Drive
Reston, VA 22091

American Vocational Education Association
1410 King Street
Alexandria, VA 22314

Association for Educational Communications and Technology
1800 N. Stonelake Drive, Suite 2
Bloomington, IN 47404

Association for Childhood Education International
11141 Georgia Avenue, Suite 200
Wheaton, MD 20202

Business Professionals of America
5454 Cleveland Avenue
Columbus, OH 43231

Council for Exceptional Children
1920 Association Drive
Reston, VA 22091

International Council for Computers in Education
University of Oregon
1787 Agate Street
Eugene, OR 97403

International Reading Association
P.O. Box 8139
Newark, DE 19714

Music Teachers National Association
2113 Carew Tower
Cincinnati, OH 45202

National Art Education Association
1916 Association Drive
Reston, VA 22091

National Association for the Education of Young Children
1509 16th St. N.W.
Washington, DC 20036

National Association for Gifted Education
4175 Lovell Road, Suite 140
Circle Pines, MN 55014

National Conference on Parent Involvement
579 West Iroquois
Pontiac, MI 48341

National Council for the Social Studies
3501 Neward Street NW
Washington, DC 20016

National Council of Teachers of English
1111 Kenyon Road
Urbana, IL 61801

National Council of Teachers of Mathematics
1906 Association Drive
Reston, VA 22091

National Middle School Assoociation
2600 Corporate Exchange Drive, Suite 370
Columbus, OH 43231-1672

National Science Teachers Association
1742 Connecticut Avenue NW
Washington, DC 20009

The student teacher should be knowledgeable about the philosophy of the school; a copy is usually available in the administrative office, or the cooperating teacher can tell the student teacher where to locate such a document. As schools prepare for visits by visiting accreditation teams, such documentation is updated for the current student population of the schools.

Given the philosophy of the school, the student teacher can integrate the statewide scope and sequence plan for the particular discipline and grade level. For instance, the state plan may indicate that eighth-grade English is to include particular elements of thought processing, grammar, composition, and literature. However, state guidelines are much more explicit. Merging the state plan with needs of the school population gives the student teacher a baseline for beginning specific planning.

Writing course goals for the year and dividing such goals into objectives for units for each grading period (6 weeks or 9 weeks) gives the student teacher a readily available starting point for writing unit plans. Units do not all need to be of the same time frame; however, the total of the time for all the units should total the number of weeks available in the school year. A functional approach is to develop units that end simultaneously with the grading period. Such planning gives both the student teacher and the students a feeling of closure and relief as well as the opportunity for a fresh new start with the beginning of the new grading period and the new unit.

Each unit should be developed by setting the goals for the unit and then writing the objectives to be met by the end of the unit. Daily lesson topics and objectives naturally emerge from such unit planning. The sequencing of activities to meet the unit objectives causes the daily lesson plans to fit together. Compare this planning to a fence, with the daily lesson plan being the fence post and the unit theme being the wire of the fence. Without the daily lesson plan (the fence post), the unit theme (the fence wire) loses its support and direction and leads nowhere.

The planning of an effective lesson is an essential skill of teaching very much in the mind of the cooperating teacher. Concern always exists about the level of readiness the student teacher has developed in the area of planning prior to reporting to the student teaching assignment.

It is critical that during the early stages of student teaching there is extensive collaborative planning between the cooperating teacher and the student teacher. As planning skills improve, the student teacher depends less and less on the cooperating teacher, who in turn has much more confidence in the student teacher. Of course, the cooperating teacher must continuously evaluate the lesson plans of the student teacher and provide necessary guidance.

A specific lesson does not develop in a vacuum; it must fit into a sequential and relevant pattern of development. This concept is often difficult for some inexperienced teachers to realize and requires assistance from the cooperating teacher. Such items as planning classroom activities, the scope and sequence of the subject matter to be used, the units to be taught, and methods of evaluation are primarily the responsibilities of the cooperating teacher, but they are shared to a greater extent with the student teacher as the term progresses.

Student teachers should have been trained to write unit and lesson objectives prior to their student teaching. Such objectives may take a number of formats, but they should include the knowledge, skills, and attitudes to be learned, the activities that enhance that learning, the degree to which the learning should occur, and methods for evaluating the extent and quality of the learning.

Student teachers should show a strong professional growth as both they and their cooperating teacher evaluate the student teacher's lesson plans. The university supervisor can be most helpful in the planning of instruction. Some colleges and universities require a student teaching seminar concurrently with student teaching, and topics such as unit and lesson planning are high-priority topics for such seminars.

Most plans may need some last-minute revisions on the basis of the previous class. To ensure the effective organization of teaching, plans should be ready far in advance. By using total-year planning, the student teacher has the entire picture in mind. If the need arises, the lesson plan for the day can move forward or can include alternate activities that were planned for the future.

The future plans can easily be revised. A good guide to use with a lesson plan is to consider whether, with adaptation, it could be used with another group of students.

Although the student teacher is not in the school for the total year, the involvement in such extensive planning enhances planning skills for future years and gives a surprising amount of self-confidence in the actual classroom teaching performance. Few things contribute to a person's self-confidence as much as understanding the gestalt involved and knowing the total picture.

GUIDELINES FOR THE STUDENT TEACHER

- **Prior to student teaching, determine which grade levels and general topics you are expected to teach.** Preparation of the necessary groundwork before the development of a teaching unit or special project is helpful. Of course, your cooperating teacher expects to approve all of your plans prior to your teaching.
- **What works for the cooperating teacher does not necessarily work for you.** In fact, your plans should be more detailed. Your teaching style also may differ from that of the cooperating teacher. Although this is to be expected, learn as many

effective teaching techniques and strategies as you possibly can from your cooperating teacher. Keep a notebook on this topic. As important as this material seems at the moment, you may forget by next year when you are in your own classroom and need to recall these techniques and strategies.

- **As you become more experienced, the detail required in lesson plans may decrease.** However, the thoroughness of planning should not decrease.
- **Obtain and organize your materials before executing your lesson.** Students become very restless if this has not been done. Your lack of strong organization plays into their mischievous nature.
- **You need to make sure that you are on task and teaching the material required.** This is particularly important because of local and state minimum skills on which many students are required to show mastery.
- **You need to budget your activities and materials to meet your time allocation.** It is probable that you will have difficulty with the timing of your lessons. Most of the time you will probably have more plans than you can complete, but there will also be times when you run out of materials. As you gain experience, you achieve skill in budgeting your time considering the activities to be completed.
- **Your teaching environment must be given consideration.** For example, if you are going to need a listening center, it must be established prior to the lesson. If you are planning to do research in the library, you should check with the librarian or media specialist and schedule this while you are still in the planning stages. Large art, science, and technology projects should to be located in an area where they will be protected.

GUIDELINES FOR THE COOPERATING TEACHER

- **Make it clear to your student teacher at the beginning that you have high expectations in the area of planning.** Under no circumstances should the student teacher be permitted to teach without your having approved the unit and daily lesson plans.
- **At the beginning of student teaching, you should assist your student teacher in making and using unit and daily lesson plans.** You may help best by asking questions and assisting the student teacher to focus more clearly on precisely what is to be done.
- **Assist in making materials accessible to the student teacher.** Student teachers cannot be completely responsible for finding all the materials they use and need guidance from you and other school personnel. Inform the student teacher about additional materials and resources that may be used with specific units and daily lessons.
- **Timing may be a problem area for student teachers,** who may spend too much time with a specific lesson or group. Most student teachers need guidance in this

area. Suggest that your student teacher overplan rather than fail to plan enough. Student teachers can always delete material, but it is difficult to add material and activities on the spur of the moment. Few experiences are more horrifying to a student teacher than to be in front of a class and to have used up all the material with 20 minutes still remaining in the class period. Help your student teacher plan alternatives for such an occasion.

- **Give your student teacher guidance in judging how much can be taught within a specified time and how much time should be spent on a particular skill development or area of study.**
- **A conversation concerning the learning levels of your students is valuable for your student teacher in preparation for planning.** It may be difficult for some student teachers to realize that not all students are eager to learn. Help them to recall their own school career and feelings about some of their classes.
- **Student teachers must learn to be flexible with planning because of potential interruptions.** Provide a schedule listing coming activities not included on lesson plans, plus classes that rotate on various days. Help the student teacher to see the total picture; the learning strand does continue even though some students are excused for one reason or another. Sometimes student teachers feel that their classrooms are just revolving doors for their students. Help them remain centered in what they are doing.
- **It is helpful if both you and the student teacher jot down notes during the day on concerns and questions to be discussed during the next conference.** Many important points are forgotten if there is not an organized method of recording these concerns as they arise (see Appendix J for suggested format).

CASE STUDIES

C A S E

20-1   Jan a fifth-grade student teacher, wanted to teach a unit on poetry because this was her favorite subject. Her cooperating teacher encouraged her and suggested that she teach this unit but only for 15 minutes per day. She explained that the unit would have to be limited because of work on the state minimum skills that needed to be covered at this time. The cooperating teacher was out of the room during the 40-minute language arts period; Jan spent all of this time on her poetry unit. Later, when the test was administered for the minimum skills, the cooperating teacher discovered that certain skills had not been taught.

1. Should Jan have been aware of the importance of minimum skills at this stage in her career?
2. How should the cooperating teacher handle Jan's failure to follow instructions?
3. Would a conversation concerning the importance of minimum skills be helpful?

4. How serious is this mistake of Jan's?
5. Should the university supervisor be informed of this situation? What could he do to help Jan?

C A S E

20-2   Malik was enjoying his student teaching in a seventh-grade social studies class and was teaching full-time. His major problem was that he could never remember to watch the clock. Every day his class before lunch ran late; he could never get his 5th period students to physical education class on time. Malik was warned by the cooperating teacher that this was creating serious problems with the other teachers and the principal.

1. What could cause a student teacher to be negligent in this way?
2. Why would this negligence be considered a serious problem?
3. What could be done to ensure that Malik got his students to the right areas on time?
4. Is there any way that the students could help?
5. What suggestions would you give Malik to avoid his having problems of this nature as he begins his career as a permanent teacher? What personality characteristics could he develop that would help this kind of situation?

C A S E

20-3   Mary had greater expectations of her sixth-grade students than her cooperating teacher had. She always included more activities than were necessary in her lesson plan and rushed to complete them. The cooperating teacher noted that certain students were becoming quite tense about Mary's lessons. When she discussed the matter with the student teacher, Mary explained that she was afraid she would run out of materials within a specified time block. She also indicated that she wanted to be certain that the students were challenged.

1. What level of tension needs to be present for a lesson to be challenging?
2. How could the cooperating teacher make Mary feel more at ease?
3. In what way could the cooperating teacher help Mary to see that her behavior is being reflected in the student stress?
4. How could this conflict be resolved to the benefit of both Mary and her students?
5. How could the personality characteristics such as the ones causing Mary's difficulty be dealt with in teacher education methods classes prior to student teaching?

C A S E

20-4   Joy is a creative student teacher assigned to a high school English class. Her cooperating teacher was quite impressed with her ideas and encouraged her to incorporate them into her teaching. Joy was scheduled to take over her first English class on Monday of the 3rd week and planned to initiate some creative dramatics. Joy's cooperating teacher wanted to see her first lesson plan a week before delivery and expected a very creative plan. Four days before the lesson, Joy still had not handed in a lesson plan. It appeared that she did not begin planning sufficiently early and, according to another student teacher, had the reputation of not carrying her tasks to completion.

1. What should the cooperating teacher do at this point?
2. Would it be unfair not to allow Joy to teach without a prior lesson plan? Explain.
3. Under what conditions would it be appropriate for the cooperating teacher to discuss his student teacher with another student teacher in the building?
4. What kinds of time lines should the cooperating teacher set for Joy?
5. At what point should the university supervisor be called in?

C A S E

20-5   Jonathan was completing his 3rd week as a student teacher in an eight-grade science class. He had taken over the science class and thought he was doing a good job. According to his cooperating teacher, however, Jonathan had one major problem. His lesson plans were much too general. Because he was just teaching one class at this time, his cooperating teacher expected much more detailed plans. Jonathan's attitude was that he did not feel it was necessary to write detailed plans because he had noticed that his cooperating teacher's plans were quite brief.

1. What is wrong in this situation? Explain.
2. Was it unfair to expect Jonathan to produce detailed plans? Explain.
3. How could this problem be resolved?
4. Why would it be permissible for a cooperating teacher to have only brief plans?
5. How can the university supervisor and the cooperating teacher assist Jonathan in understanding the difference between his stage in professional development and that of his cooperating teacher?

C A S E

20-6   Rudy had completed his 7th week in a 10th-grade social studies student teaching assignment. His major weakness appeared to be in the area of planning. He had five consumer economics classes but prepared only one lesson plan to cover all five classes. His cooperating teacher insisted on one lesson plan with modifications for each class, but Rudy continued along the same pattern. In disgust, the cooperating teacher called the university supervisor.

1. Why did the cooperating teacher insist on modifications for each class?
2. Why do you think that Rudy thought he was doing a satisfactory job of planning?
3. What should be the university supervisor's plan of action to help resolve this situation?
4. What are some of the major difficulties in teaching several sections of the same course simultaneously?

5. What options for teaching classes with other teachers in the building would be available? Would this be professionally advisable for Rudy?

C A S E

20-7   Ashley had completed her 4th week of student teaching. She had the feeling that her teaching was going well and had been told so by her cooperating teacher. Ashley was concerned, however, because she had not had any feedback concerning the lesson plans. Her cooperating teacher told her during the 1st week that he would leave the planning up to her. He said that he did not want to see her plans but would tell her if the lessons were not going well.

Ashley had prepared detailed plans for every day that she had taught and kept them in a notebook. She was happy that she had done this, especially when her university supervisor asked to see her plans before his first observation. When she told him about the attitude of her cooperating teacher toward her plans, he was disturbed.

1. Why would the university supervisor react this way?
2. Was Ashley wise in preparing thorough plans even though they were not requested? Explain.
3. Was she justified in wanting feedback on her lesson plans? Why or why not?
4. In what way should the format of a student teacher's lesson plans change as the number of lessons to be taught increases?
5. The university supervisor realized that Ashley may have a stronger professional commitment than her cooperating teacher. To what extent should she confide in Ashley? What professional guidelines should the university supervisor use in this situation?

REFERENCE

Armstrong, D. G., Henson, K. T., & Savage, T. V. (1997). *Teaching today: An introduction to education.* (5th ed.) Upper Saddle River, NJ: Merrill/Prentice Hall.

RECOMMENDED READING

DeLandsheere, V. (1988). Taxonomies of educational objectives. In J. P. Keeves (Ed.), *Educational research methodology and measurement: An international handbook* (pp. 345–354). New York: Pergamon Press. *This article presents the taxonomies of Bloom, Gagne-Merrill,* *Gerlach and Sullivan, Krathwohl, and others. Also included is Guilford's model of the structure of the intellect.*

Doll, R. C. (1996). The planning process. In *Curriculum improvement: Decision making and process* (pp. 357–414). Boston: Allyn & Bacon.

Doll presents a thorough review of appropriate strategies for curriculum planning. He offers problems, trends, and suggested steps in curriculum planning, extending this to planning for restructuring. This material is useful background information to share with the student teacher.

Henderson, J. G., & Hawthorne, R. D. (2000). *Transformative curriculum leadership.* Upper Saddle River, NJ: Merrill/Prentice Hall. *These authors assist in the reflection on emancipatory constructivism and deliberative artistry. Based on a critique of the Ralph Tyler rationale, this text offers the educational professional a method for developing curriculum that truly is transformative for students.*

Hottenstein, D. S. (1998). *Intensive scheduling: Restructuring America's secondary schools through time management.* Thousand Oaks, CA: Corwin Press. *This book provides a valuable resource in changing school schedules to accommodate increased student achievement.*

Marzano, R. J., Brandt, R. S., Hughes, C. S., Jones, B. F., Presseisen, B. Z., Rankin, S. C., & Suhor, C. (1988). *Dimensions of thinking: A framework for curriculum and instruction.* Alexandria, VA: Association for Supervision and Curriculum Development. *This book discusses in depth the kinds of thinking skills to be developed and used in the teaching/learning process. The relationship of various levels of thinking skills to content area knowledge is discussed, giving examples and models. A glossary and summary outline in the appendixes are most helpful in the instructional planning process.*

Mosston, M., & Ashworth, S. (1990). *The spectrum of teaching styles: From command to discovery.* White Plains, NY: Longman. *This text can assist the student teacher to understand how the teaching process fits into a pattern of a chain of decision making. Although the spectrum model is very detailed, an awareness of this model helps the student teacher to understand how the fragmented parts of the process of teaching fit together.*

Robbins, P., & Herndon, L. E. (1998). *Thinking inside the block: Strategies for teaching in extended periods of time.* Thousand Oaks, CA: Corwin Press. *This material will assist both the preservice and experienced teacher to work effectively in extended instructional periods. Topics include delivering instruction, working with special-needs students, planning for substitutes, and dealing with student absences.*

Roblyer, M. D. (1999). *Integrating technology across the curriculum: A database of strategies and lesson plans.* Upper Saddle River, NJ: Merrill/Prentice Hall. *Containing 250 lesson plans and strategies to integrate technology into the K–12 curriculum, this text contains diagrams and handouts and links lesson plans to national standards to enable teachers to reach national curriculum goals.*

P A R T

Classroom Organization and Management

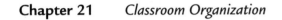

21

Classroom Organization

As the cooperating teacher and the student teacher prepare to work together, one of the main areas of concern is classroom organization. Student teachers are usually concerned about whether they will be able to develop an effective plan for classroom organization. The cooperating teacher is usually concerned with the quality of classroom organization the student teacher will maintain. For most student teachers, the student teaching experience is the first opportunity to put together all the components of teaching experienced during their training.

Frequently field experiences prior to student teaching give the student only a portion of the responsibility, and although the assignment may be well done, there may be difficulty with trying to meld the entire program for a classroom into one picture.

This melding process is one of the most anxiety-laden experiences for the novice teacher. Prior to developing a comprehensive and realistic feel for teaching, the student teacher must experience this synthesis of the many theories and the relatively small amount of practice experienced in the training program. While working with this synthesis, the meaning of teaching changes for the student teacher.

Student teachers must operate within the organizational framework of their assigned classrooms. Dr. Gordon Eade, Professor Emeritus of the College of Education at the University of West Florida and long-time student teaching coordinator, compares the student teaching assignment to operating within a balloon. Student teachers should be able to push out here and there but must stay within the confines of the balloon. When the student teacher pushes out in a certain direction, other parts of the balloon have to make adjustments, thereby changing shape. Keeping fresh air in the balloon and not breaking through are cautions to keep in mind by both the student teacher and the cooperating teacher.

Well-organized classrooms have rules and principles set up concerning use of facilities, space, materials, and time. If the room is organized properly, following these principles diminishes problems in student conduct and promotes learning.

Although the cooperating teacher can suggest, advise, and warn, only experience can bring reality to the student teacher concerning the many facets of classroom activity labeled "teaching." The value of such advice depends in part on the receptivity of the student teacher.

As the student teacher divides teaching into such components as planning, delivering the lesson, evaluating, and reteaching, he or she has a vague realization that something is missing. That difficult-to-pin-down element is classroom organization, not a separate component of teaching, but rather a pattern or matrix that falls across the entire teaching spectrum from the 1st day of kindergarten until graduation.

Classroom organization is not something that is to be done in a classroom; it is not an end unto itself. It is, rather, an approach given to those activities involved in the learning process.

A student teacher does not "do" classroom organization. Use of the best efforts of the students, school materials and their effects, the training and background of the student teacher, resources, and current time usage contribute to classroom organization. When these resources are well utilized, the teacher is acclaimed for having good classroom organization. When they are ill used, the teacher is said to have poor classroom organization.

The attitude that forms the basis for effective classroom organization is one in which the teacher-to-be likes himself or herself, likes people in general, and enjoys working with students in a helping relationship. The teacher who loves subject matter and does not like students will be a poor teacher and may have many organizational problems. A friendly and helping attitude exerts positive forces in the classroom. A positive action on the part of the beginning teacher is more likely to produce a positive action on the part of the students in the classroom.

Once the attitude has been analyzed, the cooperating teacher and the student teacher can consider applying that attitude throughout the learning activities in the classroom. This is the "rule" stage. In considering what activities to undertake in the classroom, this positive, personal attitude should be applied in an objective way to facilitate the highest quality possible of learning in the classroom. The student teacher and the cooperating teacher can break down the classroom activities into academic processes and physical activities, carefully maintaining the attitude that is to be infused into the teaching process.

Specificity begins at this point. The physical classroom can be divided into those properties of the classroom itself (desks, windows, heat, light) and those properties of the students (physical distance between students, pathways in the room, behavior patterns based on the seating arrangement, access to materials, books, learning centers, and pencil sharpeners).

The appearance of the classroom gives an indication about the extent to which the teacher cares for the environment in which the class operates. It is evident that no two classes are alike. Each one has its own environment (Eby, 2001).

The academic processes involve those nontangible actions in the classroom through which students encourage or discourage each other. The development of internal motivation can be considered a product of effective classroom organization. The teacher who can successfully develop internal motivation within students has few classroom organization problems. This again reflects the basic attitude of the teacher whose class is responding.

Considerations that should be discussed by the student teacher and the cooperating teacher include organizing the interaction and the art of questioning. The use of praise and feedback, when necessary and appropriate, should also be discussed.

GUIDELINES FOR THE STUDENT TEACHER

- **Carefully observe your cooperating teacher during the early part of your assignment.** Inquire about anything you do not understand. Your cooperating teacher is your model.
- **Keep in mind that the best organization requires rules.** You should know when to do what with what. Also, keep in mind that no set of rules fits all circumstances. The needs of students must have priority over organization.
- **Student teachers should be flexible and experimental in nature.** Be sure to stay "within the balloon."
- **You are probably now ready for the specificity mentioned earlier in the chapter,** provided that you have examined your professional attitudes and this has led to a discussion with as many teachers as you can interview or observe.
- **Make as many physical arrangements in the classroom as possible before the arrival of the students.** Never suggest that students rearrange their own chairs; bedlam may result.
- **Adjust the lights, window shades or blinds, and air or heat before the arrival of the students.** This necessitates that you arrive at the school sufficiently early so that you do not appear rushed. You may have to make additional adjustments as your lessons progress.
- **Have work ready for students to begin immediately upon their entering the room and being seated.** Develop within the group a desire to come in and get to work on materials for ongoing projects. When all students are in the room, that particular work can be put away for a time as other classwork begins. Having a few self-directing assignments on the board helps the early arrivals and those students finishing their other work early.
- **Develop a plan for pencil sharpening and other routines.** This should include an emphasis on courtesy and expediency. Do not allow students to leave their seats at just any time to sharpen a pencil. Warn them ahead of time so that they may plan ahead and bring a spare pencil. Have extra sharpened pencils ready in a mug on your desk so that students may silently borrow and return them without interrupting the class by announcing the lack of a pencil.
- **Prepare videotapes, projectors, and filmstrips before the time you will need to use them.** Set them up before class begins or while students are working on something else. Students have been known to become disorderly while waiting for audiovisual equipment to begin.

- **Be sure the students know what is to be done when their work is finished, where to put their work, and what to do next.**
- **Be specific in your own plans for record keeping and student procedures,** such as going to the restroom, lining up for lunch, and distributing materials.
- **Space the desks so that natural pathways through the room assist traffic to flow easily and do not cause crowded areas.** Be sure there is a wastebasket in the classroom.

GUIDELINES FOR THE COOPERATING TEACHER

- **As a beginning teacher launches into the world of the classroom in student teaching, you can be of great service by helping the student teacher to identify the various composite parts of the totality of teaching.** Being able to see the total picture helps many student teachers find confidence and perform better both in planning and in presentation.
- **The student teacher must understand that effective classroom organization is imperative and profitable in the teaching/learning process.**
- **Throughout the term, as you identify for the student teacher the major components of classroom organization, bits and pieces of information and advice should be exchanged.** Such information is more than a list of things to do to get the classroom ready or a list of things for students to do or to avoid doing.
- **Encourage your student teachers to use those methods that work best for them as long as they operate within your "balloon."**
- **If there is time in the schedule, arrange for the student teacher to observe other selected teachers' classrooms** for directed observation and later to visit those teachers for a discussion of effective classroom organization.
- **Offer the student teacher a wide variety of experiences in seeing how classrooms are run.** Discuss the variations between classes and point out social, economic, cultural, and maturational differences and social patterns. The experience with you will be of immeasurable value to the student teacher.
- **One of the most important factors in a student teaching program is your modeling.** Student teachers are watching for you to do the right thing at the right time.
- **Help your student teacher learn to pick up clues from your students.** For example, if a student refuses to do work assigned, the student teacher must learn to seek solutions to the problem.

CASE STUDIES

C   A   S   E

21-1   After Michelle began her full-time student teaching in the fourth grade, her cooperating teacher breathed a sigh of relief that the classroom was proceeding normally. She liked Michelle's approach to planning and her teaching methods with the students. Something kept nagging at the back of her mind, however, and as she thoroughly reviewed Michelle's progress, she became aware of the problem.

Michelle had allowed the children to keep their desks messy. Some books and materials were scattered on the floor under the desks; books inside the desks were disheveled. Before Michelle's arrival, the students had been required to keep their desks clean and neat with no books or materials on the floor. The cooperating teacher knew something must be done before the children's habits got worse.

1. Should the cooperating teacher speak to the children about their desks?
2. How could the cooperating teacher approach the situation without hurting Michelle's feelings?
3. What reaction do you think Michelle would have to the cooperating teacher's suggestions?
4. Is it important that fourth graders keep their desks neat? Why?
5. What is the connection between the organizational abilities of a teacher and sloppy desks of the students?

C A S E

21-2   When the university supervisor first visited the classroom where Wendy was student teaching, he realized that trouble might be brewing. Wendy had been placed with Miss Goldberg, notorious for her organization and neatness. Wendy, however, seemed to thrive on the lack of such qualities. Although Wendy had a number of qualities that could easily help her become a good teacher, she would have difficulty fitting into a classroom with Miss Goldberg.

Overnight the supervisor pondered the situation. Then he called Wendy and set up a conference with her in his office on campus after school.

1. What do you think the coordinator told Wendy?
2. What hope is there for compromise in this situation? Why?
3. How would Wendy discover the cooperating teacher's tolerance level?
4. Would you consider the cooperating teacher's neat habits a good professional role model? Why?
5. What are Wendy's chances of being successful in this assignment?

C A S E

21-3   Bill greeted the students in his new student teaching placement as they arrived the first morning. When the bell rang, his cooperating teacher began the day's assignment in high school geography. Later in the first class, the cooperating teacher introduced Bill to the class and asked him if he would like to say a few words.

Bill seized the opportunity and told the class some things about himself as an introduction. He proceeded to tell them that "some things" would change around the classroom, that he had plans for rearranging the desks, that the trash basket should be moved to another more accessible location in the room, and that the teacher's desk would be better nearer the door.

The class members looked at Bill as if they could not believe what they were hearing. The cooperating teacher interrupted Bill, thanked him, and proceeded with the geography lesson.

1. If you were the cooperating teacher, how would you introduce Bill to your other classes during the day?
2. How should the cooperating teacher react? What should she say to Bill?
3. In what way could the university supervisor be of help in this situation?
4. Should Bill be allowed to continue his student teaching in this classroom? Why?
5. What could have been done prior to this introduction to avoid this situation? By whom?

C A S E

21-4   Margie was student teaching in 11th-grade history with a cooperating teacher who did not share her philosophy of getting the students involved in the material. The cooperating teacher primarily used lecture and drill as teaching methods. Margie wondered why she had been placed with such a teacher. She realized that perhaps she could have a good influence on her cooperating teacher as well as learn from her.

At one point, Margie wanted the students to become involved in group work. When she discussed her ideas with the cooperating teacher, she was told that there was to be no group work in that classroom and that the desks were never to be moved for such foolishness. Margie was bewildered and frustrated.

1. What were Margie options?
2. Should Margie involve the university supervisor with her problem? Should she discuss this with the principal?
3. What could result from going against the cooperating teacher's wishes and using the group process?
4. What skills in diplomacy could Margie develop while getting to use her own methods of teaching? How?
5. Discuss the possibility of Margie's requesting a different placement for student teaching.

C A S E

21-5   Charlie a young aggressive student teacher, was assigned to a fifth-grade classroom. His cooperating teacher, Mr. Doyle, was delighted to have a student teacher and told Charlie on his 1st day that anything he wanted to do was fine with him. He said he would stay out of Charlie's way.

Within the first 3 weeks, Charlie completely overhauled the reading program in the classroom. He started by giving every student an interest inventory and proceeded to locate a wide variety of books at different reading levels to match those interests.

One of the first steps Charlie took was to discontinue working in the basal readers. He attempted to individualize the reading program, which included developing a listening and reading center and building individual study carrels. Parents donated some comfortable furniture, which added an informal atmosphere. The fifth-grade students were enthralled with their new reading program. Mr. Doyle was also very excited about Charlie's work and invited other teachers in the building to visit.

1. Do you feel that Charlie was out of line in this situation? Why or why not?
2. Was Mr. Doyle wrong in allowing Charlie to completely revamp this program without his assistance? Explain your answer.
3. Can you think of any circumstances that would make it permissible for a student teacher to make so many changes in such a short period of time?
4. Do you feel that the students benefited from Charlie's project? In what ways?
5. Would you prefer to have a student teacher like Charlie or one who would sit back and wait to be told what to do? Explain your preference.

REFERENCE

Eby, J. W., & Martin, D. B. (2001). *Reflective planning, teaching, and evaluation for the elementary school.* (3rd ed.). Upper Saddle River, NJ: Merrill/Prentice Hall.

RECOMMENDED READING

Bauer, A. M., & Sapona, R. H. (1991). *Managing classrooms to facilitate learning.* Englewood Cliffs, NJ: Prentice Hall. *This book presents a thorough coverage of classroom organization that would facilitate learning. Student teachers and cooperating teachers can benefit by reflecting on this information.*

Charles, C. M. (1983). *Elementary classroom management: A handbook of excellence in teaching.* New York: Longman. *This book thoroughly covers the basics of classroom organization. It is evident that the author has an extensive background in classroom teaching. The information is clear and the suggestions presented are beneficial for* both elementary cooperating teachers and student teachers.

Cohen, E. G., & Goodlad, J. I. (1994). *Designing groupwork: Strategies for the heterogeneous classroom* (2nd ed.). New York: Teachers College Press. *This edition combines theory and strategies that can be applied to multiability and bilingual classrooms, combining suggestions for dealing with the status problem, antisocial behavior, and other possible pitfalls of cooperative learning.*

Eby, J. W., & Martin, D. B. (2001). *Reflective planning, teaching, and evaluation for the elementary school.* Upper Saddle River, NJ: Merrill/Prentice

Hall. *The chapter "Planning a Healthy, Safe Environment for Learning" describes what reflective teachers consider to be a healthy classroom climate. Student teachers could profit from reading about and discussing the experiences of elementary students on their 1st day of school in four hypothetical classrooms.*

Emmer, E. T., Evertson, C. M., Sanford, J. P., Clements, B. S., & Worsham, M. E. (1984). *Classroom management for secondary teachers.* Englewood Cliffs, NJ: Prentice Hall. *This book discusses what a teacher can do to create a well-organized classroom. Checklists to help teachers organize planning activities in key areas and case studies illustrating how important concepts can be applied in classrooms should be of interest to secondary school teachers and student teachers.*

Evertson, C. M., Emmer, E. T., Clements, B. S., Sanford, J. P., & Worsham, M. E. (1989). Organizing your classroom and supplies. In *Classroom management for elementary teachers* (pp. 1–14). Englewood Cliffs, NJ: Prentice Hall. *Excellent advice is offered to student teachers and beginning teachers relative to the physical organization of classroom furniture, supplies, equipment, and student belongings. Classroom diagrams are included with suggestions. An effective set of activities and a checklist are included.*

Gore, M. C., & Dowd, J. F. (1999). *Taming the time stealers.* Thousand Oaks, CA: Corwin Press. *This text offers teachers practical, workable tips to assist in organizing the busy school day both in memory and on the calendar. Checklists, forms, charts, and rubrics are included.*

Kellough, R. D. (1999). *Surviving your first year of teaching: Guidelines for success.* Upper Saddle River, NJ: Merrill/Prentice Hall. *This text offers suggestions across the areas of responsibility of student teaching, including such details as time management, student seating, and professional dress.*

Roe, B. & Ross, E. P. (1998). Classroom management. In *Student teaching and field experiences handbook* (4th ed.) (pp. 96–121). Upper Saddle River, NJ: Merrill/Prentice Hall. *The authors discuss classroom organizational plans, grouping, scheduling, record keeping, and using time effectively. A long list of good filler activities is included; this will be valuable to the student teacher for those time gaps that occur.*

22

Classroom Management

Classroom management is uppermost in the minds of many student teachers. Some have heard horror stories and have seen examples of poor as well as good management techniques during their own schooling and during previous field experiences. They are correct in assuming that effective teaching can seldom take place without effective classroom management.

Appropriate classroom management begins with the student teacher's positive attitude and varies from individual to individual. Frequently, student teachers attempt to model after their cooperating teacher or some other idealized teacher, and they discover painfully that what works for one usually does not work for all.

Students in training to become teachers often ask such questions as, "What rules do you have for running a classroom?" and "Where do I find the answer to fill my bag of teaching tricks?" Many student teachers mistakenly use a list of rules in lieu of an attitude. This does not imply that the use of rules in classroom control is inappropriate; rules are necessary. However, rules must have a base and that base is attitudinal, derives from the personality and characteristics of the cooperating teacher and the student teacher, and is unique in each classroom.

As student teachers realize that the development of appropriate classroom management must first of all be an internal matter holistically seen, they are on their way to developing into competent professionals. Piecemeal rules may last a few weeks or occasionally a school year, but anxiety is always lurking in the beginner's mind that something is missing. When it is realized that the missing element is to teaching as the foundation is to a building, steps are usually retraced and new beginnings are made with the help of fellow teachers or instructors.

Student teachers should definitely operate "within the balloon" mentioned earlier. They can reach out but must stay within the framework that exists in their assigned classrooms.

More than we like to admit, much of the misconduct exhibited by students in the classroom is caused by inappropriate behavior of the teacher. This possibility should be considered, and behavior should be reviewed.

After student teachers reflect on their own classroom behavior, it is advantageous for them to look at various models. During student teaching, student teachers accept any model being used in their particular classrooms. It is important, however, that they continue to reflect on which model or combination of models they incorporate as they move into their own classrooms. They should develop their own discipline plan, which will be determined by their own philosophy and personality. Studying the models and ideas presented by such writers as Glasser, Dreikers, and Canter (see Recommended Reading at the end of this chapter) would be worthwhile to the student teacher.

All disciplining skill emanates from the teacher. A teacher, whether experienced or new, must be confident and maintain positive attitudes toward students before he or she can be an effective disciplinarian. A disciplined classroom is a well-ordered, systematic setting in which all who enter can sense the outcome of the planning without necessarily seeing the minute details of management.

Student teachers could also profit by reviewing the developmental characteristics of the students assigned to them. Are the students typical or atypical? What are the specific causes of noted behavior problems? Cooperating teachers should discuss such issues with their student teachers.

Specific instructions should be given to student teachers prior to their observing other classes. For example, a student teacher could be asked to observe how a certain teacher deals with the transition between one task and another. It is possible for student teachers to observe other classes but see very little if specific objectives are not articulated.

Student conduct is related to rules. A few specific rules are usually appreciated by both students and teachers. Few classrooms can operate successfully in a situation where there is no control. No behavior management system is 100% effective for every teacher. We cannot eliminate all misconduct no matter how hard we try; we can only minimize the causes and occurrences.

Some teachers believe that punishment is negatively correlated to learning. Misbehavior usually spreads if punishment continues. Very little can be accomplished by threats. However, effective use of praise for good conduct is important. We live in a "rewards" system; everyone wants to feel worthy, important, and rewarded.

Use all human resources possible to help solve behavior problems. This includes guidance personnel, district office personnel, the principal, supervisors, parents, and, probably most important of all, the students themselves.

A positive attitude and enthusiasm are important ingredients for teachers to have in establishing positive classroom management. Bad days will probably occur, but one would hope that these days are few and far between if the proper preparations are made.

GUIDELINES FOR THE STUDENT TEACHER

- **Keep in mind that you will not be fully in control until you get your own class.** Be patient; your day will come.

- **As a student teacher in a student teaching assignment, it is appropriate that you maintain the method of classroom control developed by your cooperating teacher.** Do not try to change any of the established routine. Learn from it, build on it, and when you have your own classroom, you will be better able to manage effectively from the very beginning.
- **Attempt to anticipate as many of the potential problems as you can and plan accordingly.** Think through what you would do if specific things were to happen. Discuss this with your cooperating teacher.
- **You cannot operate without rules.** This would not be fair to the students or yourself. It is easier to start with rigid and strict rules in the beginning of the year. As you get to know the students, you can easily add less rigid rules. The reverse can make life more hectic for you.
- **Be aware of the social patterns with your students and assign seating accordingly.** Do not allow any student to seclude himself or herself; seat the loner with someone who is friendly. Be aware that those students who sit near the doorway may talk with students who walk up and down the hall. Those students who sit near windows may daydream easily.
- **Never be caught off guard in responding to actions among your students.** Plan for all contingencies, and if you miss any in your planning, never let the students know. Stay on your toes at all times.
- **React calmly in all situations, keeping in mind that most of the behaviors in your classroom are normal and merely need some reshaping and self-control.**
- **Be sure that you know what comes next in your plan so that there is no lull or time for trouble.** Have every minute planned, but be flexible. Move easily from activity to activity.
- **Use your cooperating teacher!** Discuss your lesson plans prior to teaching to avoid any difficulties.
- **Prepare to make a few mistakes; just get over them and keep going.**
- **Keep in mind that some of your students are not receptive to academic pursuits no matter how hard you try.**
- **While you are student teaching, think through the discipline plan you will use when you have your own class.**

GUIDELINES FOR THE COOPERATING TEACHER

- **You serve as a model for your student teacher.** Formulate solutions to behavior problems that inevitably will occur.
- **Arrange to have your student teacher observe other teachers** who are strong in certain aspects of classroom instruction and encourage him or her to look for those particular aspects.

- **Your student teacher may also be able to discern that those teachers who continually have difficulty with students and the classroom activities** are usually people who have some personal hang-ups that the students intuitively know or are people who are weak willed, possibly wishing only to be liked by students.
- **Describe the backgrounds and characterists of your students to your student teacher.** The more the student teacher knows about the students, the easier the student teaching will be. Advise your student teacher to pick up clues from the students and attempt to get to know the students as individuals.
- **Turn over your class only when you feel that your student teacher is ready to handle it.** It is a must that student teachers thoroughly understand your organization and discipline plan.
- **Expect some mistakes from your student teacher.** Remember that she or he is a beginner in this business of teaching. Interrupt only when the situation demands it. Discuss this possibility with the student teacher early in the assignment.
- **Invite your student teacher to participate in parent conferences.** It is most important that student teachers realize the importance of listening closely to what parents have to say both verbally and nonverbally.
- **Through visitation and observation with other teachers, the student teacher will begin to understand** that those teachers who like students, who like teaching, and who know how to express it are more readily accepted by their students and have fewer student-related problems.

CASE STUDIES

C A S E

22-1   Jessica happily anticipated her student teaching assignment in middle school science. However, her cooperating teacher's class seemed to have several troublemakers. During Jessica's initial visits to the classroom and during observations at the beginning of the term, Mrs. Lewt, the cooperating teacher, noted that Jessica seemed to try to appease the troublemakers in an attempt to make them like her. Mrs. Lewt realized that Jessica would have difficulty with these particular students if she did not use a formal approach with them.

1. How should Mrs. Lewt counsel Jessica?
2. What difficulties might arise if the cooperating teacher did nothing?
3. What effects on Jessica's student teaching would such friendliness have?
4. How could Jessica successfully remedy the situation, assuming that she wishes to do so?
5. In what ways could the use of a formal approach affect the students?

C   A   S   E

22-2   Sean was the new student teacher in the first-grade class taught by Mrs. Elison. Sean enjoyed his students and liked teaching. His students seemed to like him, although they reserved some affection for their "real" teacher. During art time one afternoon, one student caused a paint spill, and Sean reacted negatively. The other students immediately began jeering. Sean was surprised how first graders could change so suddenly. Some students began dropping paint, others threw paper, and others banged on the worktables. Mrs. Elison had to act.

1. What should be the immediate reaction of Sean to the students?
2. What should the cooperating teacher do at this moment?
3. How could Sean develop appropriate relations with this class?
4. What could have been said or planned earlier by the cooperating teacher to avoid such a situation?
5. What do you think about male student teachers being assigned to kindergarten or first-grade classrooms?

C   A   S   E

22-3   Andrea was assigned to a third-grade class for student teaching. Her cooperating teacher, Ms. Estrada, had been teaching many years and was close to retirement. Her control of the classroom was quite lax, and this was a big concern to Andrea. When Andrea questioned Ms. Estrada about the rules of the classroom, she was told that there were no specific rules but that some were put in place as the need developed. Andrea was perplexed as to how she could possibly control the class with this type of organization.

1. What do you think of Ms. Estrada's plan for handling discipline?
2. What could Andrea do to enhance her success in the classroom?
3. Would it be inappropriate for Andrea to ask Ms. Estrada for permission to add specific rules for the classroom? Explain your answer.
4. How could this situation have been avoided?
5. In what ways could Ms. Estrada make Andrea feel more comfortable about this situation?

C   A   S   E

22-4   Sherrill had been working 3 weeks as a student teacher assigned to Mrs. Bennett's fifth-grade class. Everything appeared to be going well except for one problem. One of the students, Nicolette, evidently had little respect for Sherrill or Mrs. Bennett. She pouted most of the time and frequently refused to complete assigned tasks. The matter seemed to be getting worse as the days went by. Nicolette was becoming quite sassy and belligerent.

1. What could Mrs. Bennett do to help matters?
2. How could Sherrill's strengths be used?
3. What assistance could be obtained from outside the classroom?
4. One student can sometimes set the tone for a classroom. If Nicolette is permitted to continue her pouting and belligerence, what could be the effect?
5. Should a student be permitted to disrupt a class in this way? Explain your answer.

C A S E

22-5 Anne was getting along very well in her social science classes at the high school. Students had accepted her and her first 4 weeks had gone very smoothly. A new student, Amos, was assigned to her second-period American history class, and troubles began. Amos developed the habit of whistling in a low tone during the major part of the fourth period. Both Anne and her cooperating teacher, Mrs. Gambini, constantly told Amos to stop his whistling, as it was bothering them and the other students. Amos did not realize he was whistling and appeared to do it unconsciously. The other teachers who had Amos in classes reported the same problem.

1. What could cause Amos to whistle unconsciously?
2. How could such a seemingly small matter cause so much confusion?
3. What could Anne and the other teachers do to resolve this problem?
4. In what ways could class members help?
5. How could Amos's whistling be put to constructive use?

RECOMMENDED READING

Albert, L. (1989). *A teacher's guide to cooperative discipline: How to manage your classroom and promote self-esteem.* Circle Pines, MN: American Guidance Service. *The theoretical base of Cooperative Discipline has developed around the ideas of Rudolph Dreikurs and his teacher, Alfred Adler. This positive program shows teachers how to work hand in hand with students, parents, and colleagues. The self-esteem gained by the students is one of the major goals of this program. This is good reading for both the student teacher and the cooperating teacher.*

Cangelosi, J. S. (1986). *Cooperation in the classroom: Students and teachers together.* Washington, DC: National Education Association. *This book presents numerous suggestions for obtaining effective behavior management. The ideas presented are* *drawn from a variety of classroom discipline approaches. This is good reading for student teachers and cooperating teachers who are in the process of developing a discipline plan.*

Charles, C. M. (1989). *Building classroom discipline: From models to practice.* New York: Longman. *This book presents comprehensive coverage on the following eight models of discipline: Redl and Wattenberg, Kounin, Neo-Skinnerian, Ginott, Dreikurs, Jones, Carter, and Glasser. Implementation for classroom practice makes this book practical. This is beneficial information for preservice or inservice teachers who are attempting to formulate a discipline plan of their own.*

DiGiulio, R. (1995). *Positive classroom management: A step-by-step guide to successfully running the show without destroying student dignity.* Thousand Oaks, CA: Corwin Press. *This text offers strategies for managing student conduct and developing student respect and cooperation.*

Duke, D. L., & Meckel, A. M. (1984). *Teacher's guide to classroom management.* New York: Random House. *This book recommends that teachers be given the opportunity to select their own approach to classroom management. A number of strategies for encouraging productive student behavior are presented and are worthwhile reading for student teachers.*

Glasser, W. (1990). *The quality school: Managing students without coercion.* New York: Harper & Row. *Glasser contends that no more than half of our secondary students are willing to make an effort to learn and therefore cannot be taught. He goes on to recommend a Learner-Team Model, which he describes in detail. This is challenging reading for secondary school student teachers and cooperating teachers.*

Gootman, M. E. (1997). *The caring teacher's guide to discipline: Helping young students learn self-control, responsibility, and respect.* Thousand Oaks, CA: Corwin Press. *This text offers elementary school teachers ideas for helping students correct their own behavior, solve problems, use good judgement, and practice self-control.*

Hunter, M. (1990). *Discipline that develops self-discipline.* Thousand Oaks, CA: Corwin Press. *This text includes some reinforcement techniques that help students develop their own dignity and self-direction.*

Jones, F. H. (1987). *Positive classroom discipline.* New York: McGraw-Hill. *This book concentrates on teaching strategies that encourage positive behaviors from students. The author's realistic experiences in classroom discipline are reflected. Both student teachers and cooperating teachers could benefit from discussing ideas presented here.*

Jones, V. F., & Jones, L. S. (1990). *Comprehensive classroom management: Motivating and managing students* (3rd ed.). Boston: Allyn & Bacon.

This book presents a wide variety of research-supported methods used in managing classes. Ideas for dealing with disruptive students and the focus on methods that work with at-risk students are included in this edition. Student teachers and cooperating teachers could benefit by reading and discussing pertinent materials presented in this book.

Koenig, L. (1995). *Smart discipline for the classroom: Respect and cooperation restored* (Rev. ed.). Thousand Oaks, CA: Corwin Press. *The authors offer ideas for working with ADHD students and effective techniques for the toughest discipline problems.*

Long, N. J., Morse, W., & Newman, R. G. (1996). *Conflict in the classroom: The education of at-risk and troubled students* (5th ed.). Austin, TX: PRO-ED. *An ideal textbook for both preservice and inservice teachers, this text analyzes the complexity of troubled youth in the classroom.*

National School Safety Center. (1986). *School discipline notebook.* Sacramento, CA: Pepperdine University Press and the National School Safety Center. *This brief 66-page book presents a realistic approach to school discipline. Much of the information is drawn from various junior and senior high school handbooks from many states.*

Short, P. M., Short, R. J. & Blanton, C. (1994). *Rethinking student discipline: Alternatives that work.* Thousand Oaks, CA: Corwin Press. *The authors advocate a balanced discipline model that includes both punishment and positive reinforcement.*

Skinner, B. F., & Rogers, C. (1985). Does behavioral control provide the best learning environment? In J. W. Noll (Ed.), *Taking sides: Clashing views on controversial educational issues* (pp. 83–97). Guilford, CN: Dushkin. *Student teachers are interested in the topic of classroom control and could profit from reading the opposing views presented by B. F. Skinner and Carl Rogers. Skinner links learning and motivation to the influence of external forces; Rogers insists on the reality of subjective forces in human motivation.*

Strohmer, J. C. (1998). *Sweating the small stuff:*

Answers to teachers' big problems. Thousand Oaks, CA: Corwin Press. *Using suggestions from the "Try It Today" tips, this expert guide on the side will help the student teacher turn large classroom problems into small stuff.*

Weinstein, C. S. (1996). *Secondary classroom management: Lessons from research and practice.* New York: McGraw-Hill. *This companion volume to* Elementary Classroom Management *(below) offers a discussion of the research and the practical application of practices in secondary school classroom management. Case studies are included.*

Weinstein, C. S., & Mignano, A., Jr. (1997). *Elementary classroom management: Lessons from research and practice* (2nd ed). New York: McGraw-Hill. *This text presents the current research on classroom management and its practical application in elementary schools. Case studies are included.*

The Teaching Process

23

Teacher Competencies

Required teacher competencies vary from state to state and from one university program to another. Most teacher competencies are lists of teacher abilities that revolve around the planning, implementation, and evaluation of student learning situations. These competencies are based on a knowledge of student development, learning capabilities, and cultural, economic, and personality factors. Teacher competencies can be implemented through whole-group instruction, small-group instruction, one-on-one teaching, team teaching, and other group configurations. Interdisciplinary curriculum models adopted by some schools now require team teaching across curriculum areas, and the student teacher should readily get as much experience as possible with such techniques if the opportunities are available in their schools.

The Interstate New Teacher Assessment and Support Consortium (INTASC) has 10 principles relating to the knowledge, disposition, and performance that new teachers should possess and be able to do (Huntington College Education Department, 1997):

1. The teacher understands the central concepts, tools of inquiry, and structures of the discipline(s) he or she teaches and can create learning experiences that make these aspects of subject matter meaningful for students.
2. The teacher understands how children learn and develop, and can provide learning opportunities that support their intellectual, social, and personal development.
3. The teacher understands how students differ in their approaches to learning and creates instructional opportunities that are adapted to diverse learners.
4. The teacher understands and uses a variety of instructional strategies to encourage students' development of critical thinking, problem solving, and performance skills.
5. The teacher uses an understanding of individual and group motivation and behavior to create a learning environment that encourages positive social interaction, active engagement in learning, and self-motivation.
6. The teacher uses knowledge of effective verbal, nonverbal, and media communication techniques to foster active inquiry, collaboration, and supportive interaction in the classroom.

7. The teacher plans instruction based on knowledge of subject matter, students, the community, and curriculum goals.
8. The teacher understands and uses formal and informal assessment strategies to evaluate and ensure the continuous intellectual, social, and physical development of the learner.
9. The teacher is a reflective practitioner who continually evaluates the effects of his/her choices and actions on others (students, parents, and other professionals in the learning community) and who actively seeks out opportunities to grow professionally.
10. The teacher fosters relationships with school colleagues, parents, and agencies in the larger community to support students' learning and well-being.

These principles are subdivided into standards that can be related to the National Council for the Accreditation of Teacher Education (NCATE) standards. For additional information, see the Website http://www.huntington.edu/education/sholtrop/INTASC.html.

Sometimes in training programs, beginning teachers initially concentrate too heavily on teaching skills. It may be more helpful for these teachers to first become familiar with learner characteristics and motivation. Given such knowledge and a strong content background, students learning to be teachers may find that fitting their techniques to specific learning needs is relatively easy.

Implementing the competencies learned in methods classes is similar to that stage of putting together a jigsaw puzzle at which you begin to see the whole picture; you see where all the pieces fit. A major thrill in the student teaching experience is actually using the competencies previously developed and being successful in doing so. This is a moment that cooperating teachers can anticipate as eagerly as can the student teacher. This is the point at which the student teacher may exclaim, "Hey! This stuff all makes sense now!"

A good beginning activity for both the student teacher and the cooperating teacher is to review what the student teacher has learned in developmental psychology class about students at a particular age. The cooperating teacher can then add practical knowledge about the stages of physical, psychological, and social development the students are going through. Once the range of levels of development has been ascertained, the student teacher begins to develop objectives for student learning. Based on those objectives, unit plans and lesson plans can be developed.

Tyler (Madaus & Stufflebeam, 1989, p. 200) proposed a logical system of curriculum and instruction development. His rationale for such development has four major points:

1. clarification of purpose
2. selection of learning experiences
3. organization of these experiences
4. assessment of progress

Tyler further suggested that a study of the learner be done. Although Tyler referred primarily to the development of programs, the cooperating teacher can assist the student teacher in using this model in the development of unit and lesson plans (see Appendixes C through F).

Hunter (1976) has indicated that the most important factor for teachers is promoting learning in their students. Her book *Teach More—Faster* should be prescribed reading for every student who is becoming a teacher. Much of what Hunter has written in her other books is immediately useful for the student teacher. When such materials are read and discussed by both the student teacher and the cooperating teacher, both teachers learn.

A good plan for success in student teaching is for the student teacher to begin classroom teaching in an area of strength with competencies that are better developed than other areas. This lends confidence so that as the student teacher moves into those less developed competencies, she or he develops more self-confidence and performs at a higher level.

The primary competencies of teaching are planning, implementing, instructing, and evaluating. How they are done is determined by preferences of the student teacher and the cooperating teacher unless the school district or the state department of education has specified other methods.

Beginning with setting objectives and establishing how those objectives are to be met, the student teacher can plan the most effective activities and materials to help students reach those objectives.

Without seeming simplistic, this framework for developing teacher competence serves the student teacher well. The framework can easily be embellished as interests, abilities, and needs dictate.

GUIDELINES FOR THE STUDENT TEACHER

- **Keep in mind that the major purpose of student teaching is for you to demonstrate your teaching competence.** You should realize, however, that this area is one in which you are continually growing. No one ever reaches the highest plateau of any teacher competency. Even experienced teachers of 20 years or more are working toward improving teaching techniques.
- **Realize that although you may have passed a written competency test, you are not assured that you will be effective in the classroom.** Such abilities as classroom management, effective written and oral communication, and planning and teaching skills are difficult to measure adequately until you are assigned a group of students with whom to implement these skills.
- **As a student teacher, you may display idiosyncrasies of which you are unaware.** These unique traits cannot be determined by competency tests. Encourage your cooperating teacher to inform you of any problems of this nature. A videotape of your teaching may reveal such problems.

- **Various economic and cultural factors in the particular school to which you are assigned influence the selection of necessary competencies.** For example, a cutback in paper supplies in many schools may make it necessary for both the cooperating teacher and the student teacher to use the chalkboard more. Practicing writing on the board is the only way to develop effective board handwriting skills.
- **Work very closely with the cooperating teacher to make sure that you use the same system for testing and recording the students' minimum skills competencies.** Parents must be notified if students are not developing these skills. Teacher competencies pay off with greater student competencies.
- **Discuss with your cooperating teacher the competencies that you are expected to develop as a beginning professional.** These discussions should take place often to provide for ongoing evaluation.
- **Develop your professional portfolio.** Maintain samples of your professional work such as unit plans, lesson plans, tests, activities, and media materials.
- **Set aside one section of your portfolio for evaluations from your cooperating teacher and university supervisor.** Another section could contain notes and letters from students and parents recognizing your good work. An excellent method for documenting your teaching competence is to have someone videotape you as you are teaching a lesson.

GUIDELINES FOR THE COOPERATING TEACHER

- **Sometimes teachers who are effective in the classroom with their own students may not have completely articulated their position on teacher competencies.** This is the time for you to review your thinking on these competencies. Decide on your priorities so that you can more clearly express them to your student teacher.
- **Know your own teaching skills.** Being aware of your own competencies helps you be a better role model for your student teacher while sharpening your own teaching skills.
- **The review of research and current methodology in which you engage to stay current in advising your student teacher pays double dividends.** Observing, helping, and evaluating your student teacher throughout the student teaching process makes you more aware of your own level of competence in addition to helping you bring about positive critical development in your student teacher.
- **You should be aware that all your best intentions, suggestions, and help may be in vain.** Although chances for such are minimal, it is possible that the student teacher assigned to you has insufficient preparation, motivation, or ability to become a successful teacher. Occasionally, psychological or addiction problems get in the way of the success of the student teacher. Your close association with the university supervisor saves grief in such a situation. If the necessary level of

competence in teaching skills does not become evident within a reasonable time, make appropriate arrangements with your university supervisor to have the student teacher reassigned at a later date after being cycled through additional training and preparation.

- **Help your student teacher organize a portfolio that documents his or her competence in particular areas.** Such a portfolio could begin in an expandable folder and grow during the term to fit into a small file box. One method of documenting the portfolio contents is to label each file folder with a specific competency; place copies in the folder of all student-teacher-developed materials that pertain to that particular competency. By the end of the term, your student teacher will have a good collection that represents his or her ability in many areas of competency. Usually student teachers are surprised at how well prepared they really are.

- **You will be more supportive of your student teacher if you unobtrusively remain in the classroom until you are both confident in lesson delivery competency.** The beginning of the term is not the time to leave the room and leave the student teacher on his or her own. The student teacher grows a great deal with your specific input and assistance at this critical stage of her or his student teaching assignment.

- **As you assist your student teacher in competency development, you will find that you will have been a major beneficiary yourself.** Watching the student teacher begin the planning, implementation, and evaluation as a novice and helping the professional transformation occur will pay large dividends in your professional satisfaction.

- **During the time you are helping your student teacher develop teacher competencies, consider a variety of methods of pinpointing difficulties.** You may wish to come up with possible strategies such as the following:

  a. Insist upon a clear lesson plan.
  b. If your student teacher uses nonstandard English while orally communicating information, make note of the mistakes for immediate discussion.
  c. Audiotape or videotape the lesson and during playback cooperatively evaluate as to whether the vocabulary and teaching behaviors were suitable to the topic and the audience.
  d. Also evaluate the tapes as to suitability of volume and pace. If problems continue, give a demonstration lesson on how the volume and pace promote comprehension.
  e. As the videotape of a lesson is reviewed the student teacher will probably see traits that worked against the purpose of the lesson.
  f. Present a resource person, a film, and/or a written relevant example of the competencies that student teachers should.

- **Discuss all of the recommended competencies with your student teacher and together develop practical ways of mastering them.**

CASE STUDIES

C   A   S   E

23-1   Will is a student teacher in a fifth-grade self-contained class. He is impressed with his cooperating teacher, Mr. Randolph, who has made him feel welcome in the classroom. Will was quite surprised at Mr. Randolph's attitude toward the recently adopted state minimum standards program; Mr. Randolph resented spending the necessary time working on these minimum standards and was very hostile about it. Will was embarrassed when Mr. Randolph told the principal that he wanted a substitute teacher 2 or 3 days a week so that he could keep up with the minimum standards. Needless to say, the principal did not appreciate the "humor" of Mr. Randolph's request.

1. How should Will react in this situation?
2. How can he avoid getting caught up in the conflict?
3. In what ways could this situation affect his success as a student teacher?
4. What advice could the university supervisor give Will?
5. What opportunities could Will use in helping Mr. Randolph accept the state minimum standards program?

C   A   S   E

23-2   Beatrice is assigned as a student teacher in a third-grade classroom. She is confident that she can be successful in student teaching except for one competency. She has always had difficulty with English grammar, especially verb tense. This is particularly true when she is nervous. Former teachers have been trying to help Beatrice resolve this problem for years.

1. Why should Beatrice discuss this matter with her cooperating teacher at the very beginning of her student teaching?
2. How should Beatrice explain her difficulty with grammar to her university supervisor?
3. How could a college student get this far in her program with such a weakness? Explain.
4. What steps can Beatrice take to improve her competence in grammar?
5. Under what conditions should Beatrice be allowed to successfully complete student teaching if this problem cannot be resolved?

C   A   S   E

23-3   Hector has begun his student teaching in a senior high English assignment. He was somewhat worried about his voice projection because he had been criticized in previous field experience assignments about speaking in a monotone. It came as a surprise when he realized that his cooperating teacher also spoke in a monotone. Hector was not going to be able to use his cooperating teacher as a model in this area.

1. How could this problem be resolved?
2. Should Hector discuss his feelings with his cooperating teacher? How could this cause conflict?
3. In what way could the university supervisor be of assistance?
4. What other methods of presenting material to his class could Hector use?
5. Which other high school faculty could help Hector work on his vocal problem?

C A S E

23-4   Keiko was in her 5th week of student teaching and assigned to an eighth-grade classroom. She thought she was doing well but had received neither positive nor negative comments about her teaching from her cooperating teacher. Keiko was concerned that she might not be developing satisfactorily in the competencies necessary for successful teaching. The cooperating teacher changed the subject whenever Keiko brought up the topic of evaluation. It was getting to the point that Keiko was suspicious that she was not meeting the expectations of her cooperating teacher.

1. How could Keiko get this matter clarified?
2. Why do you think the cooperating teacher always changed the subject?
3. What should the university supervisor tell the cooperating teacher about the importance of evaluation?
4. What methods of self-evaluation could Keiko use?
5. What measures could be taken to make this a more profitable experience for Keiko?

C A S E

23-5   Vito was in his 6th week of student teaching in an 11th-grade mathematics class. He was disappointed when he received his midterm evaluation report from his cooperating teacher. He received high evaluations with the exception of the rating on his ability to keep adequate records, which was unsatisfactory.

The university supervisor discussed this evaluation with the cooperating teacher, who reported that Vito had taught effective lessons but was very careless in grading papers and recording grades. The cooperating teacher said she had discussed this matter with Vito numerous times, but no improvement had resulted.

1. What methods of feedback could the cooperating teacher have used prior to the midterm evaluation?
2. Should Vito have been content with his evaluation even thought he had one unsatisfactory rating?
3. Why was he so careless in his record keeping?

4. What advice should Vito's university supervisor give him?
5. If you were a principal interviewing Vito for a job, how would you express to him the importance of maintaining adequate records?

REFERENCES

Hunter, M. (1976). *Teach more—Faster* (p. 1). El Segundo, CA: TIP Publications.

Huntington College Education Department. (1997). http://www.huntington.edu/ education/sholtrop/INTASC.html

Madaus, G. F., & Stufflebeam, D. L. (Eds.). (1989). *Educational evaluation: Classic works of Ralph W. Tyler.* Boston: Kluwer Academic Publishers.

RECOMMENDED READING

Airasian, P. W. (1997). *Classroom Assessment* (3rd ed.). New York: McGraw-Hill. *This book is a guide to the full range of teacher decision making, beginning with organizing the class and moving through instruction and formal evaluation to grading.*

Arends, R. I. (1998). *Learning to teach* (4th ed.). New York: McGraw-Hill. *Arends includes a research base to his practical application, a how-to for action research, and recommendations on observation, reflection, microteaching, student performance, and authentic assessment.*

Barnes, H. (1989). Structuring knowledge for beginning teachers. In M. C. Reynolds (Ed.), *Knowledge base for the beginning teacher* (pp. 13–22). New York: Pergamon Press. *This chapter reviews current research related to the necessary elements for teachers to develop meaningful frameworks for teaching. The data furnished by this author serve the cooperating teacher well in guiding the student teacher.*

Cruickshank, D., Metcalf, K., & Bainer, D. (1998). *The act of teaching* (2nd ed.). New York: McGraw-Hill. *This is a revised edition of a popular text on teaching and classroom strategies, including patterns of learning, instructional alternatives, and problem solving.*

Etheridge, C. (Spring 1989). Strategic adjustment: How teachers move from university learnings to school based practices. *Action in Teacher Education, XI*(1), 31–36. *This article illustrates the translation of learnings from the university training to successful classroom practices. Examples of successful strategic adjustments are given.*

Evertson, C. M., Emmer, E., Clements, B. S., Sanford, J. P., & Worsham, M. E. (1984). Organizing and conducting instruction. In *Classroom management for elementary teachers* (pp. 109–125). Englewood Cliffs, NJ: Prentice Hall. *This chapter is a good review of the implementation of instructional activities. The responsibilities of the student teacher to communicate directions clearly, manage effective arrangement of activities, and provide practice and feedback are among the many topics reviewed.*

Gall, M. D., Gall, J. P., Jacobsen, D. R., & Bullock, T. L. (1990). *Tools for learning: A guide to teaching study skills.* Alexandria, VA: Association for Supervision and Curriculum Development. *Successful teaching/learning is based to a large degree on the successful study skills of the students. These authors have presented methods of identifying appropriate study skills and ways to teach them in both elementary and secondary classrooms.*

Kellough, R. D., & Kellough, N. G. (1999). *Secondary school teaching: A guide to methods and resources.* Upper Saddle River, NJ: Merrill/Prentice Hall. *Part 2 in this text deals with instructional planning, and part 3 deals with implementing instructional strategies. Although this book focuses on the secondary level, adaptations can be made to use much of the material on the elementary level. Sample formats for teaching plans are given as well as directions for developing a self-instructional package.*

Moore, K. D. (1998). *Classroom teaching skills* (4th ed.). New York: McGraw-Hill. *The skills addressed in this text are common to all subjects and all grade levels and include a minimum repertoire of teaching skills in the areas of planning, implementation, and evaluation.*

Schmuck, R., & Schmuck, P. (1997). *Group processes in the classroom* (7th ed). New York: McGraw-Hill. *The authors offer research/theory-based practical ideas on group process procedures, including multi-age classes, students as peer-conflict managers, and alternative methods of using cooperative learning.*

24

Student Teaching Communication

Communication is one of the most important elements in the success of the student teaching experience. It is a tool to be used both in the delivery of instruction and in the development of associations with all the various parties involved in the student teaching experience: the cooperating teacher, the university supervisor, the students, the school administration and staff, other faculty, parents, and school patrons.

Clarity of expression is highly relevant during student teaching. To be articulate in communication usually reflects a high quality of thinking, and because thinking is a major tool of the classroom teacher, communication is a reflection of the kinds of thinking the professional is capable of doing.

It is critical for the student teacher to understand the difference between the *mechanics* of communication and the *content* of communication. The mechanics may be nearly perfect but if the content if flawed or inappropriate, the student teacher may appear in a bad light. Likewise, if the content is good but the mechanics are incorrect, this will reflect on the student teacher's preparation.

Communication can be divided into reading, writing, speaking, and listening. During the student teaching assignment, all four of these areas of communication take on added meaning. The spoken work will be the student teacher's most-used communication tool, although listening skills should be especially developed and utilized during this assignment. The writing the student teacher does will be viewed by students, the cooperating teacher, the university supervisor, the school administrator, and parents; it must be correct and diplomatic. Reading skills used by the student teacher can save time and greatly assist with materials acquisition, lesson planning, and general professional development. For reading materials pertinent to the level and subject matter being taught, check current Websites, your university library, and the professional library of the district in which you are student teaching. State departments of education and professional organizations (e.g., the Association for Supervision and Curriculum Development, National Council of Teachers of Mathematics) are also a good source of curriculum information.

Although the student teacher has progressed through the university teacher education program with a heavy emphasis on reading ability, different aspects of that ability need attention during the student teaching assignment. Different kinds of materials are to be read.

Because the student teacher is attempting to adapt to a school setting, everything related to that school setting should be read carefully. The daily bulletin board usually located adjacent to the faculty mailboxes in the administrative office, notices from that office that are routinely delivered to the classroom, the bulletin board in the teachers' lounge, and notices from the district central office are all important for the student teacher to read carefully. Being a beginner in the school business means that a student teacher should stay current with what is being published in the daily newspaper relative to schools in the area and to all reports of school board meetings and activities. Maintaining an awareness of what is happening to students, faculty, and staff through reading the newspaper provides conversation topics with those individuals. In an era of national and state reports on the condition of education and schools, the student teacher should try to at least skim such information to keep up-to-date. Much of what has been presented in theory in the university classroom begins to take form and meaning in the everyday life of the school.

A second area of reading that suddenly looms as very important to the student teacher is the content of material to be taught. Reading this material can be a major task and should be approached in a manner that streamlines the process and helps the student teacher use time more efficiently. The student teacher should find all the material possible, glance through everything, skim through those areas that seem most appropriate, and then make a plan as to exactly how much of the material actually needs careful reading. Knowing the total picture before beginning the intense reading helps save time and frustration. Because teachers are deluged with mountains of reading material, learning how to identify the necessary reading intensity for any material is a time saver for the student teacher.

Writing is another major form of communication for the student teacher. Writing is the basis of the development of unit and lesson plans, writing directions for students, and writing notes home to parents. Writing memos (see Appendix K), writing in the student teacher's journal (see Appendix G) for the cooperating teacher and the university supervisor, writing materials for student groups, and writing notices to other teachers are all important tasks that must be carried out using proper grammar and writing style.

Additional writing tasks that usually occur during the student teaching assignment are writing letters of application writing letters of requests for materials and composing resumes. In such materials the allowable margin of error is zero. Materials with misspelled words or errors in grammar can cause applications to be rejected.

Just because written materials must adhere to high standards is no reason to fail to use writing as a method of communication. The student teacher should quickly become immersed in successful writing so that no matter what the challenge, it can be met!

The chalkboard or whiteboard are two of the major methods of written communication with students. The cooperating teacher has usually had years of experience to perfect such board writing; comparatively, the student teacher's writing on the board sometimes falls short. This can be remedied by practice, practice, practice, especially before or after school when no students are in the classroom. One of the things the university supervisor wants to see demonstrated is the ability of the student teacher to write legibly on the board.

Writing for overhead transparencies requires concentrated effort. It is important for the student teacher to observe how other teachers manage to stand beside the projector and avoid standing in front of the projected image on the screen. Handwriting numbers and symbols must be readable. It is helpful for the student teacher to keep in mind that such writing is meant to be read, not just to be written.

The importance of the spoken word in learning to teach cannot be overemphasized. The voice is an accurate indicator of the anxiety the student teacher may be experiencing, and although the students may not be aware of such clues, the cooperating teacher will notice them. Getting involved in the classroom activity early in the assignment and maintaining a comfortable relationship with the students and the cooperating teacher contribute to a more pleasant speaking voice for the student teacher. It is important for the student teacher to realize that the manner in which she or he speaks conveys more than the words themselves. Vocal articulation is a most important competency for any teacher. Although teachers use their voices in different modes, for example, drama coach, band director, and physical education teacher, clarity of meaning is basic to all. As the student teacher is observing other teachers during the early part of the assignment, being aware of how well various teachers articulate helps the student teacher to develop further personal articulation.

To perfect vocal qualities in the classroom such as tone, degree of harshness, and volume requires practice. It is important for the cooperating teacher to stress that the differences in sophistication of presentations have a great deal to do with the differences in experience. The student teacher is there to learn how to speak well in the classroom. It is acceptable not to know how to do everything perfectly at the beginning, but the student teacher must waste no time in beginning to strive for perfection. Classroom presentations take on a professional tone as the student teacher gains practice. That is why this kind of assignment used to be called practice teaching. The student teacher's spoken communication with other faculty and staff and with the administration should be courteous, friendly, and professional.

The cooperating teacher can model and show how other faculty members model techniques of effective listening. Through listening to what students are saying, the student teacher can better plan instruction, determine where problems lie, and actually manage better classroom control. The listening equivalent to having eyes in the back of the head is having ears of the heart: to hear what people are *trying* to say in addition to hearing *what* they are saying. It is especially important to listen to parents. Student teachers must be careful to avoid falling into the trap of believing that they have the answers parents need if the parents would just listen! It is the student teacher who should listen. Frequently, in listening to parents, what we hear is what we are listening for, not what the parents are really trying to say.

Much of the student teaching experience is like mapping uncharted territory for the student teacher, and every square mile of the new terrain should be identified. During the student teaching assignment, it is critical for the student teacher to listen to the cooperating teacher and to the university supervisor. Suggestions by either of these two individuals or by the school administrator should be considered imperative. As professionals, none of these people should have to say, "You must . . ." or "This has to be done this way . . ." The student teacher should understand the professional suggestion and implement it immediately.

Any discussion of communication would be incomplete without a mention of body language. The student teacher should be made aware of how body language such as eye contact and facial expressions indicates to students such things as control, sincerity to others when they are speaking, and levels of intensity to listeners. Posture, volume, and tone say as much as the words that are chosen to convey the oral message.

The degree to which the student teacher is assisted to learn and use appropriate communication techniques is to a large measure the degree to which the student teaching will be successful.

GUIDELINES FOR THE STUDENT TEACHER

- **Become acutely aware of needed improvement in all four areas of communication.** Push yourself to improve and try new schemes of enhancing your communication skills.
- **Particularly notice the body language of people who are listening to you.** Are they saying through this language that they are not really hearing you? Are they indicating that they are listening intently?
- **Notice your own body language as you listen and speak to people.** Is your body emphasizing what you are saying, or is it discounting what you are saying? Do you look people straight in the eye when talking to them, or do you avoid eye contact? When you are seated with another and having a conversation, does your posture indicate that you have already turned off your listening?
- **If you and your cooperating teacher seem to have a problem communicating, be objective about the situation and try to understand where he or she is coming from.** If you cannot bridge the communication gap, talk with your university supervisor for suggestions that may work with your cooperating teacher. This is a delicate area and you must be successful in communicating with your cooperating teacher to have a successful student teaching experience.
- **Listen with the ears of your heart as well as with the ears on your head.** Note what parents and students are trying to tell you when they perhaps do not know how to express themselves as well as you do.

- **Listen especially carefully to your cooperating teacher and university supervisor.** Do not force them to be blatant about telling you such things as to wear pressed and clean clothes, comb your hair, or omit the body rings. Notice innuendoes and suggestions. Make life more pleasant for them as well as for yourself by picking up on hints.
- **Talk *with* people, not *at* them.** Even when you are teaching, maintain such channels of communication that students feel that you are discussing with them, not lecturing them.
- **Be careful what you say, how you say it, and to whom you say it.** You suddenly have access to information about students and the school that other people generally do not have. This is privileged information and it must be professionally guarded. Do not allow anyone to pressure you into revealing such information.
- **If you are not comfortable with your occasional discussions with the school principal, you may want to role play such a discussion with a friend.** This may help your self-confidence, and the next time you talk with the principal you may discover that you have reached new levels of successful articulation.

GUIDELINES FOR THE COOPERATING TEACHER

- **Try to anticipate the communication avenues in which your student teacher will be involved.** Help him or her approach these with an appropriate mixture of caution and confidence.
- **Point out to your student teacher where the bulletin boards are and where notices are generally posted.** Emphasize which types of notices should be given special attention.
- **Try to assist your student teacher to reach a balance** between being uncomfortable and being too relaxed so that his or her voice is not strident and tense on the one hand or sleep-inducing on the other.
- **Encourage your student teacher to read the local daily newspapers.** This keeps him or her up-to-date with school and school district news and also gives the student teacher something to discuss with the other faculty and staff at school.
- **Point out to your student teacher that through listening to a variety of sources, she or he can stay more current in what is happening to the students.**
- **Stress with your student teacher that student peer-group jargon changes as soon as adults learn it.** Advise the student teacher to try to avoid any use of it altogether.
- **Make appointments with some of your most articulate colleagues for the student teacher to observe in their classrooms.** Prior to the observations, review the kinds of things the student teacher should be looking for.
- **Share sample kinds of school memos with the student teacher.** Point out the important elements of such documents.

- **Ask your student teacher to order free information or materials from organizations that offer them.** Before mailing the initial requests, check to see whether proper form has been followed and necessary information has been included.
- **Note any areas in reading, writing, speaking, or listening in which your student teacher needs additional development.** Tactfully point out such needs. Discuss these needs privately with the university supervisor, since the university has resources that can assist in building up these areas of deficiency.
- **If the student teacher has difficulty with vocal articulation, help him or her to gather his or her thoughts through writing and then expressing them.** Some people think best through writing. This helps the student teacher develop a pattern for future use.

CASE STUDIES

C A S E

24-1 Jorge was happily assigned to Mr. Alonzo's sixth-grade mathematics and science classroom for student teaching. He felt that major contributions to the education of children could be made during the middle school years, and this was the level he had chosen to teach. He was excited about his students and their work. His preparation and presentation skills were good, and Mr. Alonzo felt that his students were getting positive benefits from Jorge's being with him to do his student teaching.

The only problem was Jorge's handwriting. Although this would not seem to be a major problem, it was a critical one. Whenever Jorge wrote notes on student papers, to the school office, home to parents, or even on the chalkboard or overhead transparencies, his handwriting was illegible. As good as Jorge was in his other responsibilities, Mr. Alonzo was disappointed in his handwriting and discussed the problem several times with Jorge, who agreed that it was a problem and that he would work on it right away. After 4 weeks and several reminders from Mr. Alonzo, no improvement was noticeable.

1. Recognition of the problem is a major step toward getting it resolved. What are the next steps that Jorge should take?
2. What kinds of limits about note writing could Mr. Alonzo insist on?
3. In what ways could a laptop computer help Jorge with this problem?
4. What activities could the university supervisor prescribe that would help improve Jorge's handwriting?
5. What kinds of screening processes in the teacher education program at the university could have identified Jorge's problem earlier in his training?

C A S E

24-2 Hu was a young Asian student who was student teaching in mathematics in the local high school. Hu had come to the United States to attend college and become a teacher. He planned to return to his home country and teach mathematics there. In the student teaching assignment, Hu related well to the high school students, and his knowledge of mathematics was outstanding. Hu's use of English in the delivery of mathematics instruction was acceptable, but outside the realm of mathematics, his English language speaking skills were relatively poor. Hu failed to understand what students were discussing in informal discussions and was frequently unable to respond to other teachers when in conversation with them. At faculty meetings, the cooperating teacher felt that Hu was not understanding the information. Her concern was that although Hu was quite knowledgeable about mathematics, he was missing important training in how schools and classrooms are run and how students get along with teachers.

1. How important is it that Hu understand more than the language associated with mathematics?
2. How effective would it be for the cooperating teacher to assign a student each period to serve as special interpreter? What problems would this pose?
3. Because Hu is going to return to his home country to teach, why should the cooperating teacher be concerned about his English?
4. What benefit would extended observations of other teachers have in this situation? Teachers of which subjects would be of most value?
5. What level of fairness is involved in expecting Hu to speak two languages?
6. What opportunities may there be to find a middle school student who also speaks Hu's first language?

C A S E

24-3   Greta was enthusiastic about her work with the third graders in Mrs. Escalente's class. She prepared extensively and her instructional skills were good and continuing to improve. She related well to the students, was always cheerful, and was happy with her assignment.

The only problem that Mrs. Escalente could not resolve with Greta was Greta's refusal to read the daily notices from the office and check the bulletin board next to the teachers' mailboxes. This had caused several mix-ups with such things as changed schedules for art and physical education classes, a new library visitation policy, and an announced fire drill. Mrs. Escalente felt that these notices were important and that Greta was not acting responsibly in ignoring them.

1. Learning to function as a member of the school faculty is an important component of student teaching. How could Mrs. Escalente impress on Greta the importance of staying up-to-date with what is happening at school?
2. In what cases could Greta's failure to read these notices cause her students to be in danger? How could Greta be guilty of negligence?
3. Why do you think there is a lack of balance between Greta's sense of responsibility for instructional delivery and her sense of responsibility for keeping closely attuned to school functioning?

4. What kind of impression is Greta making on a principal who she hopes will give her a job when she has completed her student teaching?

5. In what stage of her training in instructional methodology and teaching responsibilities should this topic have been covered?

C A S E

24-4   Erica was an enthusiastic, well-prepared student teacher in the computer lab. Her high energy level was infectious among the students and the other faculty. She knew her subject well and was more than eager to get to know everyone at the school. Her interest in conversations with other faculty and staff was high; she seemed to enjoy such conversations a great deal.

Erica had a habit that began to turn people off, however, and fewer and fewer people seemed interested in talking with her. During conversations, Erica had a tendency to interrupt others while they were speaking. This characteristic also exhibited itself during class. Erica did not wait for students to finish talking before she jumped in with something she wanted to say. Frequently, what she said was not directly related to what the other person was saying. It became apparent that Erica was not a good listener.

1. What listening skills are imperative for a teacher?
2. What do you think Erica saw as the reason that fewer and fewer people wanted to talk with her?
3. Why do some people feel that what they have to say is more important than what someone else is saying?
4. How could the use of an audiotape or videotape recorder assist in demonstrating the problem to Erica?
5. How can the cooperating teacher squelch the kinds of nonlistening interruptions that Erica is making without inhibiting her enthusiasm for her teaching?

C A S E

24-5   Pia was a quiet, studious student teacher in Mr. Benson's geography class. She had a very high GPA and was intent on helping the students learn a great deal of geography, a subject in which she felt everyone should have high levels of interest.

Her planning was well done, her presentations were articulate, and her methods of evaluation were appropriate. However, students were becoming more and more restless. Mr. Benson had the feeling that something was not clicking but he could not identify the precise problem.

At his request, Pia agreed to have a lesson videotaped. During his study of the videotape, Mr. Benson realized that Pia seldom looked at the students. She was always looking at the board, at her notes, out the window, at the floor, or at the ceiling but seldom at the students. In other words, she made little eye contact with the students; she could just as easily have been teaching in an empty room. Her subject content was excellent but she was not relating to the students well at all.

1. How do you feel about people who look away when they are talking to you? How does that make you feel about yourself?
2. What points should Mr. Benson stress with Pia when studying the videotape with her?
3. With what psychological characteristics could the university supervisor help Pia for her to feel more comfortable with the students?
4. How could extracurricular activities help Pia to relate to students better?
5. What cultural background information would be most useful to the cooperating teacher in helping to resolve this situation?

RECOMMENDED READING

Carlson, J., & Thorpe, C. (1984). Communication: Learning to give and take. In *The growing teacher: How to become the teacher you've always wanted to be* (pp. 86–104). Englewood Cliffs, NJ: Prentice-Hall. *Communication blocks, effective listening, kinds of responses, you-and-I messages, and open versus closed questions are discussed effectively. Exercises are included for reflective listening, I-messages, and open and closed responses.*

Conoley, J. C. (1989). Professional communication and collaboration among educators. In M. C. Reynolds (Ed.), *Knowledge base for the beginning teacher* (pp. 245–254). New York: Pergamon Press. *This chapter discusses the need for effective communication on the part of the beginning teacher in such areas as collaboration, consultation, and problem solving. In addition to having compiled current research, the author has included specific suggestions for improving communication within the educational setting.*

Cooper, P. J., & Simonds, C. (1999). *Communication for the classroom teacher* (6th ed.). Boston: Allyn & Bacon. *For both preservice and inservice teachers, this text covers a wide range of communication strategies for classroom use including interpersonal and small-group communication, listening skills, verbal and nonverbal communication, communication in cultural diversity, storytelling, and personal influence.*

Geddes, D. S. (1995). *Keys to communication: A handbook for school success.* Thousand Oaks, CA: Corwin Press. *This handbook provides methods for effectively communicating with clarity and without offense.*

Gutek, G. L. (1992). The school system and staff. In *Education and schooling in America* (3rd ed.) (pp. 340–362). Boston: Allyn & Bacon. *This chapter gives information that is usually understood after the teacher has been employed in a school setting. It is to the student teacher's advantage to discuss how the local school system varies from that described by Gutek. The school system hierarchy, including line and staff relationships and the roles of teachers, is explained.*

Hevener, F., Jr. (1981). Relating to the students and parents. In *Successful student teaching: A handbook for elementary and secondary student teachers* (pp. 62–69). Palo Alto, CA: R.&E. Research Associates. *Building positive relationships with both students and parents is emphasized in this chapter. Hevener suggests a number of behaviors to assist the student teacher in developing and maintaining such relationships.*

Knowles, J. G., Cole, A. L., & Presswood, C. S. (1994). Autobiographical writing: Gathering personal, internal information. In *Through preservice teachers' eyes: Exploring field experiences through narrative and inquiry* (pp. 21–44). New York: Macmillan. *The authors offer the student teacher the experience of writing personal history accounts and journals, utilizing personal metaphors, and preparing professional development summaries. Thus, an internal dialogue may be developed through which the student teacher may better understand self.*

Machado, J. M., & Meyer, H. C. (1984). Developing interpersonal communication skills. In *Early childhood practicum guide: A sourcebook for beginning teachers of young children* (pp. 107–116). Albany, NY: Delmar Publishers. *The authors have included material on how to understand what others are trying to communicate. They emphasize the value of caring, listening, and being authentic in communication.*

Morse, P. S., & Ivey, A. (1996). *Face to face: Communication and conflict resolution in the schools.* Thousand Oaks, CA: Corwin Press. *The student teacher is encouraged to maintain control and a caring attitude using these suggested techniques in difficult school confrontations.*

Podesta, C., & Sanderson, V. (1999). *Life would be easy if it weren't for other people.* Thousand Oaks, CA: Corwin Press. *The authors offer communication strategies for dealing with assertive, aggressive, passive, and passive-aggressive personalities. Knowledge of these communication skills will make life easier for student teachers throughout their professional careers.*

25

Availability of Materials

Today's economic problems also exist within the classroom. Budgetary priorities and other economic factors result in classrooms that need additional materials and supplies. Each teacher is faced with the necessity of developing curricular materials to supplement those provided by the school. Materials developed by the student teacher and the cooperating teacher are the primary source of teaching materials.

Student teachers can be of immeasurable help in locating necessary supplementary materials. A task of student teachers is to find or develop available materials. These materials should be examined thoroughly. Teachers' manuals accompany many texts and should be supplied to the student teacher for study and use.

One of the first places student teachers can look for supplementary materials is the school library or media center. They should check textbooks, teaching kits, games, trade books, books on learning centers, films, filmstrips, picture files, tape recordings, slides, maps, globes, charts, models, and lists of community resources. Catalogs listing these materials may be available in the school media center or the university curriculum library. Because teachers often have little time to devote to investigating new materials, student teachers can be helpful in finding new resources for both the teachers and themselves.

A major materials source is the Internet. Web-based materials are available through on-line computers and can be utilized by the student teacher or by the classroom students on assignment. *The CyberEducator: The Internet and World Wide Web for K–12 Education* (Bissell, Manring, & Rowland, 1999) covers many areas of educational sources that will be useful to the student teacher. It includes resources on educational psychology, methods and subject area resources, student diversity and exceptionalities, measurement and evaluation, classroom and school websites, and research. This information takes the user directly to the site for printing the materials needed.

An additional source of technological materials for curriculum use is a commercial initiative entitled "Cable in the Classroom." This is a service free to schools and provides more than 500 hours of commercial-free educational materials each month. Use of "Cable in the Classroom" is usually a school district decision made in cooperation with the local cable TV company. If your school does not participate, you may want to talk with your cooperating teacher about discussing this with the school administration.

Procedures for letting teachers and students use the library or media center vary from school to school. Some media centers are quite flexible and allow students to come in for research and study during those precious "teachable moments." Prior arrangements should be made with the librarian so that the students' time can be used wisely. The librarian can be one of the main resources for your classroom; public and university libraries may also provide needed resources.

Some school districts have a book room or central depository for books. Some books are outdated but can be quite beneficial for additional reading, for making games, and for use in learning centers. Teachers sometimes trade books with other teachers; this helps in locating books at different reading levels. Student teachers should become familiar with all of these ways to find materials.

Student teachers are encouraged to take advantage of the opportunity to visit any central media center that is available for the entire school district. Professional libraries in various schools should be accessible to student teachers. Student teachers should consult subject area specialists and supervisors in the district office.

Student teachers should become familiar with the operation of the major types of audiovisual equipment in the building. They should have basic knowledge about threading and operating such equipment but may need some special instructions. There are many different types of machines, each with its own unique characteristics, such as filmstrip projectors, overhead and opaque projectors, audiotape and videotape recorders and playback devices, scanners, digital cameras, and a variety of computer software.

It is important for student teachers to know the procedures to follow for scheduling the audiovisual equipment. Where is the equipment stored? Can the equipment be checked out to the classroom, or is there a special place for viewing? How much advance notice is necessary to make such arrangements? Are spare bulbs available for the projectors? Who can assist with repairs in case of equipment breakdown? Who is financially responsible for the equipment when it is checked out to the student teacher?

Additional equipment to be utilized are the computers in the classroom that can be used for word processing, drill and practice, research, gathering information from the Internet for projects and papers, and creative writing. Other equipment, such as a graphing calculator in the mathematics classroom, may be utilized. Handheld computer devices for immediately filing comments on students are useful and save time. Student teachers are urged to learn to use all equipment available; the payoff will come when there is no time to learn before it has to be used.

Student teachers should consider the possibility of enriching the classroom with resource people from the community. Before such people are invited to the classroom, however, they should be cleared by the cooperating teacher. If carefully selected, individuals can be found who have a specialized knowledge that will fit with the current instruction. It is helpful if the school or district has a list of people who have been used successfully. Student teachers will probably be aware of resource people from the college community. Bringing in appropriate examples from the community can do much in promoting positive public relations. The resource people have proved to be an added asset to the "real-life" interests of students. Since some resource people's presentations may not be as relevant for classroom use as others, it is wise to prepare and plan with them before their arrival at school.

Attractively arranged bulletin boards can do a great deal in both elementary and secondary classrooms to improve the atmosphere of the classroom. Displays of student work and teacher-made bulletin boards all have their place. Student teachers are often assigned to create bulletin boards on certain timely topics.

Field trips can be valuable learning resources. Teachers and student teachers considering field trips must get approval and support from the principal. If the student teacher is encouraged to participate in field trips, certain points should be understood:

1. A successful field trip requires a great deal of planning, a major element of which is the inclusion of a sufficient number of reliable, experienced chaperons.
2. The school policies concerning field trips should be studied. Check with the principal and cooperating teacher concerning legal responsibilities involved, the need for medical authorization slips, and available insurance.
3. Parental consent for your students for such a trip is imperative.
4. Students should know the purpose of a field trip and be involved in the planning.
5. Thorough arrangements for transportation should be made.
6. Trips should be well supervised with careful planning for the movement of students to and from school.
7. Beneficial evaluation and follow-up techniques should be included in the planning.

Great variation exists from school to school and classroom to classroom in the amount and types of resource materials and equipment available. Student teachers are lucky if they are assigned a school with a wealth of such resources. Criteria for judging materials and resources for use in the classroom should be jointly developed by cooperating teachers and student teachers.

GUIDELINES FOR THE STUDENT TEACHER

- **Discover the amount of emphasis placed on the use of textbooks in the classroom to which you are assigned.** Are only grade level textbooks allowed? Does your cooperating teacher favor a multimedia approach?
- **Use your influence with the cooperating teacher to include as much computer software, Website, and Internet work as possible.**
- **Examine the materials available in your classroom.** Teachers' manuals should be made available to you; these manuals are to be used as guides and not as the only sources of materials and ideas. After you survey the range of materials, you will have a general idea of the curriculum being stressed.
- **Bring in materials from outside the school.** You have attended methods classes and should be able to bring in worthwhile suppl   ntary materials.

- **Take time to visit the school library and district media center prior to your teaching assignments.** Use your time wisely; you have no excuse for not having your resources well in mind.
- **Follow the advice of your cooperating teacher concerning the use of materials.** Be a good listener and note the advice given to you.
- **Learn how to operate the audiovisual equipment.** Ask for instructions if you do not know how to operate a piece of equipment. It is not a weakness to request aid; a person who asks shows a desire to learn.
- **Preview any materials you decide to use.** Titles alone can be misleading. You must decide whether material is appropriate and determine how it is to be used.
- **If you are assigned to prepare a bulletin board, get the job done as well as possible and on time.** Take initiative and anticipate changing bulletin boards. Always get a preliminary sketch of your new bulletin board approved by your cooperating teacher before putting one together.
- **Survey the school for possible locations for group activities, committee work, and games.** Adequate space for such activities is often at a premium. Initially discuss the merits of the activities with your cooperating teacher.

GUIDELINES FOR THE COOPERATING TEACHER

- **Explain the overall organization of materials to your student teacher.** You are able to keep many teaching techniques in your mind because of past experiences, but your student teacher does not have that advantage.
- **Encourage the multimedia approach.** Student teachers are usually very cautious about bringing additional resources into the classroom unless they are encouraged to do so.
- **Give your student teacher ample time to visit the library and central media center.** Take the student teacher down yourself and introduce him or her to the media center staff. The team approach to the selection of materials is recommended.
- **Care of equipment should be discussed; this is usually a new set of tasks for the student teacher.** Showing courtesy by returning materials on time and in good condition should be stressed.
- **Discuss with your student teacher the importance of previewing audiovisual materials before using them in class.**
- **Encourage your student teacher to bring in resource people.** Make sure that anyone you allow the student teacher to bring into the classroom knows exactly what is expected.
- **Assign your student teacher the responsibility for certain bulletin boards early in the student teaching assignment.** This will show that you have

confidence in the teacher and respect her or his ideas. It might be necessary to make a few suggestions the first time around.

CASE STUDIES

C   A   S   E

25-1   Phil, a student teacher in a sixth-grade classroom, was quite excited about taking a field trip to the Naval Air Station Museum, which was 50 miles away. His cooperating teacher had explained the importance of overplanning, and Phil had taken his advice. All of the suggested precautions had been followed. One week before the field trip, in his enthusiasm, Phil decided to invite the other two sixth-grade classes to go along. The principal and cooperating teacher approved because Phil had been so well organized up to this point. They left all the details up to Phil.

When the 90 sixth graders boarded the buses to leave for the NAS Museum, it should have been evident that planning had not been completed. There were very few adults for supervision, and some of the students lacked permission slips. When the classes arrived at the museum, they learned that they had not been expected at that particular time and tours for them had not been planned. Arrangements had not even been made for all 90 students to eat lunch. To make matters worse, one of the frisky sixth graders became lost on the Navy base for a few hours. The students arrived late back at school at 5 P.M. to find a group of angry parents.

1. Who should be held responsible for these mishaps?
   a. principal?
   b. university supervisor?
   c. Phil?
   d. cooperating teacher?
2. What effect could this field trip have on the home-school relations in this community?
3. What could be done immediately to ease the situation with the parents?
4. How could new policies on implementing field trips avoid this predicament in the future? What kind of policy would you recommend?
5. How could the cooperating teacher salvage Phil's enthusiasm for continuing in his student teaching?

C   A   S   E

25-2   Serina was student teaching in an eighth-grade science class. She planned to show a videotape on sea animals when her university supervisor arrived for his first observation. The day finally came, and Serina was quite nervous. The university supervisor arrived on time and took a seat at the back of the room.

It was evident that Serina had not made the necessary preparations. Not only was the VCR not set up, but also, Serina had to go the library to get the videotape. The class became very restless. After about 15 minutes into the period, Serina turned on the monitor and began to show the videotape. She gave no introduction to the film and allowed for no discussion afterward. Serina asked the students to complete a worksheet about the film, thereby ending the lesson.

The university supervisor was upset by Serina's lack of preparation and the fact that the cooperating teacher was not in the room during the presentation.

1. Why would a student teacher be so negligent about having materials and equipment available?
2. What do you think the university supervisor had to say during the conference with Serina and her cooperating teacher?
3. Should the cooperating teacher be in the classroom during the university supervisor's first observation? Why or why not?
4. How could careful planning by Serina have made this into an interesting and exciting lesson?
5. What kinds of personal problems may have been affecting Serina to have caused such a poor performance?

C A S E

25-3   Franzi's cooperating teacher asked her to prepare a bulletin board in her fourth-grade classroom. She suggested that Franzi come up with an idea that would motivate the students to read science fiction. She asked that the bulletin board be prepared in time for the open house that was to be held in 2 weeks.

A week before the open house, Franzi had made no progress on the bulletin board. Her cooperating teacher asked her about the matter, and Franzi said she had some good ideas. The university supervisor had been invited to the open house and planned to attend. The cooperating teacher would be quite embarrassed if the bulletin board was not prepared.

The day of the open house arrived, and still no bulletin board. Franzi's cooperating teacher finally prepared a display herself. Franzi later explained that she was very much opposed to teacher-made bulletin boards, preferring displays of students' work.

1. What action should the cooperating teacher take concerning this matter?
2. How should the university supervisor react to Franzi's difficulties?
3. Why should Franzi have mentioned earlier her objections to teacher-made bulletin boards?
4. How would Franzi's failure to produce the bulletin board affect the rapport she and her cooperating teacher may have previously established?
5. Could Franzi's failure to prepare a bulletin board be just cause to withdraw her from student teaching? Explain your answer.
6. What follow-through would be effective the next time the cooperating teacher gave Franzi a responsibility?

C A S E

25-4   Kathryn, a student teacher in a third-grade class, had been a straight-A student in college and was an avid reader. Her cooperating teacher asked her to take a group of students to the school library to do research on their projects. Kathryn and her group left for the library and were asked to return in 30 minutes.

After Kathryn helped the students initiate their work, she became "lost in the stacks." She found a historical novel in which she became completely absorbed. Her students became noisy and unruly, but Kathryn was so engrossed in the novel that she completely ignored them. After an hour of tolerating the misbehaving students, the librarian finally went searching for the cooperating teacher to retrieve the students.

Finally, Kathryn came to her senses and returned alone to her classroom. Her cooperating teacher was very disturbed over the matter.

1. Do you feel that Kathryn will ever make it as an elementary teacher?
2. Should she be pulled out of her student teaching assignment because of this failure?
3. How should the cooperating teacher handle the situation?
4. How would the university supervisor react to Kathryn's problem?
5. What steps should the cooperating teacher take to ensure that this will not develop into a pattern of behavior in Kathryn's professional life?

C A S E

25-5   Andrew was in his 4th week of student teaching in a ninth-grade English assignment. He had an intense interest in mythology and obtained permission from his cooperating teacher to do a unit in this area that had not previously been covered. After surveying the school library, he found very few resources on the topic.

1. Where could Andrew go to find such resources?
2. How could he adapt his own collection for classroom use? Would the students demolish it or wear it out?
3. What precautions will Andrew have to take in teaching this unit? What community traditions and opinions might cause people to object?
4. What were the possibilities of bringing in resource people for this unit on mythology?
5. What care must Andrew use in defining whose mythology he was teaching? How would this affect the multicultural school population?

C A S E

25-6   Mark surprised his cooperating teacher by bringing in a guest speaker in his fourth-period American history class. To make matters worse, the guest talked in a monotone and was very ill at ease in front of the class. The students were considerate, although very bored and restless. The cooperating teacher told Mark that he wanted a conference scheduled at the end of the day.

1. What did Mark expect from his cooperating teacher?
2. Do you think that Mark's cooperating teacher will be critical of his bringing in the guest speaker? Why or why not?
3. How could this situation have been avoided?
4. Should the use of resource people be a matter that a student teacher should decide on alone?
5. How should Mark express his apology to the class for bringing in an unimpressive speaker.

REFERENCE

Bissell, J., Manring, A., & Rowland, V. (1999). *The CyberEducator: The Internet and World Wide Web for K–12 education.* Boston: McGraw-Hill.

RECOMMENDED READING

Buch, J. (1999–2000). *Classroom CONNECT: 1999–2000 Internet education catalog.* 431 Madrid Avenue, Torrance, CA 90501–1430. *This annual catalog offers a variety of up-to-date Internet and CD-ROM learning activities and resources for interactive curricula.*

Cable in the Classroom. 1800 North Beauregard Street, Suite 110, Alexandria, VA 22311 (1-800-743-5355). *This source offers information about the use of Channel One in the classroom.*

Cawthorne, B. (1982). Instant success: *For classroom teachers, new and substitute teachers in grades K through 8.* Scottsdale, AZ: Greenfield Publications. *Materials in this book have been developed and teacher tested for success. Although suggested for new and substitute teachers, the activities are useful for the student teacher to keep on hand. Activities are coded for grade level and permission is given for individual teachers to reproduce the worksheet.*

Ellington, H., Fowlie, J., & Gordon, M. (1998). *Using games and simulations in the classroom: A practical guide for teachers.* Sterling, VA: Stylus Publishing. *This text illustrates the use of games and simulations in nursery school through secondary classrooms and assists the teacher in designing the right activity for the appropriate level.*

Grabe, M., & Grabe, C. (1998). *Integrating technology for meaningful learning* (2nd ed.). Boston: Houghton Mifflin. *This text gives practical advice on how to integrate technology into your classroom teaching and provides how-to on computer technology: word processor, databases, spreadsheets, the Internet, multimedia applications, and sound.*

Grabe, M., & Grabe, C. (1998). *Learning with Internet tools: A primer.* Boston: Houghton Mifflin.

This brief text explains to the novice how Internet tools can be utilized in classroom learning, including learning from Internet resources and learning using World Wide Web resources.

Hensen, K. T. (1988). Using media. In *Methods and strategies for teaching in secondary and middle schools* (pp. 223–240). New York: Longman. *This chapter can be a self-taught lesson for the student teacher because it furnishes both a pretest and a posttest. A discussion of the variety of media available in most schools is presented. This reminds the student teacher of possibilities for using such media.*

Kemp, J. E., & Dayton, D. K. (1985). *Planning and producing instructional media* (5th ed.). New York: Harper & Row. *This text gives explicit, step-by-step directions for producing media for teaching from photography to computer-assisted instruction. Background reviews of learning theory and managing the media production activities are included.*

Morlan, J. E., & Espinosa, L. J. (1989). *Preparation of inexpensive teaching materials* (3rd ed.). Belmont, CA: Davis S. Lake Publishers. *This book offers a brief, useful review of the design of instruction and an extensive presentation of methods of preparing materials for teaching. Because of its explicit instructions and day-to-day usefulness, this book is one the student teacher could profitably add to his or her professional library.*

Poole, B. J. (1997). *Education for an information age: Teaching in the computerized classroom* (2nd ed.). Boston: McGraw-Hill. *Poole gives the teacher who is beginning to utilize computers an excellent overview of the research, hardware, software systems, on-line education, computer-assisted instruction, and creative applications for the classroom.*

Schurr, S. L. (1989). *Dynamite in the classroom: A how-to book for teachers.* Columbus, OH: National Middle School Association. *This text was developed to show how concepts could be demonstrated through instructional materials. Given a solid background in instructional theory, this author includes the uses of many aids and materials in the classroom, including learning centers, gaming and simulation, investigation task cards, shoebox learning, and study kits.*

Tapscott, D. (February 1999). Educating the net generation. *Educational Leadership*, *56*(5), 7–11. Materials for learning and teaching are changing with the advent of the digital generation. Tapscott's shifts of interactive learning (linear to hypermedia, instruction to construction and discovery, absorbing to navigating the Web, customized learning, learner centered learning, learning as fun, and teacher as facilitator, and lifelong learning) offer practically limitless sources of materials on the Internet.

26

Implementation of the Classroom Process

Implementation! This is where it is for teachers! As student teachers approach the first attempts at putting it all together, they experience a number of emotions that characterize the implementation of the actual classroom teaching process.

First, the student teacher probably experiences an interest in the class of the cooperating teacher. The student teacher appropriately wonders at the magnitude of the class and the aggregate of individual lives and the vast amount of subject material to be covered. By doing so, the student teacher becomes aware of the need for objectivity and organization.

Second, the student teacher is motivated by the needs of the students in the cooperating teacher's class and is stimulated to develop plans and write projects that fit those needs. Previous classes at the university now take on new meaning in the framework of the real needs of the assigned classroom.

Third, intensive planning takes place as the student teacher adds the finishing touches to plans and makes adjustments to provide for the varying needs of the individual students. This intensity of purpose can be labeled as devotion, which is one of the facets of teaching referred to by some as the "art" of teaching.

Fourth, after the interest, the motivation, and the intensive planning, the student teacher begins teaching. The emotion often accompanying this portion of training is panic. Some student teachers conceal it rather well, but some are obviously anxious and ill at ease. Recognizing the likelihood of such anxiety is half the battle in overcoming it. Even the best prepared, most self-confident student teacher has many questions before taking over the entire class for that first exciting lesson. Most student teachers mentally catalog a list of possible alternatives for use in case of a perceived failure of the lesson. During those few minutes just before the first class, some student teachers become very tense; this is normal. Planning for this specific occurrence helps in alleviating it.

To avoid the development of anxiety, the student teacher should make plans to keep busy with the students until the time to begin the lesson. This helps the transition from the previous activity with the cooperating teacher, and the motivation of the students at the beginning of class is more easily established. By helping the students with new activities, the student teacher forgets self and is concerned more with the students' needs. Once the student teacher gets into the lesson, an awareness develops and teaching that lesson to that class can be totally engrossing.

During the initial full-class lesson, the student teacher finds that the lesson really does fit together after all and that the students really are just regular people. During those few seconds while waiting for students to think and respond, the student teacher silently thanks the cooperating teacher for insisting on thorough planning and giving specific suggestions for implementation of the lesson. As the lesson continues, the student teacher begins to breathe normally again and senses a satisfaction at the opportunities encountered during the lesson.

As the student teacher begins to assemble classroom plans and activities and as successes, even small ones, are won with particularly difficult individuals, the students are delighted with the challenge offered them by the student teacher. This delight may or may not be overtly shared with the student teacher and the cooperating teacher but both should be aware that good things are happening. The effect the student teacher's plans have on the social and emotional learning of the individual students (Elias et al., 1997) is critical and should receive the attention and reflection of the student teacher.

After the first class on the 1st day, the student-teacher's anxiety usually dissipates and the pleasures of teaching begin. The importance of effective planning is now pre-eminent; from this moment until the end of student teaching, classroom instruction is the major activity of student teaching. The student teacher becomes more aware of pacing the lesson, questioning skills based on Bloom's taxonomy (Bloom et al., 1956), and pulling all the parts of the lesson together prior to the beginning of the lesson. The issue of what to do when you do not know what to do becomes less of an issue as contingency plans are more carefully developed and aligned to the thematic or lesson topic.

Flexibility in adapting the previously planned activities and materials is crucial. Accepting changes at the last minute is frequently necessary. Sometimes these changes come in the form of suggestions from students on better ways of getting to the same objective. Individuals with an inclination toward perfectionism sometimes enter the teaching profession; their characteristics have a tendency to make students needlessly uncomfortable. The classroom is not a place to expect perfection, and the student teacher should be satisfied with a realistic level of performance by the students in his or her classroom.

It is important for the student teacher to include as many techniques as possible to enhance student learning. In addition to using direct instruction, the student teacher should incorporate problem-solving strategies, cooperative grouping, the use of taxonomies, role play, simulations, and class discussion.

The cooperating teacher is there for support of the student teacher, and that support should be obvious during the classroom lesson. By planning ahead, both teachers can develop a system of signals to indicate that the student teacher would like some assistance from the cooperating teacher. Intervention under such circumstances is not only acceptable but also much appreciated. In addition, it causes the flow of classroom activity to proceed uninterrupted, a major benefit to the students both academically and emotionally. Such an arrangement also increases the probability of maintaining positive classroom control.

Arrangements for various types of intervention by the cooperating teacher should be made before the very first lesson. There are times that the cooperating teacher should intervene for the protection of the students, for clarity in case of incorrect information, and for the self-confidence of the student teacher. Such intervention should be established as a part of the teaching arrangement so that the students in the classroom do not identify it as a negative factor toward the student teacher.

Student teachers should be patient. They have worked nearly 4 (and in some states 5) years to get to this point. They have stored much knowledge, made lesson plans, practiced vocal delivery, adjusted themselves psychologically, and made all the preparations necessary for teaching. They are ready to implement the plans put together by them and their cooperating teachers.

GUIDELINES FOR THE STUDENT TEACHER

- **Self-confidence is a major key to success for the beginning student teacher.** Some student teachers may laugh at the idea of self-confidence, due to a lack of it. However, you can profit from convincing your students that you have self-confidence, and once you have convinced them, you will find you have nearly convinced yourself. If you have good plans and feel well-prepared, self-confidence comes more readily.
- **Be as prepared as possible.** Be sure your plans are workable and realistic in terms of time.
- **Retain poise, calmness, and dignity.**
- **Be realistic about the situation.** You are placed in the classroom to learn how to teach.
- **You may make a few mistakes.** Even the most seasoned pro does that, so do not allow the possibility of mistakes to bother you. Instead, use your time efficiently by developing methods of handling your errors. Think positively and stand tall.
- **Be yourself.** Students can see right through a person. Be consistently genuine with them.

GUIDELINES FOR THE COOPERATING TEACHER

- **Your student teacher is probably anxious about that first full-class lesson.** You cannot eliminate that anxiety, but you could help alleviate it somewhat by being kind.

- **Let the student teacher know about particular problems with difficult students.** You may want to remove certain students from this first class by involving them in an activity with you during the first lesson.
- **Insist on thorough planning.** It pays huge dividends for you to be a difficult taskmaster.
- **Mentally prepare your student teacher for lesson implementation by verbally walking through it together.** The student teacher may consider this a waste of time, but insist on it.
- **Offer any materials, props, resources, and suggestions that you feel enhance the student teacher's lesson implementation.** Later, the student teacher may seek them as their importance in the lesson delivery is realized.
- **Finally, when you have done all you can, avoid the impression of watching the student teacher teaching until you feel a comfortable security that the position as teacher has been achieved.** Plan an appropriate seating area at the back of the classroom and blend into the background. You must release the student teacher with your class to allow growth.

CASE STUDIES

C A S E

26-1   Mrs. Atkins felt that her student teacher was not sufficiently concerned about planning, especially her first series of lessons. She hesitated to use fear as a motivator but her suggestions were unheeded. Finally, Mrs. Atkins phoned the university supervisor and discussed the situation. The next day, the university supervisor visited the classroom and discussed the problem with the student teacher who agreed to plan effectively. No sooner had the university supervisor left than the student teacher reproached Mrs. Atkins for calling the university supervisor.

1. What should the cooperating teacher have done initially?
2. What options are open to Mrs. Atkins now?
3. How should she continue to seek the advice of the university supervisor?
4. How should she proceed on her own?
5. What would happen if the cooperating teacher were to allow the student teacher to fall on her face before the class as a result of poor planning? To what extent would this be allowable?

C A S E

26-2   Zac was student teaching in Mrs. Rashad's high school English classes. As Zac began his first full-class teaching, he resisted using notes. Although he had a well-developed lesson plan, the plan was apparently not practical. Zac insisted that he really did not need notes for reference as he taught the class. He convinced Mrs. Rashad that he had prepared sufficiently and that he would remember everything.

Well, Zac did not remember everything. When he stood before the first class of the day, after the bell had rung and he had closed the door, as he turned to the class, his mind went blank!

1. Mrs. Rashad was aware of the situation. Should she do anything? If so, what?
2. Do you think Zac learned his lesson about using notes?
3. How would the class react to him next time?
4. What long-range measures should Mrs. Rashad take?
5. What implications does this situation hold for all student teachers?

C   A   S   E

26-3   Sixth-grade time was valuable, and Mr. Wilson hoped that his student teacher would be well organized and would use student time wisely. Mr. Wilson had talked with other teachers with whom his student teacher had served field experiences. The student teacher had a propensity for ad-libbing and wasting time. Mr. Wilson tried to tactfully express his concern about this to the student teacher but it apparently was not effective. The student teacher wrote well-developed plans and professed a high degree of organization, yet when he began teaching the full-class lessons, he was easily distracted from the subject and much student time was wasted.

1. What caused the gap between the planning by the student teacher and the teacher's delivery of the lesson material?
2. How could a videotape of a class assist in analyzing this situation?
3. Should the cooperating teacher interrupt the lesson at the point of diminishing returns?
4. Because tact had not worked earlier, what should Mr. Wilson try next?
5. As observation by the university supervisor during the very early stages of taking over the class could easily make the student teacher more nervous, what benefit would there be from such an observation?

C   A   S   E

26-4   Coach Elroy felt that lesson plans were a waste of time and shared this philosophy with Jeff, his student teacher. However, the department chairperson communicated to Jeff that he expected to see his lesson plans 1 week before his first full-class teaching.

1. Without Coach's cooperation, how could Jeff write effective lesson plans?
2. What responsibility did Jeff have to the department chairperson?
3. Should Jeff discuss the coach's feeling about lesson plans with someone? With whom?
4. What other people in the school could Jeff use for assistance in unit and lesson planning?

5. In a case such as this, Jeff has the opportunity to learn more than most student teachers through his involvement with the department chair & possibly teachers other than his cooperating teacher. What are some of the things he will be learning about personalities of teachers?

C A S E

26-5   Lily loved biology and thought she would enjoy student teaching—until it was time for her to plan her first full-class presentation. She seemed overwhelmed and initially planned too little material. After conferences with the cooperating teacher, her replanning was grossly overdone. Still filled with anxiety, Lily asked the cooperating teacher to leave the classroom for the first presentation. She assured the teacher that she would feel more confident and would be able to teach better. The cooperating teacher had some doubts about leaving her class with a beginner for the entire period.

1. As the student teacher, why would you make such a request?
2. As the cooperating teacher, how would you react to such a request?
3. What legal constraints operated for the cooperating teacher?
4. Would the student teacher actually make a better presentation to the class without the cooperating teacher present? Why or why not?
5. What approaches could the cooperating teacher take in this situation other than leaving the classroom during the initial lesson?

C A S E

26-6   Dennis had already announced to the math classes in which he was assigned to student teach that he was a retired military officer and that teaching was for him just something to do for a few years before he completely retired. He had already explained to several of the students that they could call him Captain. Students had expressed to the cooperating teacher that Dennis really did seem impressed with himself but that they were unimpressed.

The cooperating teacher was concerned that the students would become antagonized by Dennis and make his student teaching difficult for him and disrupt the positive classroom climate. The actual presentation of the lessons could be the most likely time for bad feelings to develop into inappropriate actions. During announcements and short presentations, Dennis had been overly authoritarian and the students had openly resented his attitude.

1. What action should the cooperating teacher take in helping Dennis assess the situation?
2. How should the students be prepared to deal with the situation?
3. In what ways could the university supervisor assist this cooperating teacher?
4. What options does Dennis have at this point? What is the best way to help him understand his options?
5. What kind of screening could have occurred in the teacher preparation program at the university to assist Dennis in coping with students' antagonistic behavior?

REFERENCES

Bloom, B. S. et al. (1956). *Taxonomy of educational objectives.* New York: Longman.

Elias, M. J., Zins, J. E., Weissbery, R. P., Frey, K. S., Greenberg, M. T., Haynes, N. M., Kessley, R.,

Schwab-Stone, M. E., & Shriver, T. P. (1997). *Promoting social and emotional learning: Guidelines for educators.* Alexandria, VA: Association for Supervision and Curriculum Development.

RECOMMENDED READING

Anderson, L. M. (1989). Classroom instruction. In M. C. Reynolds (Ed.), *Knowledge base for the beginning teacher* (pp. 101–115). New York: Pergamon Press. *This chapter reviews the knowledge base on classroom instruction to assist in increasing student learning through a cognitive-mediational perspective. The instruction that increases higher order learning is discussed and advocated.*

Benson, B., & Barnett, S. (1998). *Student-led conferencing using showcase portfolios.* Thousand Oaks, CA: Corwin Press. *The combination of conferencing and portfolios will add new student and parent interest in your classroom.*

Gall, M. D., Joyce P. G., Jacobsen, D. R., & Bullock, T. L. (1990). Listening, participating, and taking notes in class. In *Tools for learning: A guide to teaching study skills* (pp. 86–109). Alexandria, VA: Association for Supervision and Curriculum Development. *This chapter deals with showing teachers how to help students improve their in-class learning by listening, participating, and taking notes in class. Twenty specific skills are explained that students can implement immediately.*

Grossnickle, D. R., & Thiel, W. B. (1988). *Promoting effective student motivation in school and classroom: A practitioner's perspective.* Reston, VA: National Association of Secondary School Principals. *This monograph was written to help teachers and administrators recognize and overcome the obstacles to student motivation. Models,* examples, and cases are used to demonstrate methods of increasing student motivation.

Heinich, R., Molenda, M., Russell, J. D., & Smaldino, S. E. (1999). *Instructional media and technologies for learning* (6th ed.). Columbus, OH: Merrill. *This comprehensive text on the use of media and technology in the classroom includes a CD to assist in developing portfolio materials, lesson plans, and evaluations.*

Johnson, E. (1987). *Teaching school* (Rev. ed.). Boston: National Association of Independent Schools. *A veteran of 30 years of teaching experience has compiled realistic suggestions for practical applications in the classroom. Johnson has assembled a how-to for the entire instructional process. It is concise and to the point and is strongly recommended for student teachers and cooperating teachers.*

Jones, B. F., Palinscar, A. S., Ogle, D. S., & Carr, E. G. (Eds.). (1987). *Strategic teaching and learning: Cognitive instruction in the content areas.* Alexandria, VA: Association for Supervision and Curriculum Development. *This book contains a wealth of information from several authors related to developing the framework for strategic teaching and for applying those strategies in the content areas. Areas included are science, social studies, mathematics, and literature.*

Morrison, G. R., Lowther, D. & DeMeulle, L. (1999). *Integrating computer technology into the classroom.* Columbus: Merrill. *In providing a teaching model for integrating computer technology into classroom teaching, this text gives practical examples of computer-integrated lesson plans and power teacher tips to assist the individual teacher in improving computer skills.*

Ortman, P. E. (1988). Keeping it up: Instructional methodology. In *Not for teachers only: Creating a context of joy for learning and growth* (pp. 27–37). Washington, DC: Author. *Ortman gives the student teacher a good review of several important teaching concepts: individual differences, discovery learning, modeling, mastery learning, transfer of learning, and reinforcement. Her suggestions are appropriate for helping the student maintain confidence through effective teaching.*

Robbins, P., & Herndon, L. (1998). *The teacher's day planner.* Thousand Oaks, CA: Corwin Press. *This effective day planner comes ready to assemble in a three-ring binder and provides space for block scheduling lesson planning in addition to creative suggestions and ideas for planning.*

Ryder, R. J., & Hughes, T. (2000). *Internet for educators* (3rd ed.). Upper Saddle River, NJ: Merrill, Prentice Hall. *This text introduces educational professionals to curricula uses of the Internet, including communicating, exploring, instructing, and evaluating. It also provides Internet etiquette and interactive sites.*

U.S. Department of Education. (1986). Research about teaching and learning: Classroom. In *What works: Research about teaching and learning* (pp. 18–43). Washington, DC: Author. *Research findings are given on a number of classroom topics, including managing time, tutoring, study skills, and student ability and effort, and on specific disciplines, such as science, mathematics, reading, and writing. Comments and references to document the research findings are of assistance to both the cooperating teacher and the student teacher.*

27

Instructional Evaluation

The evaluation of student progress and the assessment processes used by a student teacher during student teaching should be an outgrowth of the unit and lesson plans that are developed in initial planning. It may be helpful for the student teacher to keep in mind that evaluation is generally used in terms of the total picture of the student and that assessment is used to determine the correctness of discrete pieces of the learning process in which the student is participating. In methods classes at the college, the student teacher has probably been exposed to a number of types of lesson and unit plan schemes, and the cooperating teacher may be able to offer some additional types of organization for planning and evaluation that are appropriate for particular situations. Classroom teachers generally have taken the theory offered in methods classes and have adapted it to the reality of the classroom. The planning and assessment methods offered by the cooperating teacher may be valuable to the student teacher.

As objectives are developed by the student teacher in planning with the cooperating teacher, and as activities are chosen to meet those objectives, the student teacher must decide how to determine whether those objectives are being met. Once the decision has been made, the evaluation process itself progresses with little difficulty. The secret is in the appropriate planning; it is critical for the student teacher to realize that teaching can be compared to a three-legged milking stool with evaluation as one of those three legs, combined with the planning and implementation legs to maintain balance on the stool. Student teachers sometimes have a tendency to postpone developing their evaluative procedures until the last minute and then rush into an inappropriate activity for the evaluation.

Cooperating teachers should be aware that student teachers sometimes tend to develop rather monotonous assessments. Because the assessment with which the student teacher is most familiar is the paper-and-pencil test, that type may be used more frequently during student teaching if adequate guidance is not given during the planning stages. Paper-and-pencil assessment exists in more varieties than the student teacher may be aware: the selected response items consisting of two-choice, multiple-choice, and matching items, and free-response items consisting of essay and short-answer items (Gallagher, 1998).

The development of student portfolios is becoming more frequently used and can be an excellent reflection of the classroom student's progress. As materials are designed for use in a student's portfolio, a rubric should be designed for each task indicating the degree of accuracy shown in the work on that task.

Benchmarking is a valuable tool in assessment. A benchmark is a point of reference against which any improvement can be measured. This concept is an important one to consider in planning lesson materials to avoid redundancy and to be able to measure achievement.

Assessment tools come in several shapes. They can be standardized, criterion-referenced (based on the criteria), norm-referenced (based on the overall group), self-designed, or commercially printed. A variety of types of assessment will assure the most accurate evaluation of a student's progress. Assessment by observation has some inherent dangers in that one observer may miss seeing what another observer may see. To guard against such problems, it is advisable to use two observers for any observational assessment.

Good planning for assessment and evaluation is difficult and takes much time on the part of the student teacher who may be inexperienced in the use of a variety of forms of assessment. The cooperating teacher can offer advice on a wide range of evaluation possibilities, and the student teacher could profit from other teachers' experiences in evaluation.

In addition to knowing whether the assessment is valid and reliable, the student teacher must question whether it will show that the students have learned what he or she was trying to teach them. If this does not occur, the assessment is of no value. This is the key reason to plan your assessment as you plan the objectives of the lesson or thematic unit.

Among problems that the student teacher must anticipate are those of evaluating for individual personal and cultural differences. Maintaining a classroom standard, evaluating special-needs students who have been mainstreamed, dealing with students who have other teachers who use different evaluation techniques, and being able to work with parents in explaining the grades that students eventually take home are critical skills for the student teacher to develop.

Adequate record keeping is a must. There is no substitute for documentation. The student teacher must be able to explain at any time just what the classroom achievement status is for any one of the students, both to the cooperating teacher or the principal and to parents and students. It is imperative to keep records up-to-date.

Among the variety of records the student teacher must keep up-to-date are attendance records, classroom discipline records, progress records, and records of the current academic standing of students (see Appendixes L & M). In addition to keeping the written records in the grade book, the student teacher would be wise to keep information about each student in his or her head. Parents may run into the student teacher at the grocery store and ask how their child is doing. If the student teacher says the child is doing fine and the report card comes home the next week with a bad report, the parent will have questions about the qualifications of the student teacher. If the response the student teacher makes to the same question is "I don't remember. He's a nice kid, though," the parent will begin to question whether their child should be taught by this person.

Patterns of record keeping vary from teacher to teacher. It is useful to develop a code so that several entries can be made in a small space. The typical grade books furnished to teachers by most schools are designed for records of 6 or 9 weeks per section. The student names are listed on the lefthand side of the book, with the rest of the space divided into cells, one per school day for the grading period. Codes that you as a student teacher might use include A for absent. If the student comes in tardy, you could overwrite a T on the A. If the student brings in an excuse for his or her previous absence, you can mark a diagonal through the A. Thus, in a very small space, you have a record of attendance.

In that same small cell in the grade book, a record of homework can be made: a zero if no homework is turned in, a check if homework is turned in, and a check through the zero that is already there if the homework is turned in late (see Appendix L).

Special columns in the grade book should be devoted to tests, projects, and special accomplishments. As the student teacher gets to know other teachers in the assigned school, it is helpful to ask those teachers to share their record-keeping systems. People who have been in teaching for some time develop coding systems that can say a lot in a small space. The cooperating teacher already has a record-keeping system in place, and the student teacher should adopt that system for that particular class. Other records for which the student teacher shares responsibility with the cooperating teacher and the guidance office are records related to standardized testing and, for high school students, tests for various college interests and entrance such as the National Merit test, ACT, and SAT.

Methods of instructional evaluation vary greatly depending on the grade level and the subject with which the student teacher is working. In elementary school, one student teacher probably uses several methods of evaluation with the same class because of the varied subject materials and content the group will have covered.

In addition to being well planned and well recorded, evaluation must be fair, both to the individual student and to the class. As important as fairness is in evaluation, the student teacher should give the student the benefit of any doubt and temper all the grades with professional mercy. The grade book is no place to feed a grudge.

When reporting to parents is mentioned to most teachers and student teachers, they often picture either a report card or a note written to the parent in regard to some inappropriate action, behavioral or academic, on the part of the student. Communication with parents can prove to be beneficial in classroom management as well as to the academic progress of individuals in the class.

Communicating student assessment and evaluation to parents is a sensitive topic and requires precision, clarity, and diplomacy. Student teachers should plan a positive communication program with the parents and, with the aid of the cooperating teacher, take the necessary steps to ensure the establishment and maintenance of such a program (see Appendix N). Such a relationship can be developed by communicating positive messages, including student achievements and attitudes. The important message here to the parents is that lines of communication are open. Student teachers should discuss this carefully with the cooperating teacher and plan a semester-long parent communication plan that will include assessment and evaluation information that the parents will be comfortable with and will respond to. The student teacher must not be disappointed if some parents do not respond. Lack of response can be due to outside pressures, lack of interest, socioeconomic status, or fear of the school. It is not a reflection of the good intentions of the student teacher.

State laws and school district regulations mandate the report card. Student anxiety produced by the report card must be dealt with by the student teacher. One method is to encourage students throughout the term to do their best and accept themselves through positive self-concepts.

Notes from the student teacher to the parents (approved by the cooperating teacher) are another standard method of communication. These notes should convey messages of a positive nature about the student, for example, good behavior, or of some well-done work (see Appendix O). The student teacher should use praise cautiously but should give the student commendations when appropriate. In the elementary school, a good rule of thumb is to send at least one personal communication home to a student's parents during each reporting period. Spaced halfway between report cards, a note can lend reassurance to both parents and students. It need be nothing more than the following:

Dear Mr. and Mrs. Jones:

Johnny seems to be enjoying school this year. I talked with him earlier about the condition of some of his homework papers and since that time he seems to have made a real effort to improve. I appreciate his cooperation and I feel we're going to have a good term.

I will be happy to set up a conference after school at your request.

(signed)
Student Teacher in Mr. Smith's Class

Student teachers should be aware that any remark written on a student's paper is also a message to parents. Some students use a poorly worded comment written by the student teacher on a homework or test paper to the disadvantage of the student teacher if any animosity exists between the school and the parents. Notes on such papers should be well thought through and sincerely and carefully stated and proofread.

Parent conferences are a method of reporting to parents. They are usually scheduled before or after school. Some schools provide PTA meeting times or other teacher-parent contact. Care must be given to make special arrangements with those parents who cannot get to the school during school hours. Most principals will agree to meet with the student teacher, the cooperating teacher, and the parents at the school after the parents' working hours. Possible sites other than the school for such conferences are the public library or the main office of the school district. Discretion is urged on the selection of any other site as it is generally recognizable that some sites are inappropriate.

Conferences with parents can be rewarding and enlightening to student teachers. Usually such conferences are held at the request of either the parents or the student teacher based on an academic or behavior problem. Some schools routinely schedule parent conferences and the student teacher, on the advice of the cooperating teacher, may choose such a schedule.

Whatever type of reporting to parents is chosen by the student teacher, reports should be kept positive and objective and must be approved by the cooperating teacher. Care must be used so that reports are realistic. If reports are glowing, parents will be surprised if the grades are poor.

GUIDELINES FOR THE STUDENT TEACHER

- **Plan your evaluation immediately on setting your objectives.** Never wait until it is evaluation time to plan for it.
- **Your cooperating teacher may be able to help you by giving you samples of evaluation procedures used in the past.** Do not hesitate to use such materials as examples of what you can develop to fit your own material.
- **As you plan, your thinking naturally flows in terms of evaluation.** It is important to make note of these ideas when they occur to you. Experience shows that those ideas that seemed to be important can be replaced very soon by other ideas of apparently equal importance, and the former are forgotten.
- **Be flexible.** As you move through the students' work, you may find a more appropriate assessment mechanism. Never hesitate to change for the sake of improvement.
- **Be careful about the directions you give to students concerning their evaluations.** Students should be told as they begin new material just how they will be evaluated. As you develop evaluative material, think step-by-step through the classroom procedure in which you will be using that material.
- **Anticipate the questions that students might have and the actions they might take.** Prepare for these in the directions to the students by giving them a sense of security about the evaluation and by developing improved classroom control based on good planning.

- **As you develop paper-and-pencil tests, remember to consider the ease with which you may be able to grade the papers.** You may want to include all your essay questions in one section of the test. With the objective questions, you may want to place the blanks down either the lefthand or the righthand margin for the student to fill in the answers (see example in Appendix P). For essay answers, you may request that the students use lined paper and write on alternate lines on one side only.
- **Ask the cooperating teacher for permission to sit as an observer during her or his parent conferences.** Many useful interpersonal skills can be gathered through such observations. You can learn how the cooperating teacher has materials and records available, is professionally ready for meeting the parents, allows the parents sufficient time to question and discuss their child, remains pleasant throughout the meeting, and ends the meeting at the appropriate time on a positive note.
- **You may feel more comfortable in your first few parent conferences if you role play through a typical situation with a friend.** Parent conferences are rough on the beginner at first. When you stop to consider that a parent conference is sharing time for someone the parent and the student teacher are concerned about, the task becomes less difficult.
- **Keep in mind that success in teaching your class depends on what you know about your students individually.** Be careful about accepting second-hand advice and information except from your cooperating teacher who is your greatest source of information. Parents are a unique source of information about your students, both in what they say and in what they avoid saying.
- **As you deal with parents, remember to be a professional educator and keep the best interests of the students uppermost in your mind.** Always be courteous and understanding with parents; try to give them the benefit of any doubt, keeping in mind that those students with the least amount of school contact on the part of their parents usually are in the greatest need of such contact.

GUIDELINES FOR THE COOPERATING TEACHER

- **In early observations, both with you and with other teachers,** suggest that the student teacher observe specific methods of evaluation and keep notes in a professional notebook.
- **Help the student teacher to realize and practice** the concept that different methods of evaluation are sometimes good for different students covering the same material.
- **Help the student teacher to understand that those students who do not test well with paper-and-pencil tests may be better evaluated with an individual**

oral test. A major difficulty with this is the security of the evaluative situation and the time required for administering individual tests. The results, however, are worth the added time and effort.

- **As the cooperating teacher, do not allow the student teacher to proceed with teaching until you have seen and approved the methods of evaluation to be used.**
- **It helps the student teacher to have access to your grade book to be aware of current performance of students in the classroom.** The student teacher should maintain a separate grade book and should keep it well documented, up-to-date, and secure.
- **Stress the necessity for immediate feedback to students with the evaluative measures chosen.** Consider, for example, the student teacher in high school English who assigned a 6-page essay to all five of his classes. In his planning, he had not considered how much time he would need to grade those essays in addition to the time necessary to continue ongoing planning and preparation. This particular student teacher became so weighted down with the work of grading the essays that he became physically ill and was forced to stay out of school for a week to recover.
- **Discuss with the student teacher the importance of good communication between the school and the home.** Openness in this area contributes to a healthier mental state for the classroom student. Frequently, school-home communications suffer because of a lack of time on the part of the teacher and a lack of accessibility on the part of the parent. If you can aid the student teacher in identifying these problems, it will be less difficult for the student teacher.
- **A variety of methods of reporting to parents can be suggested by the cooperating teacher.** In addition to the 6- or 9-week report card, the student teacher could develop a type of periodic written memo (see the format for a Happy Gram in Appendix Q), a schedule of telephone calls to parents, a planned sequence of group or individual conferences at the school, and visits by the student teacher, accompanied by another professional, to the homes of the students.

CASE STUDIES

C A S E

27-1   Three preparations per day in English were all in a day's work for Susanna, who was student teaching in Ms. Wright's classroom. In her excitement of getting students motivated and preparing materials, Susanna frequently failed to specify her planned evaluation procedures to Ms. Wright. Knowing the critical nature of the early development of such procedures, Ms. Wright felt that she must take steps to help Susanna improve her planning for evaluation.

1. Should Ms. Wright offer specific methods of evaluation?
2. Should she merely indicate the obvious need of such methods to Susanna and expect her to follow through with her own materials?
3. How could Ms. Wright involve Susanna in obtaining evaluative methods from other teachers in the school?
4. How should the university supervisor be involved?
5. How can student teachers avoid this happening to them?

C A S E 27-2

Jamal, the student teacher in Coach Martinez's physical educational classes, had stated early in his student teaching that all physical education students should receive a grade of C no matter what they did. The coach realized that someone had to change Jamal's attitude before report cards went out and parents began calling him about their children's grades. When Coach Martinez explained the problem to Jamal, he was told: "You grade them; I'll teach them."

1. How should Coach respond to Jamal?
2. How will the evaluation practices that Jamal uses in this assignment affect his evaluation methods for the rest of his career?
3. Besides having an incomplete awareness of his responsibility in the area of evaluation, Jamal seems to have a problem in terms of his respect for Coach Martinez. How should Coach handle this?
4. What issue here is more important than the responses that Coach has to give to the parents of his students?
5. What responsibility does the university supervisor have in this situation?

C A S E 27-3

Mr. Spencer noted that his student teacher gave frequent paper-and-pencil tests and seemed to be planning his entire evaluation strategy on such devices.

Because a number of students in the class could benefit from alternative kinds of evaluation, Mr. Spencer offered several evaluation alternatives, but the student teacher insisted on continuing to use only paper-and-pencil tests.

1. How should Mr. Spencer deal with his student teacher?
2. Should he force the student teacher to use other evaluation methods? Why or why not?
3. Should he allow the student teacher to learn by experience, thus penalizing the students in the classroom?
4. How could Mr. Spencer help his student teacher to want to use different methods of evaluation?
5. How could the student teacher's insecurity be affecting him to the point that he was uncomfortable with anything except paper-and-pencil tests?

C A S E

27-4   Elise, the student teacher in Mrs. Castro's first grade, felt that true evaluations of student work were inappropriate. She felt that all reports to the home should indicate only good, positive messages. Mrs. Castro could appreciate Elise's point of view, but she felt it necessary to enlarge Elise's horizons to include those needs that the children had indicated by her evaluative data.

1. Should Mrs. Castro insist that Elise maintain the established evaluation system? Why?
2. How should she attempt to involve the university supervisor and any relevant theoretical materials available?
3. How could Mrs. Castro involve Elise in researching this topic with other teachers in the school?
4. What opportunities could be developed for this same research with those teachers who were also parents of school-aged children?
5. What experiences from her own life could Mrs. Castro give Elise to help her consider this more realistically?

C A S E

27-5   Lupe felt that everything that a child did should be reflected on the evaluation report. During her student teaching, she attempted to record every response, written and oral, and make anecdotal records on each of the third-grade children. Mrs. Packard, the cooperating teacher, realized that this was ineffective and could not continue. During the midpoint of the term, Lupe seemed to be wearing down somewhat, but instead of finding a better solution to the evaluation situation, she was beset with guilt feelings, as if she were incompetent. Mrs. Packard was concerned about the immediate problems Lupe was experiencing, the effect of those problems on her students, and the long-range effect on Lupe's professional life.

1. How could the cooperating teacher help Lupe?
2. What resources on the university campus might help in this situation?
3. What role should the university supervisor play in resolving this problem?
4. Is there any hope for people such as Lupe to become effective teachers?
5. What responsibility does Lupe have to help herself without creating further guilt feelings?

C A S E

27-6   Seaton loved his student teaching in the advanced biology classes. He was a live wire in the classroom and the students seemed to be making progress. The cooperating teacher was satisfied with Seaton's work and the only complaint was that Seaton worked too hard.

In an effort to move the students along as fast as possible and keep them interested, Seaton assigned to five sections of biology classes, at the same time, 10-page compositions to accompany the students' major project. This was done without a prior discussion with the cooperating teacher. When she discovered what Seaton had done, it was too late to revise the work schedule for the students. Seaton was unable to visualize the problem until the day the papers and projects were due and he began grading them. He seemed to get nowhere fast. As his grading took most of his time, his planning suffered, as did his classroom performance. Yet Seaton felt driven to return the compositions and projects promptly.

1. How could the cooperating teacher help Seaton, aside from grading the compositions and projects for him?
2. Should the teacher take over the class temporarily while Seaton gets back on his feet? Why
3. What constructive assistance could the university supervisor offer?
4. How could this situation have been avoided?
5. How can student teachers plan their time as realistically as possible?

REFERENCE

Gallagher, J. D. (1998). *Classroom assessment for teachers.* Upper Saddle River, NJ: Merrill.

RECOMMENDED READING

Anrig, G. R., Daly, N., Futrell, M. H., Robinson, S., Rubin, L., & Weiss, J. G. (1987). *What is the appropriate role of testing in the teaching profession?* Washington, DC: National Education Association. *This book contains the proceedings of a cooperative conference sponsored by the American Association of Colleges for Teacher Education, the Center for Fair and Open Testing, the Educational Testing Service, and the National Education Association. In addition to a wide range of the uses of testing and the place of testing in the pedagogical training of teachers, the moral as well as the political imperatives of testing are discussed.*

Baker, F. B. (1989). Computer technology in test construction and processing. In R. L. Linn (Ed.), *Educational measurement* (3rd ed.) (pp. 409–428). New York: Macmillan. *Baker includes an extensive review of the technology involved in using microcomputers for item development and test development. Steps in processing the material such as item writing, test construction, scanning, scoring, and reporting are explained. The chapter is excellent information for both the cooperating teacher and the student teacher.*

Brown, J. H., & Shavelson, R. J. (1996). *Assessing hands-on science: A teacher's guide to performance assessment.* Thousand Oaks, CA: Corwin Press. *This text provides step-by-step instructions and work samples to measure student progress in science.*

Choppin, B. H. (1988). Objective tests. In J. P. Keeves (Ed.), *Educational research, methodology* and measurement: An international handbook* (pp. 354–358). New York: Pergamon Press. *Objective tests and test items are defined. Areas of application and item formats in addition to the advantages and disadvantages of objective tests are discussed. This material is important for the beginning teacher to understand.*

Cole, D., Ryan, C., & Kick, F. (1995). *Portfolios across the curriculum and beyond.* Thousand Oaks, CA: Corwin Press. *These writers share examples of how to maintain an accurate picture of what each student is learning by subject and grade.*

Evertson, C. M., Emmer, E. T., Clements, B. S., Sanford, J. P., & Worsham, M. (1984). Evaluating your classroom's organization and management. In *Classroom management for elementary teachers* (pp. 147–162). Englewood Cliffs, NJ: Prentice Hall. *This chapter covers some major indicators of the effectiveness of classroom organization and management. Methods for improving the management of instructional activities are offered.*

Fischer, C. F., & King, R. (1995). *Authentic assessment: A guide to implementation.* Thousand Oaks, CA: Corwin Press. *This text takes the teacher through the assessment process from goal selection to portfolio management to reporting to students and parents.*

Herman, J. L. (1988). Item writing techniques. In J. P. Keeves (Ed.), *Educational research, methodology and measurement: An international handbook* (pp. 358–363). New York: Pergamon Press. *The range of current item-writing techniques for objectives measures is given. Item-writing algorithms and linguistic-based approaches to item development are discussed. Rules and examples are included.*

Mabry, L. (1998). *Portfolio plus: A critical guide to alternative assessment.* Thousand Oaks, CA: Corwin Press. *This text shows the teacher how to design an assessment program and make assessment a positive part of the learning process for students.*

Perrone, V. (Ed.). (1991). *Expanding student assessment.* Alexandria, VA: Association for Supervision and Curriculum Development. *This book is a collection of writings by 13 authors who propose that those of us in education seriously review our educational goals and then determine how we can effectively assess those goals. Each chapter is a good reading assignment for the cooperating teacher to give the student teacher.*

Reineke, R. A. (1998). *Challenging the mind, touching the heart: Best assessment practices.* Thousand Oaks, CA: Corwin Press. *The author stresses the link between assessment and curriculum and instruction, offering practical suggestions on teachers' teaching and students' learning.*

P A R T

8

The Next Professional Step

28

Certification

Becoming certified to teach is one of the last major steps that teachers-to-be take in their career preparation; it is a part of the final process of becoming a professional educator.

Consideration of the certification process should occur as the teacher trainee first begins the college program. However, because most students are not aware of or concerned about the certification process until graduation, the term of student teaching is a good time to take a long, hard look at the process. Although national certification to teach currently exists, state certification requirements will vary from state to state. The National Board for Professional Teaching (NBPT) has as its mission "to establish high and rigorous standards for what accomplished teachers should know and be able to do, to develop and operate a national voluntary system to assess and certify teachers who meet these standards, and to advance related education reforms for the purpose of improving student learning in American schools" (NBPTS, 1997). For information on national certification through the National Board for Professional Teaching, write NCAE, 700 Salisbury Street, Raleigh, NO 27611, or call 1-800-662-7924.

Although some states require a degree in each area in which a new teacher is to be certified, many states bestow certification on application following the completion of state department of education approved teacher education degree programs. Some states allow additional areas of certification to be added by a person using the "course counting" method. That is, in addition to receiving the initial certification covered by the degree in the approved program, an individual can take specific courses for a specified number of hours and be certified to teach that subject also.

Some states require, in addition to a bachelor's degree, specific activities such as competency tests, student teaching, extended internships, and beginning teacher programs. There are states, such as Alabama, Georgia, Florida, New York, North Carolina, and Oklahoma, that have developed their own tests for certification. These tests vary from state to state, and test scores are not reciprocal. For instance, if the candidate wishes to be certified in Florida, passing scores on a test on the generic teaching competencies and on a test on the special subject matter area are both required. Other states, for example, Louisiana, Mississippi, Tennessee, and West Virginia, require the National Teachers Examination. For the testing schedule and information, write to

National Teachers Exam, Educational Testing Service, Box 911-P, Princeton, NJ 08541. Usually the application deadlines for any of these tests are rather early; determine which tests, if any, are needed. The candidate should contact the state department of education of the state in question for specific information.

The Interstate New Teacher Assessment and Support Consortium (INTASC) has 10 principles relating to the knowledge, disposition, and performance that new teachers should possess and be able to do. For additional information, see the Website http://www.huntington.edu/education/sholtrop/INTASC.html (Education Department, Huntington College, 1997). These principles are subdivided into standards that can be related to the National Council for Accreditation of Teacher Education (NCATE) standards.

If a teacher-to-be is otherwise qualified and applies to be certified in a state requiring either a test or an extended internship, that state's department of education usually grants a temporary certificate under which the graduate may teach and allows a certain amount of time during which the test is to be passed. It is possible and practical for the student teaching requirement to be satisfied by actual on-the-job classroom teaching.

If student teachers plan to teach within the state in which they are trained, the college will probably furnish certification information regularly throughout the training program. In some states, the department of education automatically awards the appropriate certificates to graduates of the state-approved teacher education degree programs. In other states, the graduate must submit an application, transcript, and processing fees to the department of education. Some states are now requiring all certification applicants to submit fingerprints to be processed through state police and Federal Bureau of Investigation files.

Students who graduate in one state and apply for certification in another should be aware that certification requirements vary from state to state. It is also normal procedure for the state department of education in the state in which certification is sought to write to the graduating institution for an institutional recommendation.

Your university may be accredited by NCATE, a national organization composed of constitute members across the curriculum that establishes standards, reviews programs, and makes recommendations as to the worthiness of a university's program of teacher education (National Council for Accreditation of Teacher Education, 1995). If your professional education unit program is accredited by NCATE, your certification potential across the nation is greatly enhanced. Most likely the only hindrance to your certification in any state would be that the state requires a course in the history of that state or has some related kind of requirement. Should this occur, the state department of education would probably issue a temporary certificate and allow a specified time, usually 12 months, in which to complete the requirement.

A student teacher can easily become confused with the variety of certification information and it is important to know whom to ask for information. The student teacher should be concerned about what questions are to be answered and may wish to actually make a list such as the following:

1. What is the appropriate source of certification information?
2. What are the requirements for certification in the state in which I want to be certified?
3. Will my bachelor's (or master's) degree satisfy all the certification requirements?
4. Does my state participate in the Interstate Reciprocity Agreement, in which member states agree to accept for certification those who complete state-approved teacher education degree programs in other member states? These states currently include Alabama, Alaska, California, Canal Zone, Connecticut, Delaware, District of Columbia, Florida, Hawaii, Idaho, Indiana, Kentucky, Maine, Maryland, Massachusetts, Nebraska, New Hampshire, New Jersey, New York, North Carolina, Ohio, Oklahoma, Pennsylvania, Rhode Island, South Dakota, Utah, Vermont, Virginia, Washington, and West Virginia.
5. Is my institution accredited by NCATE? Graduates of colleges and universities that are NCATE accredited are accepted in most school districts across the nation as certifiable.
6. Can I be certified in a related area of study by "course counting" and taking additional coursework without an additional degree?
7. Is a competency test required in my state? If so, should I take it before or after graduation?
8. Is an extended student teaching required in my state? If so, can I work this off while I teach with a temporary certificate?
9. What about the actual certification process?
   a. To whom do I apply?
   b. When do I apply?
   c. Where do I get my application?
   d. Is there a fee? How do I pay? To whom?
   e. Are there any papers I need to send with my application? Some states require fingerprints submitted with applications; information on this is available where you get the certification application forms.

Each college or university with a teacher training institution usually has a person designated as the certification adviser, and it is to this person that the student teacher should direct specific questions. Your college library reference section may have certification materials from other states; ask the reference librarian. For more detailed information about certification in any state, write the Department of Education in that state as shown in the following list (Boydston, 1998). Many states also have websites to give additional information.

Alabama: State Department of Education
            Teacher Placement and Recruitment
            Gordon Persons Building, Room 5202
            P.O. Box 302101
            Montgomery, AL 36130-2101
            Phone: 334-242-9935

Alaska:	Teacher Certification Administrative Services 801 West 10th Street, Suite 100 Juneau, AK 99801-1894 Phone: 907-465-2831
Arizona:	Department of Education Teacher Certification Unit 1535 West Jefferson Phoenix, AZ 85007 Phone: 602-542-4367
Arkansas:	Department of Education Teacher Education and Licensure 4 Capitol Mall Little Rock, AR 72201-1071 Phone: 501-682-4342
California:	California Commission on Teaching Credentialing 1812-9th Street P.O. Box 944270 Sacramento, CA 94244-2700 Phone: 916-445-7254
Colorado:	Colorado Department of Education Educator Licensing Unit 201 East Colfax Avenue Denver, CO 80203 Phone: 303-866-6628
Connecticut:	State Department of Education Bureau of Certification and Professional Development P.O. Box 2219 Hartford, CT 06145-2219 Phone: 860-566-5201
Delaware:	Department of Public Instruction Professional Standards and Certification The Townsend Building P.O. Box 1402 Dover, DE 19903 Phone: 302-739-4688 or 800-433-5292
Washington, DC:	Teacher Education and Licensure Branch Logan Administration Building 215 G Street NE, Room 101A Washington, DC 20002 Phone: 202-724-4249 or 800-TEACHDC

Florida:

Florida Department of Education
Bureau of Teacher Certification
Florida Education Center
Tallahassee, FL 32399-0400
Phone: 904-488-2317 (out of state); 800-445-6739 (in state)

Georgia:

Georgia Professional Standards Commission
1452 Twin Towers East
Atlanta, GA 30334
Phone: 404-657-9000 or 800-869-7775

Hawaii:

Office of Personnel Services
Certification and Development Section, Room 301
P.O. Box 2360
Honolulu, HI 96804
Phone: 808-586-3276

Idaho:

State Department of Education
Teacher Education and Certification
P.O. Box 83720
Boise, ID 83720-0027
Phone: 208-332-6880

Illinois:

State Board of Education
Division of Professional Preparation
100 North 1st Street
Springfield, IL 62777-0001
Phone: 217-782-2805

Indiana:

Indiana Professional Standards Board
Teacher Certification Program
251 East Ohio, Suite 201
Indianapolis, IN 46204-2133
Phone: 317-232-9010

Iowa:

Iowa State Board of Education
Examiners
Grimes State Office Building
Des Moines, IA 50310-0147
Phone: 515-281-3245

Kansas:

Kansas State Board of Education
Certification and Teacher Education Section
120 SE 10th Avenue
Topeka, KS 66612-1182
Phone: 785-296-2288

Kentucky: State Department of Education
Division of Certification
1024 Capital Center Drive
Frankfort, KY 40601
Phone: 502-573-4606

Louisiana: State Department of Education
Bureau of Higher Education and Teacher Certification
P.O. Box 94064
Baton Rouge, LA 70815
Phone: 504-342-3490

Maine: Department of Education
Certification Office
23 State House Station
Augusta, ME 04333-0023
Phone: 207-287-5944

Maryland: Certification Branch
200 West Baltimore Street
Baltimore, MD 21201
Phone: 410-767-0412

Massachusetts: Department of Education
Office of Certification and Credentialing
350 Main Street
P.O. Box 9140
Malden, MA 02148-5023
Phone: 617-388-3300, Ext. 665

Michigan: Michigan Department of Education
Office of Teacher/Administrator Preparation & Certification
Box 30008
Lansing, MI 48909
Phone: 517-373-3310

Minnesota: Department of Children, Families and Learning
Teacher Licensing
616 Capitol Square Building
St. Paul, MN 55101
Phone: 612-296-2046

Mississippi: State Department of Education
Office of Educator Licensure
P.O. Box 771
Jackson, MS 39205-0771
Phone: 601-359-3483

Missouri:	Department of Elementary and Secondary Education Teacher Education and Certification P.O. Box 480 Jefferson City, MO 65102-0480 Phone: 314-751-3486
Montana:	Office of Public Instruction Certification Division P.O. Box 202501 Helena, MT 59620-2501 Phone: 406-444-3150
Nebraska:	Department of Education Teacher Education and Certification P.O. Box 94987 Lincoln, NE 68509-4987 Phone: 800-371-4642
Nevada:	Nevada Department of Education Teacher Licensure 1820 East Sahara Avenue Las Vegas, NV 89104-3746 Phone: 702-486-6458
New Hampshire:	State Department of Education Bureau of Credentialing 101 Pleasant Street Concord, NH 03301 Phone: 603-271-2407
New Jersey:	Department of Education Office of Licensing and Academic Credentials CN503 Trenton, NJ 08625-0503 Phone: 609-292-2070
New Mexico:	Department of Education Professional Licensure Unit 300 Don Gaspar Santa Fe, NM 87501-2786 Phone: 505-827-6587
New York:	New York State Education Department Office of Teaching Cultural Education Center, Room 5A-11 Albany, NY 12230 Phone: 518-474-3901

North Carolina: Department of Public Instruction
                     Licensure Section
                     301 North Wilmington Street
                     Raleigh, NC 27601-2825
                     Phone: 919-733-4125

North Dakota: North Dakota Department of Public Instruction
                     Education Standards and Practices Board
                     600 East Boulevard Avenue
                     Bismarck, ND 58505-0440
                     Phone: 701-328-2264

Ohio: Ohio Department of Education
                     Division of Teacher Education and Certification
                     65 South Front Street, Room 416
                     Columbus, OH 43215
                     Phone: 614-466-3593

Oklahoma: Oklahoma Department of Education
                     Professional Standards Section
                     2500 North Lincoln Boulevard,
                     Room 211
                     Oklahoma City, OK 73105-4599
                     Phone: 405-521-3337

Oregon: Teacher Standards and Practices Commission
                     255 Capital Street, NE, Suite 105
                     Salem, OR 97310-1332
                     Phone: 503-378-3586

Pennsylvania: Department of Education
                     Bureau of Teacher Preparation and Certification
                     333 Market Street, 3rd Floor
                     Harrisburg, PA 17126-0333
                     Phone: 717-787-2967

Rhode Island: Department of Education
                     Office of Teacher Certification
                     255 Westminster Street
                     Providence, RI 02903
                     Phone: 401-222-4600

South Carolina: Department of Education
                     Teacher Licensure Section
                     1600 Gervais Street
                     Columbia, SC 29201
                     Phone: 803-734-8466

South Dakota:	Department of Education and Cultural Affairs Teacher Education and Certification 700 Governors Drive Pierre, SD 57501-2291 Phone: 605-773-3553
Tennessee:	Tennessee Department of Education Office of Teacher Licensing/Career Ladder Certification 710 James Robertson Parkway, 5th Floor Nashville, TN 37243-0377 Phone: 615-532-4885
Texas:	Texas State Board for Educator Certification 1001 Trinity Austin, TX 78701 Phone: 512-469-3001
Utah:	Utah State Office of Education Teacher Certification Section 250 East 500 South Salt Lake City, UT 84111 Phone 801-538-7740
Vermont:	State Department of Education Licensing Office 120 State Street Montpelier, VT 05620 Phone: 802-828-2445
Virginia:	Department of Education Office for Teacher Education and Licensure P.O. Box 2120 Richmond, VA 23218-2120 Phone: 804-225-2022
Washington:	Department of Education Professional Education and Certification Office P.O. Box 47200 Olympia, WA 98504-7200 Phone: 360-753-6773
West Virginia:	Department of Education Office of Professional Preparation 1900 Kanawha Boulevard, East Building 6, Room 337 Charleston, WV 25305-0330 Phone: 304-558-7010 or 800-982-2378

Wisconsin:	Department of Public Instruction
	Teacher Education and Licensing
	125 South Webster Street
	P.O. Box 7841
	Madison, WI 53707-7841
	Phone: 608-266-1027 or 800-441-4563
Wyoming:	Professional Teaching Standards Board
	2300 Capitol Avenue
	Hathaway Building, 2nd Floor
	Cheyenne, WY 82002-0050
	Phone: 307-777-6248

It is essential for student teachers to realize that certification is for a limited period and that renewal requirements vary from state to state. Once a certificate is obtained, maintaining it is important. Various infractions of criminal and civil law as well as of state school board rules can lead to certificate suspension or revocation. A number of states routinely check for revocation in other states before issuing a certificate.

GUIDELINES FOR THE STUDENT TEACHER

- **As you consider certification, you may think that another roadblock to becoming a teacher has been put in your path.** The purpose of certification is to help you in your professional development. Try not to be discouraged.
- **Begin asking questions about certification early in your college career.**
- **Find the appropriate person on campus or in the school district in which you are student teaching to assist you with certification information and keep yourself up-to-date on certification requirements and on any impending changes.** Promptness pays off. Do not be shy or assume that someone will tell you when the time is right to apply for certification. Someone may but do not wait.
- **Accept your professional responsibility early and know what is expected of you in the process of getting certified.** If you do not know the answers to the questions presented earlier find someone who does.
- **Seek information from a qualified person so that you can be assured of factual information.** Do not depend on rumors. You will be more comfortable in your student teaching classroom if you are confident about your certification process.

GUIDELINES FOR THE COOPERATING TEACHER

- Since firsthand information is often the best, it is important that you discuss certification with your student teacher.
- Feel free to relate how you became certified and how you renew and extend your certificate.
- Relate any special problems relative to certification that fellow teachers have experienced.
- If your state requires the development of certain classroom competencies, relate this information to your student teacher and assist him or her in the development and improvement of these competencies.
- Assure your student teacher that certification is to ensure that the students in the classroom have qualified teachers who are knowledgeable, trained, and worthy of the students' respect.

CASE STUDIES

C A S E

28-1   Stephanie was unaware that certification was a part of her professional preparation until her cooperating teacher referred to it one day in a conference. The cooperating teacher was surprised that the process had not been covered in Stephanie's courses at the university. Knowing that Stephanie needed the information about obtaining a certificate to teach as soon as possible, the cooperating teacher considered suggesting that Stephanie visit the school district personnel office.

1. Should the cooperating teacher call the college to find the name of the certification adviser, or should she leave this up to Stephanie? Why?
2. How could she suggest that this kind of information be included in the methods courses prior to student teaching?
3. What action should she suggest Stephanie take?
4. How could the university supervisor assist Stephanie in this situation?
5. What kinds of information do you think Stephanie would recommend to be included in the teacher education program in the future prior to student teaching?

C A S E

28-2   Kurt was working toward a teaching degree in English and was student teaching in the high school. Someone had told him that if he took 12 additional semester hours in speech and drama he could be certified in speech and drama. Kurt felt that this would be a professional asset and would improve his marketability when he went job hunting. He could not recall who had given him the information, and he felt a vague need to verify whether he could really add speech and drama to his certificate. In discussing this with his cooperating teacher, he was told, "You don't need anything but English!" Kurt relayed this to his university supervisor, who felt the need to tactfully counsel the cooperative teacher, as she did not want to come between the cooperating teacher and the student teacher.

1. Should the university supervisor give both the student teacher and the cooperating teacher the name of the university's certification adviser? Why?
2. What other steps could be taken to improve the situation?
3. How can Kurt obtain the information he needs without offending his cooperating teacher?
4. What problems could develop if Kurt tries to get his cooperating teacher to understand his desire for additional certification areas?
5. What lessons can Kurt store for future reference when he is a cooperating teacher?

C A S E

28-3   Mr. Kaiser was concerned about the professional attitude of his student teacher, Gabriel It seems that Gabriel had discussed certification requirements with the campus certification adviser and had found that with the addition of a few courses here and there, he could be certified in mathematics, science, and social studies, as well as in his major, technology education. Gabriel was interested in pursuing as many certifications as possible. Mr. Kaiser's concern was that although Gabriel might get the certifications, he really would not be prepared to teach all those subjects.

1. How could Mr. Kaiser voice his objection to Gabriel?
2. Why did Mr. Kaiser have the right to object to Gabriel's plan?
3. How could Mr. Kaiser explain this professional dilemma to the university supervisor without betraying Gabriel's confidence?
4. How could it be possible to be certified in so many subjects?
5. How can such varied certification be justified on sound professional grounds?

C A S E

28-4   Dana, a student teacher in Mrs. Crumpton's first grade, was excited about teaching and getting her own classroom following graduation and certification. Uncle Sam had other plans, however; he transferred Dana's husband to a military base in Europe. Although no problems arose about her graduation date, Dana was unable to decide whether she should apply for certification before she left for Europe.

1. Should Dana wait until she and her husband are transferred back to the United States?

2. Suppose the requirements changed in the interim? What would she do if that happened?
3. Would Dana want to teach on the military base in Europe?
4. Would she need certification from the Department of Defense Dependent Schools or from the state in which she was living at the time of transfer?
5. Since Mrs. Crumpton felt unable to help answer these questions, to whom should she refer Dana?
6. What advice would you give Dana as to taking tests for certification such as state competency tests or the National Teachers Exam?

C A S E

28-5   Marcella loves teaching. Her student teaching had been a successful experience and she was looking forward to her first job in high school home economics.

After looking through the openings for home economics teachers at home and across the nation, Marcella decided to avoid waiting for a job in her home district and to take a position in a neighboring state. During her interview with the school administrator, her certification was discussed. For the first time, Marcella realized that her home state certification would not be sufficient in the state in which she wanted to teach. She was perplexed. At this point in her life, she had completed a university degree in teacher education and fulfilled what she thought were all the requirements for her to become a teacher. With disappointment in her heart, she considered her alternatives.

1. How could Marcella become certified in the state in which she wished to teach?
2. How could she find out whether her new state requires a teacher certification test?
3. Would there be a probationary period for her to teach prior to her receiving a regular certificate in that state?
4. Was it worth the effort? So much paperwork was involved. Should Marcella just wait in line for a job in her home state?
5. How could Marcella's dilemma have been solved earlier in her university program?

C A S E

28-6   James was proud of being a teacher and was enjoying student teaching in physics. He felt that teachers should be as well prepared as possible for their noble profession.

During his student teaching, he became aware of a teacher on the faculty who had been hired primarily to coach football but also to teach a few classes in math. The coach had laughingly said that he had no certification in mathematics and did not intend to get one, that he had a winning football team, and that that was what really counted. James was astounded that the administration would allow this.

1. With whom should James discuss this situation?
2. What, if anything, should he try to do about it?

3. How should the university supervisor and the cooperating teacher respond to James's complaints relative to the situation?
4. In what ways could James help the coach to understand his feeling about certification?
5. How should James feel if the coach continues to rebuff him?
6. How would you react under the circumstances?

REFERENCES

Boydston, J. E. (1998). Teacher certification requirements in all 50 states, 1998–99, (16th ed.). Sebring, FL: Teacher Certification Publications.

Huntington College Education Department. (1997). http://www.huntington.edu/education/sholtrop/INTASC.html

National Board for Professional Teaching Standards. (1997).
http://www.ncae.org/pod/ nbcgen.html.

National Council for Accreditation of Teacher Education. (1995). *Standards, procedures, and policies for the accreditation of professional education units.* Washington, DC: Author.

RECOMMENDED READING

Armstrong, D. G., Henson, K. T., & Savage, T. V. (2001). Legal concerns of teachers. In *Teaching today: An introduction to education.* Upper Saddle River, NJ: Merrill/Prentice Hall. *The authors discuss certification and other topics that student teachers often have questions about, including the hiring process, teacher contracts, tenure, and continuing employment*

Association of Teacher Educators. (1986). Qualifications and responsibilities of affiliated supervisory personnel. In Association of Teacher Educators (Ed.), *Guidelines for professional experiences in teacher education: A policy statement* (pp. 17–18). Reston, VA: Author. *This material speaks to the qualifications and responsibilities of the individuals who are to be involved as affiliated supervisors. Criteria are to be jointly established by the institutional affiliates to ensure the maintenance of high-quality professionals. The entire set of guidelines (pp. 1–21) are standards that are highly regarded in the teaching profession.*

Boydston, J. E. (1998). *Teacher certification requirements in all 50 states, 1998–99* (16th ed.). Sebring, FL: Teacher Certification Publications. *The author provides detailed specifics about certification requirements in every state; he includes types of certificates, endorsements, fees required, and web pages for most state departments of education. Included are a list of the members of the Interstate Certification Agreement Contract (36 states, DC, and Puerto Rico) and a list of members of the Northeast Regional Compact (9 states).*

Cronin, J. M. (1983). State regulation of teacher preparation. In L. S. Shulman & G. Sykes (Eds.), *Handbook of teaching and policy* (pp. 171–191). New York: Longman. *Cronin reviews the reasons for regulating teacher preparation programs, including concerns in the areas of accreditation, certification, and licensure for teachers. He speaks specifically to the issues of current reforms, an overreliance on testing, the overextension of teacher training, the overatomization of teaching competencies, and the costs of screening and selection.*

Feistritzer, C. E. (1990). *Alternative teacher certification: A state-by-state analysis 1990. Washington, DC:* National Center for Education Information. *This article includes comprehensive data on the location of alternative certification programs across the United States. State listings and requirements for certification for those who hold a bachelor's degree and data on certificates issued are also presented.*

Floden, R. E. (1988). Analogy and credentialing. In J. Sikula (Ed.), *Action in teacher education, the journal of the Association of Teacher Educators: Tenth-year anniversary issue, commemorative edition* (pp. 13–19). Reston, VA: Association of Teacher Educators. *Floden speaks to the purposes of credentialing and to the similarities and differences between other professions, such as law and medicine, hand education. He responds to critics of certification and points out that education has a better system of credentialing than does the health or the legal profession.*

Huling-Austin, L. (1988). Factors to consider in alternative certification programs: What can be learned from teacher induction research? In J. Sikula (Ed.), *Action in teacher education, the journal of the Association of Teacher Educators: Tenth-year anniversary issue, commemorative edition* (pp. 169–176). Reston, VA: Association of Teacher Educators. *The author discusses the characteristics of some alternative certification programs, their populations, and the potential for induction and retention. Also discussed is the beginning teacher research at the Research and Development Center for Teacher Education at the University of Texas at Austin.*

Westerman, J. E. (Summer 1989). Minimum state teacher certification standards and their relationship to effective teaching: Implications for teacher education. *Action in Teacher Education, 11(2),* 25–32. *This article presents a review of the potential for a relationship between state department of education standards and effective teaching. A knowledge of these effective teacher characteristics and professional education curriculum standards research may guide the cooperating teacher in helping the student teacher develop into a more effective teacher.*

29

Job Placement

Most education students are contemplating a future in teaching. The task of finding a teaching position at the completion of their education degree program is uppermost in the minds of the majority of education majors.

The college or university placement office is a potential resource for finding a teaching position. Personnel in such offices provide insight into such topics as supply-and-demand trends, suggested methods of making applications and resumes, and recommended interviewing techniques, as well as information about various school districts and lists of specific teaching vacancies. Computers that streamline services are available in many placement offices.

There will always be a market for good teachers. The difficulty in finding a job varies, of course, depending on a number of factors. One important factor is the school record of each candidate. Such records are summarized in sets of credentials that are housed, at the request of the student, in the placement office. These credentials may include a summary of grades, references from supervisors and professors, and other information requested by hiring officials. It is most important that education majors and teachers in the field keep their credentials up-to-date. A hiring official seldom employs a teacher without first seeing the credentials file.

The importance of maintaining an up-to-date placement file has been proved time and time again. It is wise to obtain references from your professors and supervising teacher while you are fresh on their minds. It is sometimes difficult to make contact with these people as the years go by.

A second reason for keeping credentials up-to-date is the possibility of receiving a promotion or changing jobs. If a candidate is being considered for a promotion, the hiring officials will want to see the credentials and will be impressed if they are available and current. If there is a change of jobs with the possibility of a move involved, a teacher should get immediate supervisors to send references to the placement office involved. (See sample letter of application in Appendix R.)

The letter of application is many times the first contact between teacher candidates and hiring officials. This letter is usually one page and includes information such as application request, name, address, phone number, date of graduation, present or prospective certification, including area qualified to teach, reasons for interest in school district, and availability for interview. The letter should be sent to superintendents of schools or personnel directors, whoever is responsible for the screening of teacher candidates.

Great care should be taken with letters of application. Sloppy erasures, misspelled words, or poorly constructed sentences usually result in elimination of consideration for employment. The cooperating teacher is a good proofreader and adviser for these letters. After receiving the letter of application, the personnel office usually responds by sending an application form with a request to complete and return it.

Because student teaching normally takes place at the end of college training, it is likely that student teachers will be invited for interviews during this period. Student teachers must keep in mind, however, that their first responsibility is to their pupils and classroom, and any interviews scheduled during the school day must be with complete knowledge and approval of the school principal, cooperating teacher, and university supervisor and should be done infrequently.

After applications have been sent to the personnel office, the next step is to make contact with various principals, because principals usually have the major responsibility for hiring their teachers. A short personal resume presenting the candidate's best features should be forwarded to the principals with whom the candidate wishes to have an interview. A resume contains the following information: name, address, telephone number, professional objectives, educational background, work experience, extracurricular activities, hobbies and interests, military service, related professional experiences (if any), and the names, addresses, and telephone numbers of references (see Appendix S for resume format).

Teacher candidates have found that one of the best methods of obtaining employment is through successful substitute teaching experience following graduation. Positive contacts with school personnel, no matter the form they take, should improve their chances.

All of the above-mentioned contacts will be of no use if a candidate does badly during interviews. This one-to-one conference is crucial. The importance of such things as promptness, proper dress, intelligent questions, effective eye contact, good listening ability, enthusiasm, and overall ability to sell oneself cannot be overemphasized. Hiring officials can usually be quite selective, and it is therefore imperative that candidates present themselves in the best possible way.

Availability and willingness to go where jobs develop is also a big factor in being selected. At any given time, there are teaching vacancies in large metropolitan areas as well as in remote rural areas. Good candidates who are available to move around should have little difficulty in finding a teaching position. Nationwide Job Network is found at http://www.nationjob.com

Teacher candidates sell themselves short at times. They feel that they are prepared only to teach. This is not true! In fact, many businesses, industries, and governmental agencies are interested in employing good teacher candidates, regardless of their major areas. The traits that make a good teacher are the same traits that enhance success in other areas. The necessary training programs are usually provided after employment. Successful teacher candidates can have numerous opportunities for employment in areas other than actual teaching if they desire. Each candidate should consider this possibility and, if interested, make the necessary contacts. Here again the placement office can assist.

GUIDELINES FOR THE STUDENT TEACHER

- **Register with your placement office before becoming a student teacher.** You will have little time for such tasks after student teaching begins. You should not only register with the placement office but also use its services.
- **Become acquainted with all the principals in the schools where you are doing fieldwork.** Express your interest in employment to the principal of the school where you are student teaching. Even though there may not be vacancies in that particular school, the principal meets periodically with other administrators who may know of vacancies.
- **Make applications for employment early.** One does not have to complete university work before applying for a job.
- **Be very careful in the preparation of your letters of application, school district applications, and personal resumes.** Brevity and careful proofreading are two necessities.
- **Use your cooperating teacher as a reference.** Hiring officials are most interested in this particular reference.
- **Prepare for your job interviews just as you would plan for a teaching lesson.** You must project yourself at your very best. In preparing for these interviews, consider the following suggestions:
  a. Have good questions in mind. This shows interest and concern on your part.
  b. Arrive at your interviews on time; in fact, it is best to be early. If you are late for interviews, you would probably be late for school as a teacher.
  c. During the interviews, try to emphasize what you could do for the school district if you are employed. Special talents and interests should be mentioned.
  d. Be a good listener; you will get your chance to talk.
  e. At the close of the interview, inquire about the next step. Will you be contacted, or should you check back periodically? Some hiring officials consider it a lack of interest if you do not keep in contact.
  f. Write the interviewer a letter expressing thanks for the interview (see Appendix T for sample letter). Reaffirm your interest in the job.
  g. Do not settle for one interview; keep making contacts.

GUIDELINES FOR THE COOPERATING TEACHER

- **Take an interest in the concerns your student teacher has about finding a teaching position.** If you are working with top-notch teaching prospects, you can make a contribution to the education profession by making employment contacts for them.

- **Encourage your student teacher to register with the college or university placement office.** This results in the availability of credentials that can be sent to potential hiring officials.
- **Report the successes of your student teacher to your principal.** If you feel that this student teacher would be a definite asset to your school as a professional employee, make this known to your principal.
- **The references you write for your student teacher are a most important contribution in the student teacher's quest for a job.** Accentuate the positive but at the same time be honest about the potential of your student teacher.
- **Keep copies of your letters of recommendation.** The student teacher may request a recommendation again in years to come at which time your memory may be dimmer.
- **Encourage your student teacher to make contacts for employment.** Finding a teaching position is very difficult in certain geographic areas and requires an all-out effort

CASE STUDIES

C   A   S   E

29-1   Student teaching was drawing to a close for Richard, a student teacher assigned to a middle school. Richard had begun his last 2 weeks of full-time teaching and was progressing very well. One of his fraternity brothers received an offer to teach in a nearby community. Suddenly, Richard appeared to lose interest in his student teaching and began leaving school early to contact principals concerning employment.

Richard's cooperating teacher was quite upset. The last 2 weeks were crucial for the rounding out of Richard's student teaching experiences. The time at the end of the day after the students left was needed for necessary revision of plans and conferences.

1. What steps should the cooperating teacher take to revitalize Richard's enthusiasm previously shown to his teaching assignment?
2. If a change in attitude does not take place, should Richard be allowed to pass his student teaching? Explain.
3. Should the university supervisor be called?
4. How will this affect the desire on the part of the cooperating teacher to help Richard find a teaching position?
5. Could Richard be jealous of his fraternity brother's job offer and be beginning to panic that he has not received one?

C A S E

29-2   Adriana is a second-semester student teacher assigned to a high school English classroom. She is very concerned about finding a teaching position for the following school year.

Adriana had been successful in her student teaching, and her cooperating teacher was quite concerned about her finding a job. She suggested that Adriana register with the college placement office and was surprised at Adriana's response: "I prefer to get my own job! I don't need help from the placement office."

1. How can the university supervisor convince Adriana that placement is a lifetime service?
2. Why do you think Adriana had this attitude about getting a job without any assistance from the placement office?
3. What are the advantages to having your records available at a central repository?
4. What does the attitude Adriana shows here tell you about her?
5. What impression might Adriana's response have on the cooperating teacher?

C A S E

29-3   Ben had completed his student teaching assignment in a fifth-grade classroom. He was interested in setting up his placement credentials and was in the process of obtaining references. Ben refused to get a reference from his cooperating teacher. He was successful in his student teaching but was afraid that his cooperating teacher would give him a poor recommendation. He and his cooperating teacher did not communicate well, and he really did not know where he stood. Ben felt that his selection of references was to be his decision.

1. What should be his university supervisor's advice concerning this matter?
2. What chance would Ben have to get a teaching position without a positive reference from his cooperating teacher?
3. Would a negative reference from his cooperating teacher keep him from getting a job?
4. Should Ben discuss this with the placement office?
5. Should Ben consult with his cooperating teacher about whether or not he would receive a positive reference?

C A S E

29-4   Lisa completed a successful student teaching experience in a third-grade classroom. She worked very well with her third graders but always felt ill at ease around adults. At the final conference with her cooperating teacher and university supervisor, the topic of employment came up. The cooperating teacher pointed out that Lisa might not be successful with personal interviews because of her bashfulness. Lisa agreed and asked whether there was anything she could do to have a successful interview.

1. What suggestions could the university supervisor and cooperating teacher give Lisa?
2. Would mock interviews be helpful? If so, how could they be arranged?
3. Could a person as shy around adults as Lisa be happy and successful as an elementary school teacher?
4. How could Lisa have received constructive help with this problem during her teacher training?
5. What are Lisa's chances of overcoming her shyness with adults after several years of teaching?

C A S E

29-5 Jennifer was very concerned about the possibility of getting a job in the high school where she was doing her student teaching. She was assigned in business education and was doing a very good job, according to her cooperating teacher.

A vacancy for an accounting teacher developed at another high school in the district, and Jennifer thought this was her chance. She scheduled an interview with the principal to discuss this vacancy. The interview went well until the principal asked Jennifer what questions she had about the job. Jennifer's mind went blank; she could not think of one question to ask. She was afraid that the principal considered this an indication of a lack of interest on her part.

1. Do you think the principal would eliminate Jennifer as a candidate because she had no questions?
2. Give examples of appropriate questions Jennifer might have asked.
3. What follow-up procedures could Jennifer take to show her interest in the vacancy?
4. Should Jennifer request help from her cooperating teacher?
5. What sources of assistance could Jennifer have used prior to the interview?

C A S E

29-6 Daniel was in his next-to-last week of student teaching in an eighth-grade mathematics assignment. He was quite elated when he was offered a job to teach in a nearby community 20 miles away. It was his hope that he would be permitted to complete his student teaching in the school where he would be teaching. He suggested this to his cooperating teacher who did not think it was a good idea at all. Daniel decided to call his university supervisor.

1. If Daniel's request is granted, what effect would it have on his present class?
2. Why would the cooperating teacher veto Daniel's request?
3. Would Daniel have any problems in transferring to another school district for the final days of his student teaching?
4. How should the university supervisor react to Daniel's situation?
5. What could be the legal implications if Daniel were to serve as both a student teacher and a contracted teacher?

RECOMMENDED READING

Connotillo, B. C. (Ed.). (1984). *Teaching abroad.* New York: Institute of International Education. *This is a good source of information on schools abroad. Schools are listed by country. The book also includes addresses of embassies and education-related employers who hire for worldwide vacancies.*

Edelfelt, R. A. (1988). *Careers in education.* Lincolnwood, IL: VGM Career Horizons. *The author reviews job descriptions and educational requirements for specific careers in education. Patterns of preparation, benefits, and details relevant to specific careers are included.*

Fine, J. (1985). *Opportunities in teaching careers.* Lincolnwood, IL: VGM Career Horizons. *The author reviews the career opportunities in teaching and related fields. She includes suggestions on how to plan and get started toward a career in teaching.*

Kniker, C. R., & Naylor, N. A. (1981). Career preparation and employment opportunities. In *Teaching today and tomorrow* (pp. 61–83). Columbus, OH: Merrill. *Important concerns of student teachers include nonclassroom job opportunities. This chapter discusses the following options: business and industry, government agencies, nonpublic teaching, overseas opportunities, adult education, agencies, and service groups. This material includes the steps for applying for a position and provides a set of questions to assist candidates in deciding whether being an educator is the right thing for them.*

Krannick, R. (1991). *The educators' guide to alternative jobs and careers.* Manassas Park, VA: Impact Publications. *Krannick explores career opportunities for educators outside of the field. This should be a rich resource for student teachers who are restricted to locations offering few vacancies in teaching.*

Machado, J. M., & Meyer, H. C. (1984). Resumes, applications, and interviews. In *Early childhood practicum guide: A sourcebook for beginning teachers of young children* (pp. 295–312). Albany, NY: Delmar Publishers. *This chapter helps the student teacher to immediately begin the job search. A resume outline is included with directions and advice on preparing it. The content of cover letters is illustrated with samples; suggestions on how to prepare for a successful interview are included.*

Machado, J. M., & Meyer, H. C. (1984). The search: Choices and alternatives. In *Early childhood practicum guide: A sourcebook for beginning teachers of young children* (pp. 281–294). Albany, NY: Delmar Publishers. *Material in this chapter assists the student teacher to think through questions about future employment, including short- and long-range career goals, career ladders, and ways to find job openings.*

Moody, D. (Ed.). (1990). *Patterson's American educator.* Mount Prospect, IL: Educational Directories. *Part I presents addresses of secondary schools, territories of the United States, diocesan superintendents of Roman Catholic schools, and superintendents of Seventh-Day Adventist schools. Part II lists postsecondary schools and educational associations and societies. This is helpful information for student teachers not restricted to a particular location.*

Moody, D. (Ed.). (1992). *Patterson's elementary education.* Mount Prospect, IL: Educational Directories. *This book lists addresses of elementary schools, diocesan superintendents of Roman Catholic schools, and superintendents of Seventh-Day Adventist schools. This is a helpful resource for student teachers looking for vacancies & school addresses in various locations.*

Nation Job Network. http://www.nationjob.com provides an opportunity to search a national database of preschool through college/university teaching vacancies.

O'Hair, M. (Spring 1989). Teacher employment interview: A neglected reality. *Action in Teacher Education, 11*(1), 53–57. *The author discusses the importance of training the new educator in employment interview techniques. Factors given that affect the outcomes of interviews include communication, stereotypes, demographics, atmosphere, enthusiasm, and psychological factors.*

Appendixes

APPENDIX A

Line and Staff Organization

Principal

Assistant Principal

School District
Supervisors ---

School Secretary

Noninstructional Staff   Teachers

Copyright © 1994 by Macmillan Publishing Company. All rights reserved.

APPENDIX B

Student Teaching Evaluation

Key: 1 = Outstanding
        2 = Good
        3 = Acceptable
        4 = Needs help
        5 = Not observed

I. Personal qualities
   A. Dedication to teaching
   B. Personal grooming
   C. Enthusiasm
   D. Flexibility
   E. Creativity
   F. Acceptance of students as worthy individuals
   G. Other:

II. Instructional qualities
   A. Knowledge of principles of teaching and learning
   B. Planning and preparation
   C. Instructional skill
   D. Lesson variety
   E. Appropriate questioning techniques
   F. Reflective learning techniques
   G. Higher level thinking skills
   H. Evaluation techniques
   I. Knowledge of subject matter
   J. Group management and organization
   K. Other:

III. Professional qualities
   A. Understanding of student growth and development
   B. Communication skills
       1. Written
       2. Verbal
       3. Listening
   C. Understanding of student socialization patterns
   D. Ability to utilize criticism and suggestions
   E. Organizational ability and timeliness
   F. Other:

Copyright © 1994 by Macmillan Publishing Company. All rights reserved.

APPENDIX C

Lesson Plan Format A

1. Objectives:

2. Teacher activities and materials:

3. Student activities:

4. Evaluation of student work:

5. Evaluation of lesson:

Copyright © 1994 by Macmillan Publishing Company. All rights reserved.

APPENDIX D

Lesson Plan Format B

Subject: Period: Date:

1. Name of unit and purpose of the lesson:

2. Teacher procedures to use:

3. Elements of lesson and time required for each:

4. Materials/equipment needed:

5. Methods of evaluating student progress:

6. Method of evaluating lesson effectiveness by teacher:

7. Notes for future planning:

Copyright © 1994 by Macmillan Publishing Company. All rights reserved.

APPENDIX E

Lesson Plan Format C

1. Comprehensive objectives:

2. Behavioral objectives:

3. Sequence of lesson (with approximate time):

4. Materials needed:

    A. By teacher:

    B. By students:

5. Evaluation of student learning:

6. What changes could improve this lesson next time?

Copyright © 1994 by Macmillan Publishing Company. All rights reserved.

APPENDIX F

Lesson Plan Format D

1. Primary objectives of the lesson:

   Expanded objectives of the lesson:

2. What materials/activities will be used:

   A. By teacher:

   B. By student:

3. List of procedures in lesson with approximate times:

4. Evaluation of student work:

5. Evaluation of lesson implementation:

6. What changes would you make next time in this lesson?

7. What could be added to this lesson if you see that you are about to run out of material?

8. What could be omitted in this lesson if you see that you are beginning to run out of time?

Copyright © 1994 by Macmillan Publishing Company. All rights reserved.

APPENDIX G

Student Teaching Journal

Date:

What happened in class today:

How I felt about what happened:

Implications of what happened:

Next steps (what I need to do):

Copyright © 1994 by Macmillan Publishing Company. All rights reserved.

APPENDIX H

Two-Way Conference Log

Date: Time:

Participants:

Points made in discussion:

Recommendations/suggestions:

Other:

Copyright © 1994 by Macmillan Publishing Company. All rights reserved.

APPENDIX I

Three-Way Conference Log

Date: Time:

Participants:

Points made in discussion:

Recommendations/suggestions:

Other:

Copyright © 1994 by Macmillan Publishing Company. All rights reserved.

APPENDIX J

Format for Daily Notes

(Steno Pad)

Student Teacher   Cooperating Teacher

Copyright © 1994 by Macmillan Publishing Company. All rights reserved.

APPENDIX K

Memorandum Format

MEMORANDUM

DATE:

TO:

FROM:

SUBJECT:

Copyright © 1994 by Macmillan Publishing Company. All rights reserved.

APPENDIX L

Student Record-Keeping Form

Code: s absent; s $_E$ excused absence; s $_T$ tardy; + homework turned in; − no homework; * see notes; test scores to be written in numerically.

Student Names	Days										Notes
	1	2	3	4	5	6	7	8	9	10	

Copyright © 1994 by Macmillan Publishing Company. All rights reserved.

APPENDIX M

Classroom Management Record Form (10-Day Period)

Code: + motivated, working; — not motivated; \ not working; O minor misbehavior; X major misbehavior.

Student Names	Days										Notes
	1	2	3	4	5	6	7	8	9	10	

Copyright © 1994 by Macmillan Publishing Company. All rights reserved.

APPENDIX N

Parent Phone Log

1.

     Date   Phone #   Person called

Purpose of call:

Summary of discussion:

2.

     Date   Phone #   Person called

Purpose of call:

Summary of discussion:

Copyright © 1994 by Macmillan Publishing Company. All rights reserved.

APPENDIX O

Interim Report to Parents

Name of Student   Name of Teacher

Subject   Date

Dear Parent or Guardian:

    Work is satisfactory in most areas.

    Needs particular help in such areas as _____

_____

    Seems to be enjoying school.

    Your child may wish to discuss with you problems related to _____

_____

Copyright © 1994 by Macmillan Publishing Company. All rights reserved.

APPENDIX P

Objective Test Format

Name of Course
Test #
Date

Directions:

Write the answer to each question in the blank to the left of the question. Read the questions carefully.

_____ 1. (Write short answer or fill in the blank for question here.)

_____ 2.

_____ 3.

_____ 4.

_____ 5.

_____ 6.

_____ 7.

_____ 8.

_____ 9.

_____ 10.

_____ 11.

_____ 12.

_____ 13.

_____ 14.

NOTE: Answers are to be written in the blanks to the left of the questions, enabling the grader to check the answers much more quickly. In the case of multiple-choice questions, the answer blank can be shorter because only the selected letter will be written in the blank.

Copyright © 1994 by Macmillan Publishing Company. All rights reserved.

APPENDIX Q

Happy Gram

Date:

To:

From:

The GOOD news is:

Copyright © 1994 by Macmillan Publishing Company. All rights reserved.

APPENDIX R

Letter of Application

March 15, 2002

Dr. John Smith
Director of Personnel
Harrisburg Unified School District
3086 Main Street
Harrisburg, FL 33209

Dear Dr. Smith:

Our university placement office has posted a notice of anticipated vacancy for an English teacher in your school district for next school year. Please consider me an applicant for this position.

I will graduate in May from Middletown University with a bachelor's degree in Education with a major in English and a minor in Spanish. While attending the university, I was active in the Future Educators' Club, serving as secretary during this school year. I also participated in an intramural volleyball league and was a student ambassador for the university for three years. My enclosed resume lists other pertinent data.

I will be happy to come for an interview and can be reached at the above address or by phone: (317) 555-5555.

Sincerely,

Molly Young
2220 University Drive
Middletown, IN 47304

Copyright © 1994 by Macmillan Publishing Company. All rights reserved.

APPENDIX S

Resume Format

Name
Address
Phone

Brief statement of qualifications:

Educational history:

Work experience:

Nonwork-related experience:

Honors and awards:

Activities, interests, and hobbies:

References:

Copyright © 1994 by Macmillan Publishing Company. All rights reserved.

APPENDIX T

Follow-Up Thank You Letter

May 4, 2002

Dr. James R. Smith
Director of Personnel
Escambia District School System
412 North Avenue
Byrneville, NC 28400

Dear Dr. Smith:

I appreciate the opportunity you gave me yesterday to visit with you and to discuss the teaching vacancy in English in your school district. I enjoyed the discussion about the new 10th-grade English curriculum that is being implemented next year.

The professional opportunity that this position offers is exciting; I hope that I will be seriously considered.

Thank you.

Sincerely,

Molly Young
4220 Pine Street
Byrneville, NC 28400

Copyright © 1994 by Macmillan Publishing Company. All rights reserved.

About the Author

Dr. Patricia J. Wentz has worked with students in field experiences and student teaching since 1972. She has served as Director of Pre-Student Teaching Field Experiences, Assistant Director of Student Teaching, Assistant Director of Clinical Studies, Director of Clinical Studies, Director of Teacher Certification and Field Experiences, Director of Teacher Education Student Services, Associate Dean, Interim Dean, and Dean of the College of Education at the University of West Florida (UWF). As chair of the Department of Educational Leadership, she directed administrative internships with students pursuing their specialist degrees. As Director of the Educational Research and Development Center (ERDC) at UWF, she supervised doctoral graduate student assistants and faculty involved in grant proposal writing and implementation and worked extensively in service to the schools through the ERDC. Most recently, Dr. Wentz has been selected as State Director of the Florida Committee of the Secondary and Middle Schools Commission of the Southern Association of Colleges and Schools (SACS). The State Office of the Florida Committee of SACS Secondary and Middle Schools is housed in the Educational Research and Development Center at the University of West Florida.

Dr. Wentz received a B.S. in English and a M.A. in Counseling at East Carolina University; she received her Ph.D. from Texas A&M University in Educational Psychology and Curriculum & Instruction. Dr. Wentz has served extensively in staff development activities related to student teaching. Her public school teaching experience includes being a junior high school librarian, teaching English and U.S. history at the junior high and high school levels, and serving as a high school guidance counselor. Prior to her public school experience, Dr. Wentz worked at the D. H. Hill Library at University of North Carolina at Raleigh and as a newspaper reporter for North Carolina's *News & Observer.*

Index